Realist Christian theology
in a postmodern age

This book brings together for the first time traditional Christian
theological perspectives on truth and reality with a contemporary
philosophical view of the place of language in both divine and
worldly reality. Patterson seeks to reconcile the requirements that
Christian theology should take account of postmodern insights
concerning the inextricability of language and world as well as
taking God's truth to be absolute for all reality. Yet this work is
not simply about theological language and truth as such. Instead
Patterson asks: where does language fit in divine and human
reality?

Patterson's discussion straddles realist, liberal–revisionist and
postliberal theological schools, and analyses their various
positions before going on to develop and apply a theological
model of 'language-ridden' reality. This model affirms that
worldly reality has a radical dependence on God. Finally, the book
explores the theological and ethical implications of the model it
proposes.

SUE PATTERSON is Lecturer in Ethics and Applied Theology at
Trinity College Bristol. She gained her Ph.D. from the University
of Otago, New Zealand and is a member of the Center of
Theological Inquiry, Princeton. Dr Patterson has been an
ordained minister of the Anglican communion since 1988.

Cambridge Studies in Christian Doctrine

Edited by
Professor COLIN GUNTON, *King's College London*
Professor DANIEL W. HARDY, *University of Cambridge*

Cambridge Studies in Christian Doctrine is an important new series
which aims to engage critically with the traditional doctrines of
Christianity, and at the same time to locate and make sense of
them within a secular context. Without losing sight of the
authority of scripture and the traditions of the Church, the
books in this series will subject pertinent dogmas and credal
statements to careful scrutiny, analysing them in light of the
insights of both Church and society, and will thereby practise
theology in the fullest sense of the word.

Titles published in the series
1. Self and Salvation: Being Transformed · DAVID F. FORD
2. Realist Christian Theology in a Postmodern Age · SUE PATTERSON

Titles forthcoming in the series
Theology, Music and Time: The Sound of God · JEREMY BEGBIE
Church, Narrativity and Transcendence · ROBERT JENSON
Doctrine of Sin · ALISTAIR I. McFADYEN
The Trinity and Truth · BRUCE D. MARSHALL
A Political Theology of Nature · PETER SCOTT
Remythologizing Theology: Divine Action and Authorship
    KEVIN J. VANHOOZER

Realist Christian theology
in a postmodern age

SUE PATTERSON

CAMBRIDGE
UNIVERSITY PRESS

PUBLISHED BY THE PRESS SYNDICATE OF THE UNIVERSITY OF CAMBRIDGE
The Pitt Building, Trumpington Street, Cambridge, United Kingdom

CAMBRIDGE UNIVERSITY PRESS
The Edinburgh Building, Cambridge CB2 2RU, UK   http://www.cup.cam.ac.uk
40 West 20th Street, New York, NY 10011–4211, USA   http://www.cup.org
10 Stamford Road, Oakleigh, Melbourne 3166, Australia

First published 1999

Printed in the United Kingdom at the University Press, Cambridge

Typeset in 9/13 pt Lexicon (*The Enschedé Font Foundry*), in QuarkXPress®   [SE]

A catalogue record for this book is available from the British Library

Library of Congress cataloguing in publication data

Patterson, Sue M.
Realist Christian theology in a postmodern world / Sue Patterson.
        p.   cm. – (Cambridge studies in Christian doctrine)
Includes bibliographical references and index.
ISBN 0 521 59030 2
1. Philosophical theology.   2. Language and languages – Philosophy.
I. Title.   II. Series.
BT55.P37   1999
230′.01–dc21   98–35099   CIP

ISBN 0 521 59030 2 hardback
ISBN 0 521 66806 9 paperback

Contents

Acknowledgments

viii   Throughout what proved to be a much longer-drawn-out process than I ever anticipated I have been helped and sustained by a number of people. Alan Torrance not only originally pointed me in the direction of the issues but kept fuelling me with his own inimitable enthusiasm. Thomas F. Torrance was a brief but fruitfully goading correspondent. Janet Soskice and George Lindbeck showed forbearing generosity of spirit in debate. My colleagues at the Center of Theological Inquiry in Princeton during 1993–5 challenged me to see where and how further thought was required. I was grateful for Colin Gunton's constructive comments on the first complete draft. Daniel Hardy's discerning and patient reading of what in the end proved to be three penultimate drafts over three years has been invaluable. Needless to say, the remaining limitations or confusions of thought or expression are entirely my own.

I must thank the Center of Theological Inquiry, Princeton, the Fulbright Foundation, and the Trinity College Theological School, Melbourne, for generous funding and other resources that have made this book possible, and my editors at Cambridge University Press, Alex Wright, Ruth Parr and Kevin Taylor, for their efforts in seeing it through various obstacles. I am grateful to friends and colleagues, Hilary Regan and John and Michaela Wright, for their unstinting and unobtrusive hospitality during its second phase of revisions. Finally, and not least, I would like to thank my husband John and daughters Felicity and Eleanor, for their forbearance and support over what proved to be more of a marathon than any of us could have anticipated, and which were crucial to my reaching this point.

Introduction

This inquiry's twin concerns are the nature of theology and the nature of reality, where the issue that links them both is the role of language – not the content of language as in theological language, although that is part of it; rather, language as an entity in itself. The scope of the inquiry is the combined context of contemporary realist, postliberal and liberal revisionist theology. It straddles all these schools to a greater or lesser extent in that it arises out of the awareness that, while their various preoccupations and insights are different and potentially complementary, their shortcomings are essentially similar.

The nature of theology

Contemporary theological realists (such as T. F. Torrance) tend to operate with what might be termed a linguistic-window-on-reality model, however much the view from that window is acknowledged to be partial, theory-laden and in need of progressive revisions.[1] While this window on reality is clouded by the limitations and distortions of human concepts, it becomes clearer if not transparent in the search for the truth as the truth gives itself to us to be known. Theological realists accordingly regard theology as having a scientific character in that, like scientific observation and theory-building, it is governed by its object. The being of God reflected in contingent creaturely being has an intrinsic rationality which the human knower comes to know in the same way that he or she comes to know worldly reality – that is, by 'grasping it in its depths' through participating in the given (revealed) structures of its

1. See, for instance, T. F. Torrance, *God and Rationality* (Oxford: Oxford University Press, 1971).

being.[2] This approach, therefore, asserts a universal rationality which is in the first place divine and in the second place, contingently, cosmic or worldly. The argument is that our concepts become true concepts as they come to be coordinated with the rational structure of reality (whether divine or worldly) through our indwelling of that reality.

Liberal revisionists (such as Werner Jeanrond) operate with what might be described as a multifaceted one-way mirror model in which a general anthropology mediates divine transcendence through a myriad of human images.[3] The resulting ambiguity requires that religious beliefs, while all assumed to be pointing to the one truth, must be treated as fallible and held tentatively. Human thinking and experience must be tested according to reason, just as, reciprocally, reason must answer to a linguistically mediated experience, for our knowledge of God is not confined to the overtly religious but is present in all truth. A corollary is that theology should always interrelate the experience and rationality of its own time and place with the Christian past in a dialectic that allows each to make a reciprocal contribution to the formulation of Christian claims. Of course, this then poses the dilemma of how to balance this dialectic so that both are taken seriously and entered into fully. The suggestion is that stories common to humanity and Christian text should both be taken as primary sources, each acting reciprocally as critic for the other, each essentially as a story read by the other, where, however, the foundational Jesus story is the 'classic' that is able to transform human existence.

For postliberal theologians (such as George Lindbeck) Christian traditions are in effect mirrors which reflect God holistically *to the extent that* their faithfulness to handed-down and doctrinally ruled uses of the normative text corresponds to the being and will of God.[4] According to the postliberal cultural-linguistic model, 'religions are systems containing both discursive and non-discursive idioms connecting intentionalities with action; they also provide regulative structures which guide reflection, feeling and conduct'.[5] On this view, our humanness is

---

2. Ibid., pp. 16–17; also T. F. Torrance, *The Christian Doctrine of God* (Edinburgh: T. & T. Clark, 1996) p. 90, and *Reality and Scientific Theology* (Edinburgh: Scottish Academic Press, 1982) pp. 26–7.

3. See, for instance, W. G. Jeanrond, *Textual Hermeneutics: Development and Significance* (New York: Crossroad, 1991).

4. Postliberal theology's central architect has been George Lindbeck, lately of Yale; see G. A. Lindbeck, *The Nature of Doctrine: Religion and Theology in a Postliberal Age* (Philadelphia: Westminster Press, 1984).

5. K Surin, *The Turnings of Darkness and Light: Essays in Philosophical and Systematic Theology* (Cambridge: Cambridge University Press, 1989) p. 160.

acquired and shaped in a particular communal reality. As this particular reality or world is primary, and accordingly any purportedly generic view must rest on the axioms grounding the viewer's standpoint, there can be no non-linguistic or universal experience. All human experience comes historically and contextually shaped, in this case Christ-shaped. In this regard, Scripture is taken as encompassing 'both the times and stories of the text and those of the reader', who 'must fit his or her own experience into Scripture's cumulative narrative, thus becoming a "figure" of the text. Christian reality claims (mediation) and the formation of the Christian life (application) follow from and are normed by the explicative shape of biblical narrative.'[6]

A key difference between these perspectives is their view of truth which reflects their understanding of the role of language. Realist theology asserts that Christian truth claims only make sense if they correspond to an extra-linguistic reality beyond inherited traditions of belief and practice and the claims of human religious experience. Being true to Christianity's incarnational revelation of God in Jesus Christ means taking its associated truth claims as absolute. On the other hand, postliberal theology views truth in terms of faithfulness to the norm of Scripture as interpreted by a tradition. In both cases truth may be a matter of revelation and reality a matter of givenness, but according to very different models. The pragmatically based postliberal view of truth seems to be restricted to received truth expressed in traditional patterns and as such it would appear unable to explain the dynamic and innovative character of a Christianity that is always renewing itself in new and surprising ways. In this regard, the theological realists maintain that the formulation of our concepts requires constant revision and reconstruction with reference to 'the objective source that gave rise to them . . . for that is the only way in which they can be renewed in their original force and rationality'.[7]

On this realist reckoning, the dynamic and innovative character of Christian thought and practice is a function of its participation in a reality transcendent of human formulations, whereas on the revisionist view it is a function of our ('classic' text-enabled) engagement with the 'limit-character of common human experience' through which we encounter and are able to interpret divine transcendence. That is, if theological realism and liberal revisionism are both able to account for

6. Ibid., pp. 203–4.   7. Torrance, *God and Rationality*, pp. 19–20.

new truth, they differ on whether this is an external truth which we discover as our concepts are brought into line with it and are able to grasp it, or whether this is at least in part an internal truth (correlated with an external truth) which we construct as a function of our God-endowed and God-enabled creaturely experience and creativity. The pragmatic and strongly christological focus of postliberal theology may point to a way of uniting these oppositions.

Of course, conversely, the revisionist recognition of the creative human contribution to God's ongoing work tends to be too generally anthropocentric to take the particular revelation of God in Jesus Christ as absolute; thus Jesus is required to function as exemplary instance or 'classic' and Christian truth claims are interpreted according to what is perceived to be transformative about *this* 'classic' for *this* experience in *this* context. There again, the postliberal theology that recognizes the text-and-tradition-groundedness of Christianity renders propositional Christian truth claims internal to that tradition, so that, again, their absoluteness appears qualified. Where for postliberals this simply reflects the inescapably historical and traditional nature of life (and may in fact allow for a human contribution to Christian truth), it can also be construed as a fideistic form of relativism which privatizes truth in the face of those truths' universal claims.

Accordingly, for each of these perspectives the others may serve as prophetic 'voices of disorder' in a reciprocal pointing up of shortcomings and confusions. Where realists are able to demonstrate how a postliberal bracketing of propositional truth is fundamentally destructive of Christianity, both postliberals and revisionists have contended that realists have been unable to accommodate adequately the implications of the theory-ladenness of all observation and description. At first glance, several pairings suggest themselves: first, postliberal and revisionist theology share an acceptance of the culturally and linguistically conditioned nature of human existence, although they differ in the degree of particularity they assign to this. Where they are at odds is where, secondly, realist and postliberal schools agree, namely on the givenness of a Christian reality that absorbs and judges all human formulations (although they differ on the nature of that reality). While the similarities are to do with linguisticality on the one hand and criteriality on the other, the differences come down to the differences between what Hilary Putnam terms 'external' realism (in which facts are context free) and 'internal' realism (in which facts are context determined).[8] Again, these differences may rest on assumptions that indicate the inadequacy of the present models.

Disorder may be an essential stage of reordering, as Daniel Hardy points out.[9] Both the complementarities and the conflicts in the above approaches indicate the need for a synthetic understanding able to combine insights from them all without departing from what is recognizably (even if revisably) the core of Christian belief. In response to this, some theologians from opposing schools have moved closer to each other in their awareness of the need to address Christian truth claims in the face of the complex nature of worldly existence.[10] If these theologies are all true in part (and false in part), it may be that their models are at fault – it is just as likely that their frameworks are too limited as that the insights are off-track. What is required is a hybridizing master model that is able to account for all the key insights and resolve some of the conflicts.

The aim of this inquiry is to come up with just such a synthesis, recognizing that to fill the bill such a model would need to be both content-relating and methodological and accordingly operate on two reciprocal levels. At the first-order level, it will aim to maximize the comprehensiveness of Christian theology through the incorporation of supplementary explanatory models that are able to account for, relate and extend the insights of the various schools of theology, in particular the insights concerning the nature of language, truth and reality. This is to be achieved without doing violence to the christological centre of Christianity while at the same time bearing in mind that logic also demands a doctrinal self-consistency which has been expressed classically in the trinitarian 'doctrine of doctrines'.

The imperative of self-consistency becomes methodological in requiring a second-order or meta-level exploration of the relation between models or paradigms. The relation of Christian theology to the models with which it interacts may be expressed in terms of relative power or priority, dynamics and stability (the maintainability of priority). The issue of comprehensiveness also enters at this level in connection with reductionist (for instance, dichotomizing) and synthetic interactions. A loss of

8. See, for instance, H. Putnam, *Reason, Truth and History* (Cambridge: Cambridge University Press, 1981).
9. D. W. Hardy, 'The Spirit of God in Creation and Reconciliation', in H. Regan and A. J. Torrance (eds.), *Christ and Context* (Edinburgh: T. & T. Clark, 1993), pp. 237ff.
10. David Ford, Garrett Green, Colin Gunton, Daniel Hardy, George Hunsinger, Bruce Marshall, William Placher, Kenneth Surin and William Werpehowski are all arguably participants in this hybridizing movement.

comprehensiveness may occur not only when a rich model is commandeered by one that is less so, but also, conversely, when an impoverished model is utilized by a rich one. What is aimed for here is the bolstering of comprehensiveness without a concomitant loss of coherence.

What this inquiry aims *not* to do (and hopefully succeeds in) is to reject any theological position or insight out of court. Its hypothesis is that many seeming incompatibilities both between theological approaches, and between any approach and the classical doctrinal logic, are due more to confusion about how things fit together, or to the use of inadequate models, than to out-and-out wrongness. These difficulties should, therefore, be amenable to the sort of sifting and reordering of concepts afforded by the use of a new or expanded model. Methodologically, this is expressed in two ways: first, in the synthetic way indicated which requires that the critique of various approaches does not dig them up and throw them out in order to plant a new theory, but takes cuttings from them for grafting. Second, consequently, the line of argument is lateral as much as linear. The aim is to relate ideas and models to each other, exploring the dynamics of their interaction, while pursuing several lines of thought forward.

If we can assume that theologians all aim to seek the truth and to give glory to God without surrendering anything they regard as central to Christian belief and life, then the Thomist Principle of Charity should prevail in theological discourse as in biblical exegesis. We should read one another as trying to be truthful as well as Christian. What will prevent such a charitable reading is the 'in-groupness' that claims a competitive monopoly on truth for any one school. If progress is to be made in theology (or anywhere else for that matter) it will not be made by staying in old lines of thought or digging new ones deeper, but in lateral and synthetic developments. The preservation and development of what is good in the old lines may involve the questioning of some deeply rooted assumptions, but, as Fergus Kerr points out, 'If theologians proceed in the belief that they need neither examine nor even acknowledge their inherited metaphysical commitments, they will simply remain prisoners of whatever philosophical school was in the ascendant 30 years earlier, when they were first year students.'[11]

The main supplementary model this study utilizes is Wittgensteinian. To be Wittgensteinian in theology is less fashionable than it used to

---

11. F. Kerr, *Theology After Wittgenstein* (Oxford: Blackwell, 1986), p. 3.

be, perhaps because the way in which this has been pursued has given rise to certain prejudicial views about Wittgenstein's thinking. A Wittgensteinian approach has been typed (by Don Cupitt, for instance) as anti-realist or constructivist.[12] However, as Wittgenstein himself has pointed out, the edifices we build out of realist and anti-realist distinctions are themselves founded on the wrong questions.[13] This study aims to follow Kerr in the pursuit of a more helpful Wittgenstein.

A postmodern reality

This inquiry has, in its title, defined the 'age' as a 'postmodern' one, but what is meant by 'postmodern'? It is possible to advance either a strong or a weak thesis. It could be argued that local human contexts are their own watertight worlds or histories (story or narrative worlds) with a self-description and self-understanding that is particular to themselves and which, therefore, cannot be understood by anyone outside that world. Or it could be argued that they are their own worlds but not water-tightly, inclined to leak and intermingle, but that reality and truth nevertheless come linguistically and contextually nuanced. To argue the strong case is not necessarily to claim that because human beings and their contexts are 'language-ridden' (a basic premise of postmodernity), human forms of life are linguistically constructed and all is therefore language. It is possible to argue that a particular context is a self-contained world without holding this view of language's scope and origins. Yet strong thesis devotees in holding the premise that stories go all the way down – that we never get out of stories at any level of our existence – are inclined to infer that the point of the story lies only in the telling. That is, the content of the telling is arbitrary; there are no meta-narratives as there is nothing beyond the 'local networks of signs that play out their patterns against the void'.[14]

A practical consequence of the strong thesis is that '*style* is everything; with massive commercial support, cultural options – even when their roots are in would-be dissident groupings – are developed and presented

---

12. See D. Cupitt, *The Sea of Faith* (London: BBC, 1984).

13. 'We have been tempted into the habit of thinking that either *die Dinge* or *unsere Vorstellungen* must be the primary thing, but the choice between realism and idealism overlooks *das Leben*: that is Wittgenstein's suggestion' (Kerr, *Theology After Wittgenstein*, p. 133).

14. G. Loughlin, *Telling God's Story* (Cambridge: Cambridge University Press, 1996), p. 18. See, for instance, D. Cupitt, *The Long-Legged Fly: A Theology of Language and Desire* (London: SCM, 1987).

as consumer goods. Religious belief is no exception.'[15] Gerard Loughlin has this Kafka-like vision of a postmodernist society as an endless shopping mall with no exit, within which we wander about endlessly. The Church buys into the shopping mall in becoming a sort of 'Gods"R"Us' in which customers choose the religious style that fits them.

What this serves to underline is the main theological consequence of the strong postmodern thesis: that on this thesis it is questionable whether in the first place we can have such a thing as a single Christianity in which its various contexts participate because a single Christianity requires a master story, a central metanarrative. Arguably the coherence of Christianity itself requires this because it rules out taking our essential humanity, whether general or particular, as primary. Or rather, to persist with the suggestion that we might have a metanarrative and still be postmodern is to dispense with the many watertight worlds of the strong thesis. For if we are inclined to the view that metanarratives still lurk in postmodernity – that there is always an implicit metanarrative in any worldview – we are into the weak thesis.

This may be recognized as amounting to a species of critical realism. Some claim it as belonging in late modernity; others would identify it as postmodern. Helpfully it could be said to have a foot in both, as it allows us to combine their insights while rejecting their mistakes. Loughlin identifies two sorts of narrative theology that answer to the weak thesis description in placing the emphasis on the content of the story as it is told rather than on the telling itself. As Loughlin puts it, narrative theologians

> accept the ubiquity of language. They believe that our sense of the world is formed by the socially constructed discourses in which we find ourselves, and to which we contribute. We are embedded in language, as is language in us. There is a reciprocal relation between story and story-teller. As I recount my life-story, my story produces the 'I' which recounts it. I tell the story by which I am told. And since I am part of a larger community – one in which others tell stories about me, just as I tell stories about them – I am the product of many inter-related narratives, as is everyone else.[16]

In this weak thesis group the postliberal narrativists are to be distinguished from the liberal-revisionist ones such as David Tracy.[17] For

---

15. R. Williams, 'Postmodern Theology and the Judgment of the World', in F. B. Burnham (ed.), *Postmodern Theology* (San Francisco: Harper & Row, 1989), pp. 92ff., 99–100.
16. Loughlin, *Telling God's Story*, p. 18.
17. See, for example, D. Tracy, *Plurality and Ambiguity: Hermeneutics, Religion, Hope* (San Francisco: Harper & Row, 1987).

the latter any text can be a reality-revealing 'classic', in which to be human is above all to have a story – for being storied is integral to a general theory of human experience as primary. In this situation, if the Gospel is metanarrative, it is subject to another metanarrative, the human story, which is a collection of many local and particular human narratives or histories. The paradox of this type of postmodern theology – and this is a paradox that shows up the paradox in postmodernism generally – is that it takes a general theory of storied humanity to validate a model of religious experience as local and self-validating.

On the other hand, the postliberal narrative theologians take a christological metanarrative as the master story, the story within which we find all our stories, which determines the shape of our true reality. As Lindbeck puts it,

> the canonical Scriptures provide the basic narratives for how the Church imagines the world and itself in the world. The Church imagines itself within the narrative-world of the Bible, a written-world into which people can be 'inscribed'. Rather than understanding the Bible in worldly terms, the Christian understands the world in biblical ones; the Christian takes the biblical narratives, above all the narratives of Christ, as the fundamental story by which all others are to be understood, including his or her own story. 'The cross is not to be viewed as a figurative representation of suffering nor the messianic Kingdom viewed as a symbol for hope in the future; rather suffering should be cruciform, and hopes for the future messianic.[18]

Loughlin argues that this postliberal position is postmodern – and that it views Christianity itself as postmodern – because it sees Christianity as

> not founded on anything other than the performance of its story. It cannot be established against nihilism by reason, but only presented as a radical alternative, as something else altogether. It is also postmodern because its story – God's story – imagines a world 'out of nothing', a world of becoming, in which people are not fixed essences but life-narratives with a future.[19]

Certainly the postliberal position seems consistent with the weak postmodern one that allows metanarratives but insists that they are always contextually nuanced. And this position allows us to argue that Christianity without a master-story, a metanarrative, ceases to be Christianity while at the same time arguing that it is too uncritically

---

18. Lindbeck, *The Nature of Doctrine*, p. 118, quoted in Loughlin, *Telling God's Story*, p. 18.
19. Loughlin, p. 21.

realist, too simplistic to hold that in sharing the one Gospel all Christian confessions and contexts proclaim the same reality. For this amounts to treating our own context as invisible or transparent. To accept the weak postmodern thesis is to be prepared to accept both the necessity of a Christian metanarrative and the existence of many small local worlds to which the Gospel is to be proclaimed and within which therefore it is to be Gospel.

Yet it is not quite as simple as that either. If theology is to be post-modern in the weak sense – that is, more in a critical-realist sense – then the dialectic between Scripture and tradition ceases to be self-contained. There is a reality outside of texts and their interpreting traditions, a reality which awaits conversion to the text and the tradition, but which itself brings aspects of itself into a dialectical encounter with the special revelation. Reading is world-involving; if the text reads the world, the world also reads the text. We always view the world from a particular theological place – there is no God's-eye view, system-neutral position from which we can get at the truth – and yet this particular theological place is also a particular faith-traditional and particular cultural place. The theology indwells the context and the context the theology, and from this intermingling comes new facets of revelation. As Loughlin points out, the text does not become revelatory until it is read by a reader – until it connects with lives, and not merely with ecclesial doctrinal formulations. If theology is a matter of working at understanding the content of faith and the world from a position in which the truth has already been revealed specific to that context and simply requires exegesis according to a doctrinal intrasystemic logic, then it is hard to see how, if it is to be postmodern in the strong sense, theology can be anything other than sectarian.

Yet to argue that reality is language-ridden, inextricably interpreted and reinterpreted, is not the same as to claim that we cannot judge things about Christianity at all – that we just have to take each local variety as we find it. Christian theology cannot take any one facet or aspect of life in the world as being whole and adequate on its own terms for this denies the common thread, the christological metanarrative that interacts with and ultimately judges all our stories, that shows us that no one rendering of Christ is complete and undistorted. We are simply not Christian enough on our own. It *is* to say that Christianity constitutes a world, a reality, a self-defining comprehensiveness that we have to stand within to understand on its own terms, for to attempt to understand it from outside is to understand it on some other terms – which is to contain it within some other view of the world – and that the Gospel must therefore be critiqued on its own terms. There is nothing we can bring to bear in judgment upon revelation without making it subject to human judgment, which is a contradiction in terms. By definition, revelation is a brute fact. The Gospel interprets itself.[20] What post-modern thinking does for us here is to let Christianity be its own judge – to rule out of court all modernist attempts to make Christian beliefs and practices subject to a supposedly universal rationality, ethic or anthropology.

Clearly this inquiry will adopt the weak thesis on postmodernity and, as the title implies, this will be construed as a species of critical realism consistent with what will be argued to be the non-negotiably realist nature of Christianity. In the process it will become part of a theological realism that, in its ability to include the insights of postmodernity, will be arguably more comprehensively and coherently what it is.

20. H. Frei, *Theology and Narrative: Selected Essays*, ed. W. C. Placher and G. Hunsinger (Oxford: Oxford University Press, 1993), p. 40.

1

The task of theological realism

Realism makes the commonsense claim that physical objects exist independently of being perceived. 'On this perspective', comments Hilary Putnam, 'the world consists of some fixed totality of mind-independent objects. There is exactly one true and complete description of the way the world is. Truth involves some sort of correspondence relation between words or thought-signs and external things and sets of things.'[1]

The state of the art

In her essay 'Theological Realism' Janet Martin Soskice defines theological realists as 'those who, while aware of the inability of any theological formulation to catch the divine realities, none the less accept that there *are* divine realities that theologians, however ham-fistedly, are trying to catch'.[2] And Thomas Torrance observes rather more uncompromisingly that 'it belongs to the very essence of rational behaviour that we can distinguish ourselves as knowing subjects from the objects of our knowledge and distinguish our knowing from the content of our knowing. If we are unable to do that, something has gone wrong: our minds have somehow been "alienated" from reality.'[3] It is hard to argue with this imperative; suggesting how we might do this distinguishing is another matter. Torrance's view is that we can and must get past the deflecting,

---

1. H. Putnam, *Reason, Truth and History* p. 49.
2. J. M. Soskice, 'Theological Realism', in W. J. Abraham and S. W. Holtzer (eds.), *The Rationality of Religious Belief* (Oxford: Clarendon Press, 1987), pp. 105–19, 108.
3. T. F. Torrance, 'Theological Realism', in B. Hebblethwaite and S. Sutherland (eds.), *The Philosophical Frontiers of Christian Theology* (Cambridge: Cambridge University Press, 1982), pp. 169–96, 169.

distorting lenses of culture and language to 'grasp the deep structure of reality', a reality that has a structure independent of our cultural and linguistic structuring, a 'graspable' coherence independent of our various perspectives.[4]

While Soskice and Torrance both regard the relation of scientific or worldly truth to theological truth as a matter of analogy, they differ in the species of analogy posited. Soskice appears to favour a Thomist 'analogy of being' in which theologians using the metaphorical resources at hand must qualify any such use with a recognition of their qualitative remove from the reality they are attempting to 'depict'. This depiction is accordingly of a blurred and refracted divinity and must be continually revised and extended as our discoveries of the natural world extend the range of metaphors whose analogous use is enabled by grace.[5] Torrance, on the other hand, asserts a Barthian 'analogy of faith' in which our knowledge of empirical worldly reality is subsumed through revelation within a divinely determined meaning-structure, or intelligibility, so that we do not depict divine reality, rather divine reality depicts us. The radical contingence of worldly upon divine reality means, in effect, that all study of the former then constitutes the study of natural theology, a natural theology which can only be what it is in relation to the supernatural theology which reveals its ultimate meaning.

Where Soskice suggests that we cannot know whether what the theologians think and say about reality is really the way things are, Torrance accords our ability to 'grasp the deep structure of reality' the status of a necessary truth, for if we cannot do this, he asserts, then the whole basis of rationality is in jeopardy. The difference between the tentative pragmatism of Soskice and the unequivocality of Torrance is more than a difference in personality and theology; it exemplifies the difference between critical and postcritical realism. This is a difference which, while at heart a difference in analogies, also concerns the nature of rationality. Critical realism retains the direct-realist commonsense belief in independent physical things, but in the face of the verification problem inherent in correspondence theories of truth, admits that these are not directly and homogeneously presented to us in perceptual situations. It concedes to idealism that whenever something is perceived it is an object for a mind, but insists that it does not follow from this that a

---

4. See Torrance, *God and Rationality*, pp. 16–17; also *The Christian Doctrine of God*, p. 90, and *Reality and Scientific Theology*, pp. 26–7.
5. J. M. Soskice, *Metaphor and Religious Language* (Oxford: Clarendon Press, 1985), p. 152.

given 'something' has no existence except in its being perceived. Critical realism has taken note of the Kantian 'turn to the subject' from which we gain the insight that the world is necessarily the world under a certain description, while noting that although the world may be conceptually mediated, this does not mean that our concepts (or apperceptions) constitute reality.

Postcritical realism moves back a step from the tentative subject-riddenness of critical realism in maintaining that rationality is not a possession of the human intellect alone but is also present as an inherent intelligibility in the object which 'gives itself to be known'. Hence Torrance's insistence on a universal rationality; knowledge is not to be centred on the knowing subject. Instead we indwell that which we perceive and in so doing are absorbed into and participate in its reality. Knowledge and reality, therefore, are personal, but in a way that turns the tables on subjectivity in that the subject becomes recipient and channel of a transcendent rationality. Our images and concepts are tools of discovery rather than tools of creation, for they are true images and concepts only when they truly correlate with reality.[6]

For Torrance, contingent worldly rationality necessarily reveals and is revealed by transcendent divine rationality. This is the nature of the relation between the transcendence of Creator and the contingence of creation and is the given upon which the analogy of faith rests. We may be critical realists within this relation in recognition of the fact that our grasp of reality is incomplete, but only in the knowledge granted by faith that the inherent intelligibility of that reality will continue to revise and complete our graspings. On a Torrancean view, therefore, there can be no distinction between 'ordinary' or worldly realism and theological realism. They must be one and the same. As mentioned, the radical contingence of worldly upon divine reality means, in effect, that all study of the former including the study of its rationality according to philosophical theories of truth constitutes the study of natural theology within the framework of revealed theology.

Torrance employs a theory of Michael Polanyi's in working out the nature of this theological realism. On a Polanyian model of perception, we displace meaning away from ourselves in a bipolar semantic relation. This displacement renders the mediating sign transparent.[7] For 'when

---

6. Torrance, *Reality and Scientific Theology*, p. 27.
7. See T. F. Torrance, *Theological Science* (Oxford: Oxford University Press, 1969) and M. Polanyi, *The Tacit Dimension* (London: Routledge, 1966). But see S. W. Need, *Human*

we adopt something, sensible or intelligible, as a sign for something else our attention does not rest upon the sign but on what it indicates or points to: it is, so to speak, a transparent medium through which we operate. That is to say, the natural orientation of the human mind is, in this sense at least, quite "realist".'[8] Accordingly, a sign, if it is to do its job properly, must be to some extent arbitrary, detached from the signified, incomplete or discrepant, or it will be confused with the thing it is supposed to be representing. On the other hand, a complete arbitrariness in which the sign has 'no natural bearing on the reality for which it is said to stand' renders it 'semantically useless'.[9] In other words, it is necessary to be able to distinguish between sign and signified, but not to the extent that the connection is purely arbitrary (except presumably in the case of catachrestic first-uses). A middle way must be trodden between nominalism and the idealist consequence of the total substitution of concept for object, which is the logical conclusion of correspondence.[10] That we take the sign as transparent is a necessary part of our making sense of the world. That it is *not* transparent – that it is contaminated by its previous uses so that the map gets mixed up with the world – is a fact of the inseparability of the world as it is to us from its accretion of interacting descriptions. Torrance concedes the context-and-language-boundedness of the situations in which sign and signified occur:

> while what we know and how we know, subject-matter and method, cannot be finally separated from one another, no true knowledge can be explained by beginning from the knower himself. We do not really know anything unless we can distinguish in some measure how our knowing is determined by the nature of what we know, as we are all conditioned by the activity of the knowing subject. On the other hand, it is also evident that we cannot think of, speak of what we know cut off from our knowing of it. In some sense, therefore, our knowing of a thing constitutes an ingredient in our knowledge of it, or at least in the articulation of our knowledge of it. The recognition of this fact can have the salutary effect of preventing us from making inordinate claims about the objectivity of our knowledge, but it also helps to remind us that what we know has a reality apart from our knowing of it.[11]

Language and Knowledge in the Light of Chalcedon (New York: Peter Lang Publishing, 1996) for a different interpretation of Polanyian epistemology to be examined in chapter 5.
8. Torrance, 'Theological Realism', p. 169.   9. Ibid., p. 171.
10. Ibid., p. 172. Torrance observes that if such an idealism leans towards objective reality it can become a form of realism.   11. Torrance, *Reality and Scientific Theology*, p. 1.

It is in a particular context of language use that the sign appears transparent. Critical realists towards the postmodern end of the realist spectrum, such as Putnam, would maintain that what something means, or what a term represents, depends in large part on the context in which it occurs. It may even be said, as Torrance says, that the separation of object and interpreting subject and the impression given of language's 'transparency' between the two are themselves concepts which find their home in the modern Western philosophical tradition.[12] We are immersed in a rationality that is transparent to us but is nevertheless a particular form of rationality.[13] The point to be made is that the whole discussion of sign and signified and their necessary distinctness is not somehow universally objective and value free, but takes place within a situation in which all the time we are referring to *this-thing-plus-its-previous-description-in-this*-context. As noted, Torrance does not deny this yet frequently states his belief that we can, through patient and rigorous successive revisions, eliminate the preconceptions, illusions and linguistic habits that obscure our knowledge of reality and thereby progressively 'grasp' things as they are in themselves.

> The conception of inherent intelligibility means that, whether we are concerned with things visible or invisible, knowledge is to be attained only as we are able to penetrate into the inner connections and reasons of things in virtue of which they are what they are, that is, into their ontic structures and necessities. Only as we let our minds fall under the power of those structures and necessities to signify what they are in themselves do we think of them truly, that is, in accordance with what they really are in their natures and must be in our conceiving of them. On the other hand, the inner relation between *logos* and being, or the concept of the truth of being, does not reduce to a vanishing point the place or function of the human knower, but on the contrary provides the ground upon which the inseparable relation of knower and known in human understanding can be upheld. This was already made clear by St Augustine.[14]

On this understanding the concept may be part of the thing ('the inner relation between *logos* and being'), but only to the extent that it is not overreached and pulled out of shape by human hubris. For 'as the history of thought has shown again and again in later eras, no sooner has full

12. Ibid., pp. 15–19.   13. Putnam, *Reason, Truth and History*, p. 203.
14. Torrance, *Reality and Scientific Theology*, pp. 7–8. Augustine, *De Trinitate*, 9.12.18: *ab utroque enim notitia paritur a cognoscente et cognito*.

place been accorded to the agency of the human subject in knowledge than it tends to arrogate to itself far more than its share'.[15]

Torrance is convinced that 'the universe as we know it is one in which being and knowing are mutually related and conditioned, intelligible reality and intelligent inquiry belong together'. Nevertheless he poses a dichotomy. As he puts it,

> the great question still confronts us. Granted that the universe as we know it constitutes an intelligible whole, and granted that the universe exists, as we say, not only *in intellectu* but also *in re,* is the universe comprehensible to us because somehow it is *intrinsically* intelligible, because it is endowed with an immanent rationality quite independent of us which is the ground of its comprehensibility to us, or is the intelligibility with which the universe is clothed in our knowledge of it something *extrinsic* to it, which we construct out of our own mental operations and impose upon the being of the universe?[16]

He concludes that we should be guided by the 'most persistent answer to that question throughout the centuries', that 'our mental operations are steadily coordinated' with '"natural" patterns and stuctures in the universe which are what they are independent of us'.[17] The true concept is not something constructed by us but rather discovered as the noetic component of the thing that makes its inherent intelligibility accessible to us. Human construction is not a part of the deal; true conceptions of reality are discovered, not invented.

Torrance's analysis seems limited by its relegation of the human role to passivity and consequent insistence on a dichotomy between construction and discovery. Must true concepts come to our merely receptive minds from an intrinsically intelligible reality so that, while images and concepts arise in our understanding in coordination with our experience, 'there *shows through* an objective rationality which is independent of our forms of thought and speech'? It seems that only to the extent that we are able to distinguish the content from its linguistic vehicle do 'we have a firm base from which to put our forms of thought and speech to the test, to see how far they are actually coordinated with the realities which they claim to indicate and so provide an intelligible medium in which our minds come under the compulsion of those realities and take shape under their ontic necessity and intrinsic intelligibility'.[18] However, to talk of content and vehicle is to imply that our knowledge is divisible into

15. Ibid.   16. Ibid., p. 2.   17. Ibid., p. 3.   18. Ibid., pp. 27–8.

parts that we are then able to identify as factual and conventional.[19] How are we to do this by the light of naked reason, that is, without recourse to a God's-eye view? As Richard Rorty puts it,

> we can always enlarge the scope of 'us' by regarding other people, or cultures, as members of the same community of inquiry as ourselves – by treating them as part of the group among whom unforced agreement is to be sought. What we cannot do is to rise above all human communities, actual and possible. We cannot find a skyhook which lifts us out of mere coherence – mere agreement – to something like 'correspondence with reality as it is in itself'.[20]

It seems that a 'skyhook' is precisely what theological realism requires, yet how is it to be found when, as Torrance argues, the conventional agreements that underlie our systems of thought far from being creative agents may merely muddy our perception of reality? To be consistent with the classical Christianity expressed in patristic theology is to maintain that knowledge, while admittedly linguistic in character, is creative only in creating the linguistic vehicles, the images and concepts, through which we are able to grasp in its depth the intrinsic intelligibility of the reality beyond language. Yet if the world is inherently rational as patristic thinking suggests, and if this world as inherently rational includes human rationality, then why is there any need to pose this dichotomy? Perhaps we may keep the premise but alter the conclusion.

If it is 'to patristic thought that we owe the conception of an ontology in which structure and movement, the noetic and the dynamic, are integrated in the real world', then why not include human rationality, as expressed in the active conceptual patterning, structuring of the world, *in* the world's inherent rationality, *in* this 'ontology in which structure and movement, the noetic and the dynamic, are integrated in the real world'? This interpretation would seem equally consistent with the patristic insight into 'the profound integration of *logos* and being which it discerned, in a transcendent way, in the living and active God, and in a creaturely and contingent way in created reality'.[21]

As Paul Ricoeur has said of metaphor, what it creates it discovers and what it discovers it invents.[22] If we are to 'penetrate into the inner

19. H. Putnam, *Realism and Reason* (Cambridge: Cambridge University Press, 1983), p. 178.
20. R. Rorty, *Objectivism, Relativism and Truth. Philosophical Papers*, vol. 1 (Cambridge: Cambridge University Press, 1991), p. 38.
21. Torrance, *Reality and Scientific Theology*, pp. 6–7. Again, see Need, *Human Language and Knowledge*, for an argument that supports this interpretation.
22. P. Ricoeur, *The Rule of Metaphor*, trans. Robert Czerny (London: Routledge, 1978), p. 124.

connections and reasons of things in virtue of which they are what they are', this 'penetrating into' will necessarily involve describing and conceiving, as Torrance would agree. However, it may also involve not only 'minds falling under the power of these structures and necessities to signify what they are in themselves' but also minds supplying the noetic component to 'things in virtue of which they are what they are'. For why is it necessary to state that the rationality of the universe is a function of '"natural" patterns and structures in the universe which are what they are independent of us but with which our mental operations are steadily coordinated'?[23] Can it not be that it is as human knowledge participates in that knowledge that it is completed and fulfilled?[24] Putnam would say that things cannot be this way for Torrance simply because the realist definition of world excludes it (Putnam does not classify himself as a realist in the usual sense), for under this definition 'the world is . . . being claimed to contain Self-Identifying Objects, for this is just what it means to say the world, and not thinkers, sorts things into kinds'. [25]

Non-dualistic alternatives

The danger of separating construction from discovery is that in doing so we discount the inevitable local human linguistic input into what we then take to be a universal rationality. As Stephen Toulmin suggests, this mistake tends to further the assumption that a generic rationality (on which science is constructed) which claims to be independent of any metaphysical or theological baggage may apply in any context and determine the rationality of any arguments. What this means is that we think we can infer from our own situation to all others and be 'objectively correct'.[26] Yet, we subsist in a goldfish-bowl in which we already assume reasonableness in deciding what is reasonable! [27] At best, we access a universal component to rationality through various local components that constitute our template for understanding what is rational in the first place, and are therefore inextricable from what they access. What constitutes a fact about reality always depends to some extent on the community of knowledge and belief from which one is operating. An

---

23. Torrance, *Reality and Scientific Theology*, p. 3.
24. This may also be consistent with how Torrance reads Origen (see ibid., p. 5) and is also consistent with Need's reading of Polanyi in relation to patristic thought (see Need, *Human Language and Knowledge*).   25. Putnam, *Reason, Truth and History*, pp. 53–4.
26. S. Toulmin, *Cosmopolis: The Hidden Agenda of Modernity* (Chicago: University of Chicago Press, 1990), p. 21.   27. Putnam, *Realism and Reason*, p. 234.

object's inherent intelligibility is all mixed up with commitment to that communal reality-description, so that conventional considerations play a part in what we take to be facts, a point not missed by Soskice, who proposes a pragmatic variety of critical realism.

Soskice addresses the problem of how metaphorical terms can be claimed to be descriptive or fact-stating when they cannot be known to be: 'To meet instrumentalism, the realist must attempt to say how religious language can claim to be *about* God at all, given that naive realism in these matters is unthinkable.'[28] Soskice goes on to suggest that this may be done through an account of how metaphor functions in religious language. While her concern is with God-language, the question is equally relevant to terms about the world-at-hand. How do we know that a fact is indeed a fact? In other words, the problem concerns realism itself. Our inability to verify that our facts are indeed facts means that the entity to which the term refers does not have to be world-transcending in order to be inaccessible to 'definitive knowledge'.[29] Suggesting that the problem is one that scientific and theological realism have in common, Soskice advocates a move away from definite descriptions towards a more pragmatic solution along Saul Kripke's lines.

> [Kripke] argues that reference can take place independently of the possession of a definite description which somehow 'qualitatively uniquely' picks out the individual in question and can even be successful where the identifying description associated with the name fails to be true of the individual in question . . . the relevant linguistic competence does not involve unequivocal knowledge but rather depends on the fact that the speaker is a member of a linguistic community who have passed the name [e.g. Columbus] from link to link, going back to the man, Columbus, himself.[30]

In other words, accuracy, or certified truth, is not a necessary condition of reference. Rather, *reliability* is. 'The point here is that reference depends, in normal speech, as much on context as on content and that reference is an utterance-dependent notion.'[31] Kripke and Putnam argue further (although, as Soskice points out, not uncontroversially) that reference may be fixed by 'dubbing' in the case of natural-kind terms. In this pragmatic theory what matters is that the reference be

---

28. Soskice, 'Theological Realism', p. 109.   29. Ibid., p. 111.
30. Ibid., citing S. Kripke, 'Naming and Necessity', in D. Davidson and G. Harman (eds.), *Semantics of Natural Language* (Dortrecht: D. Reidel, 1972), pp. 295, 301.   31. Ibid., p. 112.

successful, that it achieve its purpose of identification. Here the suggestion is that correctness is not so important as reliability, consistency or continuity with how a reference has been made in and by a community – or rather that correctness is a function of reliability.

> The realism under discussion emphasizes rather than conceals contextuality by emphasizing that descriptive language, while dealing with immediate experience, will be language embedded in certain traditions of investigation and conviction . . . The descriptive language . . . is forged in a particular tradition of investigation and a context of agreement on what constitutes evidence and what is a genuine argument. While theories may be reality-depicting they are not free from contextuality, both historical and cultural.[32]

Therefore a fact is what its societal context says it is, or lays down, even to the extent of laying down what is to constitute a fact in addition to the content of facts. That is, logic as well as observation and description may vary with context, as Wittgenstein observed.

One may be accordingly agnostic about whether one's models describe reality and pragmatically point to the success of science or social institutions as proof that they must do so to some extent. But is reliability as measured by success able to function as a sufficient as well as a necessary condition of truth in this situation, or does it still need to be supplemented by some correspondence measure of truth? And if so, how is this to be done? Arguably, the problem with the realist insistence on separating language and world does not lie in our belief in the existence of a physical world or in our ability to predict what goes on there, but in the very idea of the 'thing as it is in itself' independently of our knowledge of it. With this premise securely anchored in our thinking, we take things designated and described by us in their 'thingness' to enjoy an existence apart from the concepts we have of them and the terms we employ to express those concepts – an existence that somehow, at least to some extent, corresponds to those terms and those concepts. The objection is then raised to the guaranteed knowability of the thing 'as it is in itself' apart from that specification.[33]

Therein lies the difficulty with the notion of correspondence as traditionally employed at least. It proves impossible to 'get behind' the linguistic mirror to check on how its image reflects the non-linguistic

---

32. Ibid., p. 114.
33. H. Putnam, *Mind, Language and Reality* (Cambridge: Cambridge University Press, 1975), p. 5. This is not to discount the distorting and false aspects of description. Obviously illusions and deception are factors to be taken into account. See chapters 6 and 7.

reality because the very getting-behind is itself conceptually framed and hence not a real getting-behind at all.

> What is wrong with the notion of objects existing 'independently' of conceptual schemes is that there are no standards for the use of even the logical notions apart from conceptual choices . . . To talk of 'facts' without specifying the language to be used is to talk of nothing; the word 'fact' no more has its use fixed by Reality Itself than does the word 'exist' or the word 'object' . . . Internal realism says that the notion of a 'thing in itself' makes no sense; and *not* because 'we cannot know the things in themselves'. This was Kant's reason, but Kant, although admitting that the notion of a thing in itself *might* be empty, still allowed it to possess a formal kind of sense. Internal realism says that we don't know what we are talking about when we talk about 'things in themselves'. And that means that the dichotomy between 'intrinsic' properties and properties which are not intrinsic also collapses – collapses because the 'intrinsic' properties were supposed to be just the properties things have 'in themselves'. The thing in itself and the property the thing has 'in itself' belong to the same circle of ideas, and it is time to admit that what the circle encloses is worthless territory.[34]

What this means is that once the premise of 'in-itself-ness' has been taken on board (and we have all taken it on board with the infrastructure of modernity), the difficulties with realism cannot be solved by agnosticism as to the extent of correspondence because it is obvious that any claim of partial correspondence is equally unjustifiable. While it seems reasonable to conclude so, we do not *know* that our concepts *in part* correspond to reality. (Which parts correspond?)

Yet total agnosticism is not only pointless; it is also Christianly unacceptable, for how can truth *not* be a consideration in Christian theology? We need to ask along with Putnam: '*can* one be any sort of a realist without the dichotomies?'[35] For if realism must always founder on the premise of correspondence, or perhaps more broadly on its implicit theory of language, perhaps we should conclude that realism has had its day and that we should agree with Derrida that everything, including Christianity, must be considered 'under erasure', afloat on a sea of linguistic relativity.

Realists of a pragmatic inclination, however, do not see this as reason

---

34. H. Putnam, *The Many Faces of Realism* (La Salle, IL: Open Court, 1987), pp. 35–6.
35. Ibid., p. 30.

to lose hope. Nancey Murphy suggests that theology needs to do more than use the failure of belief in objectivity in science post-Hanson and Heisenberg as a *tu quoque* argument to bring science down to its own less-than-objective level. Murphy also advocates the Kripkean/ Putnamian pragmatic notion of reliability as a measure of Christian truth in proposing discernment as a *replicable* (communal) way of seeking 'data' in Scripture and experience and establishing new facts in theology.[36] Reliability, of course, is a matter of degree, probabilistic and relativistic. In theology it takes the form of the reliability of Christian tradition and communal judgment as to what constitutes true Christianity. Murphy maintains that the use of Scripture as 'data' for theology must be governed by such replicable, hence reliable, judgments governed by fact-establishing auxiliary hypotheses.

Bruce Marshall proposes a theory of 'world-absorbing', or assimilative, capacity as a measure of Christianity's efficacy or worth as another pragmatic option.[37] But, as Marshall himself recognizes, this basis of comparison is akin to subjecting theology to an external coherence-comprehensiveness theory of truth, for on this basis it is always coherence relative to something else. Does Christianity provide a better way of living and explanation of human reality than, say, Zen Buddhism or Dialectical Materialism? How can this be judged, asks Marshall, except on pragmatic grounds? Yet how, then, can we be sure that certain fruits are good and others not so – what is the criterion of goodness? And if judged to offer better fruits by some humanly derived criterion, does this make Christianity more attuned to ultimate reality? When it all boils down, world-absorbing capacity simply amounts to another version of reliabilism and we are no better off than before, for of course these questions cannot be answered without having recourse to the internal criteria which define this ultimate reality. On these grounds Marshall adjudges 'assimilative power' to be a necessary but insufficient condition and suggests that it needs to be used in conjunction with a realist propositional model, such as Jesus as *veritas Patri*, to provide the baseline of Christian reality.

Torrance sees the adoption of a pragmatic theory of truth 'as an attempt to break out of . . . the oscillating dialectic between coherence

---

36. N. Murphy, *Theology in the Age of Scientific Reasoning* (Ithaca, NY: Cornell University Press, 1990), pp. 165–6.
37. B. D. Marshall, 'Absorbing the World: Christianity and the Universe of Truths', in B. D. Marshall (ed.), *Theology and Dialogue: Essays in Conversation with George Lindbeck* (Notre Dame, IN: University of Notre Dame Press, 1990), pp. 69ff., 85.

and correspondence' yielded by dualist modern thought, but considers that this pragmatic 'solution' only substitutes a form of operationalism for truth. It must be conceded that this is so. Pragmatism will not stand alone. The question is where to go from here. A way out may be suggested by the evidence that propositional truth is older than the modern dualist theories of correspondence. As Putnam observes, medieval thinking had no difficulty with realism because it held that human beings were created with a special capacity for 'rational intuition' of the nature of things in themselves.[38] Torrance inclines to this way of thinking:

> Now of course we do not proceed in this way unless we could have some initial glimpse, and some initial grasp, however tenuous, of reality, and unless reality were comprehensible in itself apart from our perceiving or knowing of it, that is, unless it had its own intrinsic relations and structure, for it is only as we are able to hook our thought on to those that we can advance in our inquiry or climb up into fuller knowledge of the reality under investigation. In so doing we presume that a correlation is possible between our human conceiving and the inner structure of reality itself, and we carry out all our operations in that belief. However, that very presumption makes us direct our critical questioning back upon ourselves to make sure that we are not moulding reality in terms of our own constructions or imposing artificial structures of our own upon it.[39]

Torrance talks of the way 'the inner relation between *logos* and being, or the concept of the truth of being, does not reduce to a vanishing point the place or function of the human knower, but on the contrary provides the ground upon which the inseparable relation of knower and known in human understanding can be upheld'.[40] Yet he also refers to the subjective element in knowledge as 'the conceptual lens through which we apprehend the rationality inherent in nature or through which the rationality in nature discloses itself to us'.[41] In other words, while he proposes an intimate interplay of subjectivities, it is nevertheless the 'inner' or 'deep' structure of the object that is the source of our conceptions of it as the sole source of its own intelligibility. It plays its tune on our linguistic keys, but the tune is its own. If our keyboard is out of tune (or if we are bad performers) we will distort reality's melody. A less lyrical analogy is the premodern view of procreation in which the male is the

---

38. Putnam, *The Many Faces of Realism*, p. 52.
39. Torrance, *Reality and Scientific Theology*, p. 27.   40. Ibid., p. 8.   41. Ibid., p. 183.

sole producer of the seed of new life and the female merely the receptacle. Both of these analogies enjoy some affinity with Torrance's own images.

> Properly regarded and pursued, scientific activity is not a tormenting of nature but rather the way in which nature pregnant with new forms of being comes to be in travail and to give birth to structured realities out of itself. Man is here the midwife, as it were, and yet rather more than that, for his own rational nature is profoundly geared into the intrinsic rationalities of nature in such a way that he is the appointed instrument under God through which the intelligible universe reveals itself and unfolds out of its crysalis, so to speak, in rational, orderly and beautiful patterns of being. Hence there is disclosed through scientific activity and intelligibility in the created universe beyond man's artifice and control, something absolutely given and transcendent, to which as man he is and must be rationally and responsibly open. That openness and responsibility are part of his human nature as rational agent. Man acts rationally only under the compulsion of reality and its intrinsic order, but it is man's function to bring nature to word, to articulate its dumb rationality in all its latent wonder and beauty and thus to lead the creation in its praise and glorification of God the Creator.[42]

Yet, are human beings in their creativity not directly (if also enablingly) part of 'the way in which nature pregnant with new forms of being comes to be in travail and to give birth to structured realities out of itself'? And as midwives-cum-piano-players, how do we know whether our piano is in tune or not – or, even if we have perfect pitch, whether it is not playing itself, pianola-style, at least some of the time? Even if our 'own rational nature *is* profoundly geared into the intrinsic rationalities of nature in such a way that [we are] the appointed instrument under God through which the intelligible universe reveals itself', what Torrance still appears to be proposing is that human concept-vehicles progressively, if partially and revisably, 'grasp' a non-linguistic reality 'in its depths' – which amounts to shifting the correspondence verification back a step. For if the ultimate incoherence of an ordinary correspondence theory of truth is to be avoided, we must anchor our partial and distorted human grasp of reality to 'an Archimedian point beyond it by which it can be steadily levered out of its own self-incarceration, and . . .

---

42. Ibid., pp. 68–9.

coordinated with the openness of all created being to the unlimited reality of God'.[43]

> What we need is such a shift in the focus of our vision that, instead of looking at the universe in the flat, as it were, we look at it in a multidimensional way in which the universe as a whole, and everything within it, are found to have meaning through an immanent intelligibility that ranges far beyond the universe to an ultimate ground in the transcendent and uncreated Rationality of God.[44]

It follows then that Jesus Christ as God's *logos*, or intelligibility, subsumes the self-disclosure of the object's deep inner coherence, so that 'objectivity' as reality-given is only so as specifically God-given. Yet then may not the *logos* as the meeting place of divine transcendence and human contingence subsume a creaturely reality of which its description knowledge is an integral part? Arguably, this is quite consistent with the patristic line that Torrance is taking. And, to pick up the procreation analogy again, this is akin to what all but possibly extreme biblical fundamentalists living an entirely premodern existence in isolation from the rest of the world have allowed modern science to put in place of the premodern theory: that the procreative function is both male and female, yet as such is still a function of the creativity of God. This issue will be returned to in later chapters.

The theistic-realist option

In the light of the preceding discussion, it is unclear how it can make sense to say that any object is able to be accessible to us 'as it is in itself' and therefore represent in itself an 'ultimate judge of the truth or falsity of our conceptions and statements about it', or how 'in the last resort scientific theories are justified by the grace of reality alone'.[45] Putnam contends that correspondence between words and objects is something that goes on within a particular conception of reality, that objects 'do not exist independently of conceptual schemes. We cut up the world into objects when we introduce one or another scheme of description. Since the objects *and* the signs are alike *internal* to the scheme of description, it is possible to say what matches what.'[46] Yet we can take an 'internal-realist' line without this being inconsistent with a revealed model in

---

43. Ibid., p. 23.   44. Ibid., p. 44.   45. See Torrance, 'Theological Realism', p. 172.
46. Putnam, *Reason, Truth and History*, p. 52.

which God is the source of all the human 'schemes of description' within which such propositions as 'objectivity' and 'correspondence' have their play. Torrance appears to be suggesting something similar when he states that

> we cannot have any knowledge of God or even faith without a conceptual relation to him ... There is no conceptual gap between God's revealing of himself and our knowing of him, for God reveals himself to us on the ground of his own inner intelligibility which is the creative ground of all rationality in the universe and as such enables us to conceive and speak of him truly in ways that are ultimately grounded in God's supreme being.[47]

As Putnam points out, we may not be able to operate from an eye-of-God perspective because we are bound up in language and context; nevertheless, 'the rightness and wrongness of what we say is not *just* for a time and a place'.[48]

Michael Dummett and Fergus Kerr have suggested that realism's coherence might be salvaged by claiming a verification transcendent of human possibility.[49] If some notion of correspondence stubbornly lingers on in realism and is seen to be immanent in local forms of human thought and practice then, logically, any correlation of these correspondences with a transcendent reality cannot be verified within those local forms themselves. Accordingly, because 'one cannot talk about the transcendent or even deny its existence without paradox, one's attitude to it must, perhaps, be the concern of religion rather than of rational philosophy'.[50] We cannot avoid correspondence in the realism required by Christianity, but it is not the correspondence we thought it was. We are talking, rather, of a correspondence between God's world-under-God's-description and a regenerated, redeemed world-under-human-description. The name and the means of the correspondence is incarnation, where this is taken to embrace the whole of human history and rationality, including its eschatological judgment and fulfilment.[51] Its method of verification is revelation.

Consistent with this position, Torrance notes that '*contingent* creaturely

---

47. Torrance, 'Theological Realism', pp. 177–8.   48. Putnam, *Realism and Reason*, p. 247.
49. See Kerr, *Theology After Wittgenstein*, and M. Dummett, *Truth and Other Enigmas* (London: Duckworth, 1978). Also see chapter 5 for an extended discussion of this.
50. Putnam, *Realism and Reason*, p. 226.
51. As Torrance puts it, it is 'the incarnation of God himself in Jesus Christ which constitutes the dynamic centre from which the whole pattern and history of created reality is to be discerned': cf. T. F. Torrance, *Divine and Contingent Order* (Oxford: Oxford University Press, 1981), p. 68.

being and *intelligibility* require a sufficient ground and reason beyond themselves in order to be what they actually are'.[52]

> Contingent being cannot explain itself, otherwise it should not be contingent. Nevertheless it does have something to 'say' to us, simply by being what it is, contingent *and* intelligible in its contingency, for that makes its lack of self-explanation inescapably problematic, and it is precisely through that problematic character that it points beyond itself with a mute cry for sufficient reason. What the intelligible being of the universe has to 'say' is thus something which by its very nature must break off in accordance with the utterly contingent existence of the universe. This may be expressed more positively: the fact that the universe is intrinsically rational means that it is capable of, or open to, rational explanation – from beyond itself.[53]

In this, as suggested earlier, the world's inherent rationality (which is grounded in Christ) must include human rationality, for if not, another dualism is being proposed. If the universe is inherently intelligible, then humanity is a part of that intelligibility. As Torrance puts it, 'Since the universe includes man, it includes his knowing of it within the full process of its reality', so that the universe 'is the cosmos of created being in which the relation between knowing and being falls within being. Thus the knowing of being is to be acknowledged as an operation of being itself, for it is through being known that the structure of the universe manifests itself.'[54]

As suggested, while Torrance restricts human involvement to the role of cosmic knower, interpreter and communicative vehicle, at the same time his endorsement of the patristic integration of knowing and being opens the way to a human role in creation. If knowing (and therefore conceiving) is a part of being, then knowledge not only discovers but also in part constitutes reality.[55] This seems inescapable logic. As Rorty puts it, while the notion of things 'as they are in themselves' and the distinction between 'as they are' and 'as we describe them' are both vacuous, nevertheless it is not 'mirrors all the way down', for there are 'objects which are *causally* independent of human beliefs and desires'.[56] Yet the theological-realist disinclination to engage with some of the implications of this logic of human involvement seems to stem from the conviction that these are quite antithetical to a theistic realism. This is not

---

52. Torrance, *Reality and Scientific Theology*, p. 44.   53. Ibid., p. 52.   54. Ibid., p. 2.
55. See Need, *Human Language and Knowledge*, pp. 185ff.
56. Rorty, *Objectivism, Relativism and Truth*, p. 101.

necessarily so. Theological realists such as Torrance retain a correspondence view (even if it is described as 'correlation' or 'coordination') because it is inherent to realism and because, accordingly, they cannot see how an adequate theory of truth can be worked any other way. And yes, correspondence to and verification by an external reality are inherent in realism, but not according to *our* lights, and not, as shall be argued, in a way that relies on a fundamental dichotomy between linguistic and non-linguistic reality.

Critical realists have opted for a partial correspondence in recognition of the inevitable contamination by prior concepts any description of reality represents. Critical realism's strength is that it incorporates aspects of both modernity and postmodernity. It is a strength that is expressed in its being still concerned with truth while grasping the nettle of reality's 'language-riddenness'. It loses this painful grip the moment it either adopts a postmodern nihilism or sidesteps the issue of language. Yet it also loses coherence if it does not seek a revelatory (incarnational) solution to and grounding of correspondence.[57] While such a revelatory verification of correspondence must ultimately be humanly external (although at the same time incarnationally internal) in being grounded in God, it may be humanly internal within that ultimacy which is its final judge. Correspondence does not have to be 'windows all the way down'. It is arguably possible for a 'by their fruits ye shall know them' reliabilism coupled with a 'things are what we agree they are' conventionalism (if not a 'things are what we make them' constructivism) to set the local correspondence terms that underpin our propositional truths subject to a 'higher' ultimate correspondence to which all these systems must answer. It may be consistent with this theistic realism to maintain that our intuitions as to the nature and shape of reality in so far as they are correct are recognized as participatory in a divine creativity transcendent yet inclusive of our own. In later chapters this line of argument will be pushed further.

It follows that there is no need for a realist theology to ignore the evidence that revelation takes place in a context- and language-ridden world; that knowledge and rationality are all caught up with the way language is used in various contexts; that consequently meaning and

---

57. This is consistent with Torrance's argument that 'incarnation as a whole provides . . . the intersectioned vertical dimension which gives the horizontal coordinates of the universe the integrative factor providing them with consistent and ultimate meaning': see *Divine and Contingent Order*, pp. 24–5.

logic may vary with context; that the theory-ladenness of observation does not pursue linear paths but makes holistic leaps in various directions. There are many theories, stories and language-games outside the rules of scientific practice and discourse so that, whereas in science one theory may be replaced by another in a given field because it is more comprehensive, more coherent and not yet falsified (although here there are also holistic leaps in which a whole paradigm replaces another),[58] this orderly linear progression is not necessarily typical of theories and observation in the world at large.

Daniel Hardy suggests that both the sciences and Christianity

> are now being judged for their adequacy by reference to a new situation. While presented as in many respects utterly new, the new situation combines many of the features of the scene which has been emerging for the past two hundred years. What is this new 'postmodern' situation? It defies generalization, and in actuality resists any synthetic picture. But even at the risk of generalizing, it is above all a picture of plenitude, consisting of an endless complexity and dynamism of meaning at every level. Imagine any connection that appears in the history of knowledge, and then imagine that connection being seen as a complexity of interrelations; the picture thus obtained would not be inappropriate. Hence, so-called 'correspondence' notions of knowledge and rational agency, in which a simple one-to-one relation is drawn between words or concepts and realities, are vastly oversimple; all such relations are multiple and complex. The same argument affects all supposed affinities, emphasizing their 'difference', 'deconstructing' the simplicities on which they are founded. The consequence is that all that gives a solid foundation for knowledge and rationality, particularly the 'onto-theology' of the Western tradition, and its 'logocentrism', are dissolved. And with them go conventional notions of knowledge and rationality.

A further indication of the immensity of the changes implicit in these suggestions can be given by referring to a problem in topology. If one cuts a hole in the inner tube of a bicycle tire where the valve is and begins to put the rest of the tube through the hole, what happens? The issue with modern understanding – though hardly appreciated yet – is that one can repeat the exercise at an infinite number of points on the tube, drawing the tube through *after* it has been drawn through at an infinite number of other points. That is a

---

58. See T. S. Kuhn, *The Structure of Scientific Revolutions*, 2nd edn. (Chicago: University of Chicago Press, 1970).

> fascinating prospect, not only a testimony to the amazing creativity of human understanding but an indication of the possibility of an endlessly multiplying complexity in knowledge. If such major endeavours as those which have to do with the factors of materiality ... provide more and more holes through which other endeavours – and even their own – can be drawn, then knowledge becomes fuller and fuller, with no limit in sight. It is, as we said, an indefinite plenitude.[59]

As Hardy comments, the things that self-destruct in Christianity under this postmodern analysis 'are in fact not the Christian tradition at all but the product of various kinds of rationalism imposed on Christian faith ... Christian faith at least has the means by which to rediscover the possibility of knowledge and rationality in the new situation.'[60] The general theory is the enemy, not only of a coherent realism, but of Christianity as well. Realist insistence that postmodern theologies come up with general theories of language and truth is done in ignorance of realism's own problem with general theories – in particular the general version of the correspondence theory of truth – and in ignorance of general theories' subjection of the particularity of Christianity to an illusory universal. Accordingly, the only *general* theory Christianity should adopt, and then adopt in terms of its own particularity, is its own fundamental claim of the ultimacy and universality of God's reality and truth. In the service of this theory and not dictating to it, what is needed is a *theistic-realist* (and therefore incarnational) theory of both language and truth that takes account of the 'plenitude' and 'plurality' of human reality.

Conclusion

Christian theology's internal logic is such that it is required to be realist, in that its self-consistency requires the upholding of certain central truth claims. However, while on a realist view physical reality has an existence independent of our cultural and linguistic structuring, this view must reckon with the postmodern insight that language (and the language-user) has for good or for bad the power to construct a reality which is also an integral component of the universe, and that both

---

59. D. W. Hardy, 'Rationality, the Sciences and Theology', in G. Wainwright (ed.), *Keeping the Faith* (Philadelphia: Fortress Press/Pickwick Publications, 1988), pp. 274–309, 304–5.
60. Ibid., p. 305.

construction *and* discovery are not only inevitable and inherent in human linguisticality, but also inevitably partial, flawed, perverse and idolatrous. As the coherence of reality is arguably dependent in part on its human linguistic component, we do more than reach through our images and concepts to grasp worldly reality; we also arguably help to shape that reality with our descriptions, for all that they are partial and distorted. Yet apart from these shortcomings in description – description, moreover, which is inextricably mixed up with that which it describes – reality eludes us. For who but God is able to comprehend the whole?

This requires the correspondence element inherent in realism, however critical or postcritical, to seek a theistic resolution if it is to make any claim to coherence. The world under human description seeks verification and redemption in terms of the world under God's description, that is, in the person of Jesus Christ who is the incarnate meeting place of divine and creaturely reality. While the strength of critical realism, is its emphasis on the ongoing partiality and revisability of our knowledge, postcritical realism also offers a personal as well as dynamic understanding of reality that is particularly compatible with a theistic realism, as will be explored further later. While the complexity and thoroughness of Torrance's thinking on this subject and the related one of rationality have only been touched on here, Kerr's programmatic suggestions for a Wittgensteinian theistic realism have also been behind this chapter and remain to be examined later.

The challenge facing this inquiry is that of retaining a critical/postcritical framework for theology while finding room within such a framework for a theology that is comprehensive enough to serve a Christian reality that necessarily subsumes all of created reality, material and otherwise, including the constructivist element in human language and thought which has kept surfacing in this discussion but which is seemingly ruled out by a correspondence model, even (or especially) a theistic one. How is such a theological realism able to take account of a continuing linguistic contribution to worldly reality? Chapters 2 and 3 deal with the postliberal and liberal revisionist contributions to this search.

2

The dilemma of postliberal theology

In the last chapter it was suggested that an internal-realist model of a Putnamian kind may find a place within a theistic realism. The question was raised at the end of the chapter whether such a model could accommodate a postmodern linguistic element within the theistic framework.

The postliberal proposal

In attempting to follow the perilous path of postmodernity without leading Christian theology into the wilderness, postliberal theology[1] has faced the challenge of reconciling a biblical theology with a world in which all human reality comes historically and contextually shaped and human beings are constituted as persons in relation to a particular inherited communal reality. In maintaining the priority of first-order language in biblical narrative and Christian practice over propositional knowledge and experience and suggesting an alternative 'cultural-linguistic model', it aims to put a combination of Wittgensteinian models and Geertzian 'thick description' ethnography in place of traditional-realist and phenomenological assumptions.

In *The Nature of Doctrine*, George Lindbeck suggests a cultural-linguistic model as the framework for a 'common denominator' theory that will enable interfaith dialogue. This means, importantly, that his discussion context is initially the pre-theological one of theories of religion rather than Christian theology as such. The cultural-linguistic

---

1. As mentioned, 'postliberal theology' is the name coined by George Lindbeck for the work, centred on the Yale Divinity School (but now scattered), of the so-called 'Yale School'.

perspective is advanced as an alternative to the prevalent 'cognitive-propositional' and 'experiential-expressivist' perspectives which Lindbeck considers have hindered or inadequately served this dialogue.[2] This alternative is attractive because it does not deal in the truth claims or expressive symbols (respectively) peculiar to a given religion. From the viewpoint of this model, becoming religious is like learning a language or acquiring a culture. Like these things it is particular: 'One can in this [cultural-linguistic] outlook no more be religious in general than one can speak language in general.' Becoming religious is also primarily a matter of doing and living. While this sounds like a species of pragmatic internal realism with the parameters of truth set by the shape of the context and what works in that context, Lindbeck goes on to argue that 'languages and cultures [as such] do not make truth claims' in the way that cognitive propositionalists hold that Christian doctrinal propositions do.[3]

Lindbeck justifies his initial 'nontheological case for a cultural-linguistic approach to religion and religious doctrines' on the grounds that if this approach does not provide better historical and anthropological explanatory power in the first instance, then there is no use applying it theologically. It is therefore necessary to test it *pre*-theologically for its superior comprehensiveness and workability. In so doing, 'All that is claimed . . . is that a cultural-linguistic approach is preferable to traditional cognitive and experiential-expressivist approaches, provided the aim is to give a nontheological account of the relations of religion and experience.'[4] This does not prove hard to do. Lindbeck is able to demonstrate that experiential expressivism's assertion of a common core of religious experience is 'logically and empirically vacuous' because the core is unspecifiable, while the superior explanatory force of the cultural-linguistic model provides a general description of religion as 'a kind of cultural and/or linguistic medium that shapes the entirety of life and thought . . . a communal phenomenon that shapes the subjectivism of individuals rather than being primarily a manifestation of these subjectivities'. Just as a language, or language-game is correlated with a form of life, so a religion's doctrines are related to its practices and rituals. Accordingly, 'all symbol systems have their origin in interpersonal relations and social interactions. It is conceptually confused to talk of symbolizations (and therefore of experiences) that are purely private.'

2. Lindbeck, *The Nature of Doctrine*, pp. 16–17.   3. Ibid., pp. 21–3.   4. Ibid., p. 30.

Instead, 'First comes the objectivities of the religion, its language, doctrines, liturgies and modes of action, and it is through these that passions are shaped into various kinds of what is called religious experience.'[5]

Lindbeck is not necessarily reductionist here; the experience may be enabled by its cultural-linguistic medium but it does not follow that it is reducible to it. In this way Lindbeck does not ignore the 'logical and behavioural dimensions' of a religion but sees them as caught up with the cultural-linguistic aspects – with its 'form of life'. The cultural-linguistic model accordingly does not discount experience but 'is part of an outlook that stresses the degree to which human experience is shaped, molded and in a sense constituted by cultural and linguistic forms'. So what is 'given' are forms of life, rather than isolated, 'objective' experiences or facts. These latter instead are internal to the 'categorial' framework of the form of life, the framework of rules that tell us what the facts are in this situation.[6] If 'language creates the possibility of religious experience' rather than expressing a prelinguistic experience, doctrines therefore 'define the grammar of a linguistic system which makes religious discourse and experiences possible'.[7] It is the grammar, the doctrinal system, of the Christian world that determines what is to be taken to mean what. In other words, doctrines rule how things are to be defined or categorized ('the Bible is Christian Scripture') and what constitutes facts ('Jesus is the Son of God'). These doctrinal rules are both fed by and feed back into Scripture. As the reading-rules for Scripture, they are basic to Christian reality and determine what is Christianly possible. What is to be taken as real is laid down by doctrine.[8]

Different religions 'do not merely represent different expressions of the same experience',[9] so their content cannot be taken to be interchangeable. What they do have in common, Lindbeck suggests, is this rule-like function of doctrines. In a pre-theological (or meta-theological) sense, doctrines may be argued to function primarily as rules determining what is to be taken as what, while the matter of their own claims to right judgment in these cases is determined internally by the very material they judge. Because of this internal self-certification,

---

5. Ibid., pp. 33, 35, 39.   6. Ibid., p. 34.
7. W. C. Placher, 'Paul Ricoeur and Post Liberal Theology', *Modern Theology* 4 (1987), pp. 35f., 37.   8. Lindbeck, *The Nature of Doctrine*, p. 19.
9. Placher, 'Paul Ricoeur and Post Liberal Theology', p. 37.

comparison between religions is like comparing apples and oranges. They may only be compared as species of religious rule-systems. In respect of wider, overall claims to religious truth, on the other hand, Lindbeck decides that comparisons may be made on the grounds of 'categorial adequacy', adequate categories being 'those which can be made to apply to what is taken to be real, and which therefore make possible, though they do not guarantee, propositional, practical, and symbolic truth'.[10] Thus,

> The question of truth arises in two ways in a cultural-linguistic approach. One is that of the consistency or coherence of each part of the system with the rest – first-order community practices and beliefs must be consistent with second-order theological and doctrinal statements and vice versa. Such consistency measurements are intrasystematic or 'intratextual'. Second, one may raise a question about the 'truth' of the religion itself, but this is better expressed as a question about the *adequacy* of the system as a whole to conform its adherents in the various dimensions of their existence to what is 'Ultimately Real'.[11]

Absorbing the world

Here, then, is something like a theistic realism. On the first, internal, count the criterion of Christian adequacy is its comprehensiveness and coherence. On this, Christianity stands or falls according to its own rules. Christianity is what Christianity says it is and whether this is intrasystemically adequate depends on how well it is able to explain everything without contradicting itself. This requires that hermeneutics becomes an intrasystemic and intratextual exercise. On this count, to use Christian Scripture as 'world-absorbing' is to use it normatively. From the normative text are inferred the doctrines that rule according to that normativity.[12]

On the second, external, count, that of a religion's overall truth, the model is that of a particular religion as 'a single giant proposition', true in so far as it corresponds in its acting out to 'the ultimate reality and goodness that lies at the heart of things. It is a false proposition to the extent that this does not happen.' However, as we mostly misread or

---

10. Lindbeck, *The Nature of Doctrine*, p. 48.
11. N. Murphy and J. Wm McClendon Jr., 'Distinguishing Modern and Postmodern Theologies', *Modern Theology* 5/3 (1989), pp. 191–214, 206.
12. Frei, *Theology and Narrative*, 'Introduction' by W. C. Placher, pp. 17–18.

misinterpret what we are given, this revealed truth is likely to end up distorted into false propositions expressed in inauthentic practices.[13] Lindbeck does not suggest how we might know the extent of the categorial truth of Christianity. Presumably it is revealed to us; we are judged sinful in the light of divine truth, at the Last Judgment, if not before.[14] The unstated implication, then, is indeed a theistic realism.

Of course, theological realists will quickly point out, to the detriment of the dialogue which is Lindbeck's aim, that this ultimate truth has already been revealed within Christianity, in the person of Jesus Christ, who must define as well as enable both true God-ness and true humanity. Interestingly, and seemingly at odds with this dialogical aim, this is also arguably the result of the cultural-linguistic model's insistence on an intrasystemic criterion of truth. Such a criterion requires postliberal theology to accept the claim, central to Christianity's internal logic, of an *absolute* truth revealed in Christ and therefore within Christianity. Surely to be intrasystemically watertight, Christianity has to be true to what its doctrinal grammar has determined to be the facts. This is inescapable unless we are prepared to reclassify Christian truth claims according to an external 'as-if' metalanguage, so that we talk not about what is the case, but only about what is Christianly claimable.[15]

Lindbeck appears to be putting one foot in this direction when he suggests that, while ontological truth is not possible without intrasystemic truth, the reverse need not apply – that ontological truth, even in an intrasystemically coherent religion, cannot be assured.[16] But assured by what? For it seems that he is regarding Christian truths as either needing justification from beyond or (confusedly) as non-ontological (although propositional!) truths. This is just one means of avoiding the paradox, the means afforded by a reading of 'ontological' as 'external' which places truth in a position inaccessibly transcendent of human language and forms of life. In this Christian context, however, the divinely external must become the divinely internal according to the Christian imperative of incarnation. This affords the more adequate and consistent solution of

---

13. Lindbeck, *The Nature of Doctrine*, pp. 51–2. As Kenneth Surin (*Turnings*, p. 165) puts it, a '"categorially true and unsurpassable" religion' can then be defined as one which 'is capable of being rightly utilized, of guiding thought, passions, and actions in a way that corresponds to ultimate reality, and thus of being ontologically (and "propositionally") true, but it not always and perhaps not even usually so employed'.
14. See ibid., p. 170, and the extended discussion on this in chapter 7.   15. Ibid., p. 173.
16. Lindbeck, *The Nature of Doctrine*, pp. 63–5.

reading 'ontological' as 'revealed'. In postliberal terminology, the Christian incarnational grammar may provide us with the means of internalizing transcendent truth that allows us to accept the absoluteness of Christian truth claims while at the same time agreeing that they must be internal in their reference.

On this view, Christianity's absorption of the world extends the boundaries of what is Christianly ruled to contain all other systems. There can be no 'outside' to this world, as Lindbeck points out; so any description of how this world might relate externally to some other world or to an *externally* transcendent God must become an exercise in metalanguage 'which merely "quotes" or "conceptually redescribes" those propositions . . . designative of the convictions and practices of the believing community'.[17] In this case, when they are so redescribed it can only be in terms of Christianity's unsurpassability, for that is the premise according to which it absorbs the world. The upshot is that the notion of categorial adequacy can have no information value. We read all truth claims through the entire Christian form of life but not as requiring a justification from beyond that form of life, for there is no beyond in *this* world and whatever may await us eschatologically will also take place in Christ.

Yet, if this is how we are to read Lindbeck, it leaves open the question of why he is advancing the categorial model. Lindbeck could be suggesting that *for a Christian only*, Christian intrasystemic truth defines the whole of reality, a truth that must therefore be bracketed by an agnostic 'as if' that allows other possibilities. This seems to be supported by his assertion that

> Canonical texts are a condition, not only for the survival of a religion but for the very possibility of normative theological description . . . *For those steeped in them*, no world is more real than the ones they create. A scriptural world is thus able to absorb the universe . . . Scripture creates its own domain of meaning and . . . the task of interpretation is to extend this over the whole of reality.[18]

The qualifier, 'for those steeped in them', leaves room for uncertainty about how adequately a religious form of life or belief system mediates the 'Most Important' or the 'Ultimately Real' and this uncertainty effectively places the Christian intratextual model within a wider cultural-linguistic, study-of-religions model, where it becomes a member of the

17. Surin, *Turnings*, p. 173.   18. Lindbeck, *The Nature of Doctrine*, p. 117, emphasis added.

set {religious forms of life}. Ultimately, on this reckoning, the imperative to 'unify the canon', then 'encompass the cosmos'[19] becomes nothing more than a communally solipsistic exercise.

William Placher suggests that Lindbeck can be read in two different ways. He may be offering a 'radically consistent cultural-linguistic model' in which 'religious language does not refer to anything beyond itself and the activity of its religious community'. Any effort to ask how these relate to historical or ontological realities beyond is to discard this cultural-linguistic model for a cognitive-propositional one. Less radically, Lindbeck may be claiming that doctrines function culturally-linguistically by setting grammatical rules for Christian language. 'To accept the Doctrine of the Trinity, for instance, is to agree to speak and act in certain ways.' This makes ontological truth claims possible but restricts such claims to their use in ordinary religious language-games. Doctrines are second-order uses of language that have the status of necessary truths or tautologies. Therefore 'doctrinal orthodoxy on this point need not imply any cognitive claims about the true nature of God or any particular sort of religious experience or historical event'. What Lindbeck wants to do is to 'insist that one need not make such claims in order to affirm the relevant doctrine', so that one can be 'grammatically orthodox' 'without making metaphysical claims'.[20] This amounts to suggesting that the rules may be detached from the propositional material they rule and compared in the abstract, as it were. At the same time, truth is somehow to be both internal to the Christian form of life (and therefore not touching down in an external reality) and simultaneously external to it in the suggestion that the Christian world itself (within which the internal truths are held fast) as a whole may correspond more or less to a transcendent divine reality. Yet the provisionality of this correspondence – at least as Lindbeck states it – saws off the branch of certainty on which the internal truth sits.[21]

While this inconsistency seems to merit Placher's allegation of 'crypto-cognitivism', Lindbeck does do us the service of pointing up the logical impossibility of being both postmodernly cultural-linguistic *and* generically monotheist. It seems that to be coherently cultural-

19. Ibid., pp. 65, 117.
20. Placher, 'Paul Ricoeur and Post Liberal Theology', p. 46 (see Lindbeck, *The Nature of Doctrine*, p. 106, also pp. 66–7).
21. Yes, faith demands certainty, but uncertainty may have a place within Christianity in a way that Lindbeck implies but does not state. See the discussions on underdeterminedness in chapters 5, 6 and 7.

linguistic, while at the same time monotheist in the classical divine transcendence-requiring sense, demands a peculiarly Christian doctrine of incarnation which becomes the lynchpin linking internal and theistic realist perspectives.[22] In not stating this connection explicitly Lindbeck seems to be trading on the agnosticism he sees as inevitable in view of the failure of a traditional correspondence theory of truth to enable him to agree with those who would not accept Christian truth claims, an agreement which would be foreclosed if a Christian revelation was taken as truly and totally world-absorbing. Lindbeck wants to be able to say that just as two languages may be different but may have similar grammatical patterns, semantical and syntactical structure, so it is with religions. According to Lindbeck, what content different religions hold in common is banal (and the 'commonality' often spurious in any case as things mean something different in a different context). Content is always distinctive and often contradictory inter-religiously. Therefore if a 'nontheological theory of religion' is to be of use theologically, it 'must not exclude the claims religions make about themselves and . . . must supply some interpretation of what these claims mean'.[23] Hence the rule theory of doctrine, which would be unproblematic if Lindbeck were to stay with the non-theological theory (but as he says, he means to do theology with it). Theology must then be done with the content intact, but somehow without adjudicating on that content's truth claims.

> From the regulative perspective propositional interpretations are superfluous. If doctrines such as that of Nicaea can be enduringly normative as rules, there is no reason to proceed further and insist on an ontological reference . . . the question of the ontological reference of the theories may often be unimportant for theological evaluation . . . The theologian's task is to specify the circumstances . . . in which [the doctrine] applies [rather than] to discover what truth it enunciates.[24]

This simply begs the question of how canon is to be normative if canonical truth claims do not apply. It seems a contradiction in terms. Supposedly, 'we can agree about the rule while disagreeing about its "ontological implications"'.[25] Whereas the theologian must accept an

---

22. Need makes the comment that Lindbeck does not connect his view of language with his Christology, although this fault is by no means confined to him or to contemporary theology (cf. Need, *Human Language and Knowledge*, p. 205).
23. Placher, 'Paul Ricoeur and Post Liberal Theology', pp. 42, 46.
24. Lindbeck, *The Nature of Doctrine*, pp. 105–7.
25. Murphy and McClendon, 'Distinguishing Modern and Postmodern Theologies', p. 205.

'ontology of faith', the scholar in religions wants to be able to say that 'Doctrines can be construed nonpropositionally' but, at the same time, *may* also *possibly* be true.[26] Hence the suggestion of an inconsistent cognitivism (or externalism). If something fundamental to Christianity and couched as a doctrine is 'possibly true', it can only be so from a perspective which is outside that context and inside another, in this case an ethnographic or linguistic-philosophical one for which it is not required to operate as a true proposition and premise. If there is no 'outside' to a Christian form of life, as Lindbeck maintains and as is consistent with an intratextual approach, then it is non-negotiable that for those who inhabit that life the notion of a doctrine's being a rule and the general analysis of rule-theory must be subsumed within the particularity of Christian theology subject to the true-proposition-stating function of Christian doctrines, rather than the reverse. The necessary truths of doctrine hang on the contingent truths of the Gospel. Truth can only be both internal and external if divine truth as revealed, transcendent truth is also couched incarnationally as human truth. On this reckoning an expression of agnosticism about the degree of correspondence of internal to external truth is an attribution of unconvertedness or unredeemedness to the Church's representation of incarnational reality.[27]

If the logic of this equation is accepted, then Incarnation, as the locus of Christianity's absorbing of the world, is the context of the cultural-linguistic model. Within this context, the consistent employment of a Wittgensteinian/Geertzian cultural-linguistic model will be able to supply a description of how the propositions of the Gospel are related to the rules of doctrine and the language-games of Christian life. This is what Lindbeck's programme appears to promise in suggesting that 'part of the strength of a cultural-linguistic outlook is that it can accommodate and combine the distinctive and often competing emphases of the other two [cognitive-propositional and experiential-expressivist] approaches'. Yet, unsurprisingly in view of the above discussion, he fails to suggest how this accommodation and combination may be achieved. While he distinguishes between truth claims and 'the conceptual vocabulary and the syntax or inner logic which determine the kind of truth claims the religion can make', he fails to describe the *relation* of proposition, paradigm and syntax.[28] Lindbeck wants to stress the code rather than what is encoded, yet the two are inextricable.

26. Lindbeck, *The Nature of Doctrine*, p. 69.   27. See chapter 7.   28. Ibid., pp. 34–5, 19.

Doctrines, agreed, are second-order, but this merely means that they refer to first-order uses of language in Scripture and 'traditioned communities', where these uses participate in the incarnational reality the Church represents. The circularity resulting from an intrasystemic model of truth, in which the first-order uses to which the doctrines refer are themselves justified by the doctrines, operates within and according to the revealed fact of incarnation, namely the person of Jesus Christ. Christianity might therefore be described (rather too simplistically) as a tautology within a revelation. But then, as indicated, if Christianity absorbs the world, everything else is subsumed by that tautology and that revelation. From this standpoint, as Barth has insisted, nothing is pre-theological. If, as Lindbeck contends, 'A religion is above all an external world ... that molds and shapes the self and its world, rather than an expression or thematization of a preexisting self or of preconceptual experience', then that world has no 'outside'. Canonical truth claims, being inseparable from the rest of canonical content, are the framework within which extra-scriptural reality also lives and moves and has its being. Hence the Lindbeckian hermeneutic:

> Typology does not make scriptural contents into metaphors for extrascriptural realities, but the other way round ... it is the religion instantiated in Scripture which defines being, truth, goodness and beauty, and the nonscriptural exemplifications of these realities need to be transformed into figures (or types or antitypes) of the scriptural ones ... It is the text, so to speak, which absorbs the world, rather than the world the text ... We are to be conformed to the Jesus Christ depicted in the narrative.[29]

Consequently, Lindbeck does finally concede 'that revelation dominates all aspects of a theological enterprise, but without excluding a subsidiary use of philosophical and experiential considerations in the explication and defense of the faith'.[30] The appropriate place for this statement would have been prior to what he has termed the 'pre-theological' argument for employing rule theory within a cultural-linguistic model. Yet it would still have been contradictory to claim, on the one hand, that one is being pre-theological while, on the other hand, asserting that revelation subsumes all.

---

29. Ibid., pp. 118, 120. See following chapter.   30. Ibid., p. 131.

A postliberal theistic realism?

While this account supports Lindbeck's requirement that for Christians Christianity be the primary reality that defines all else, and agrees with him that this is best achieved through a christo-typological hermeneutic, it suggests that there are two problems with Lindbeck's postliberal theology as presented in *The Nature of Doctrine*. First and foremost, as it stands, it is inconsistent on its own terms. When the task of theology is taken to be a non-evaluative description of (presumably) classical Christianity, a regulative cultural-linguistic model of doctrine requires that an incarnational trinitarian grammar sets the terms for the relation of the Christian world to any external reality. That is, the grammar or doctrinal rule of incarnation brings the context of the meeting of an internal-realist Christian form of life and its external, transcendent justification inside that very Christian world. Of course, this is mandatory given that there is no 'outside' to Christianity as self-defined. It follows that it is incoherent then to talk of an 'outside', divine or otherwise, in any terms other than its being brought inside incarnationally. (If, on the other hand, the 'outside' is also inside this indicates the form of life's unredeemedness in part.)

While on their own, expositions of Christianity's internal logic are perfectly consistent with the argument that Christianity must absorb the world, there is a certain futility, not to mention a lack of justification, about exploring the internal logic of the world-absorbing system if that world might well be fantasy! The feeling of discordance or incredulity when it is suggested that the whole system might function in a way cut adrift from the claims of its own propositions may be taken as a sign that an inconsistency has been created, some component of the logic skewed. For the point at which Christianity, and therefore the Christian, is required to be realist is the point at which we appropriate the revelation made accessible to us in human terms, the point of conversion, of world-absorption. As Garrett Green points out, Christians use doctrines not merely as if they were true, but with the confidence that they *are* true; the truthfulness of Christian truth claims is an integral part of what Wittgenstein would term ordinary Christian language use.

> To claim that Christian believers . . . act *as if* they live in a world
> created by God and redeemed by Jesus Christ is to beg the crucial
> question. Surely most Christians, both pre- and postcritical,
> understand themselves to be making assertions about reality, about

the way things are, whether or not they can supply a second-order theory to justify that intent. They may be right or wrong in what they assert about reality, but it misrepresents their intent to describe them as producing fictions, 'useful' or otherwise . . . not '*as if*' but '*as*' is the key to the logic of religious belief.[31]

If we retain Lindbeck's dictum about Christianity as world-absorber and yet read Christianity as the truth that indeed absorbs the world and all it includes – in this case cultural-linguistic models and their theory of truth – the implication is that the ontological boundaries of the Christian world and the world at large must become one and the same. What is anticipated in the life of the convert is the point when all is redeemed and every knee shall bow and tongue confess.

If this line is taken, solutions to the problems presented by Lindbeck's work may be found at least programmatically in Hans Frei's work. It may also be possible to identify some things, more implicit than explicit in Frei's thinking, that may prove a bridge to some recent theological realist thinking.

If Christianity is read primarily either as a collection of narratives or as a system of language-using practices, then one or other of these (or somehow both) must become basic to everything else. If, for instance, 'narrativity' is primary, then Christianity cannot be 'everybody's story' (as Lesslie Newbigin terms it) because it is story as such that is basic and the particular Christian story just one member, Christian story, in the universal set {story}. Christianity is thus in effect subordinated to the primitiveness, or givenness of narrative. A model of language use by a tradition may at least offer a more comprehensive description in relating Scripture to Christian practice, but in the end the problem is the same. While aiming to be particular, the postliberal model becomes a general theory which then swallows up the specific Christian instance.

This incursion of a general theory of narrative worried Hans Frei sufficiently that he decided to subject criteria of narrativity to those of practice – the criterion of 'plain sense' biblical reading as normative Christian practice. The supposed remedy that Christianity *as narrative* might absorb the world was seen by Frei as an occult supplanting of Christianity by literary theory. In Frei's theology the theistic realism that is programmatic and ambiguous in Lindbeck is more closely and fully

31. G. Green, '"The Bible As . . .": Fictional Narrative and Scriptural Truth', in G. Green (ed.), *Scriptural Authority and Narrative Interpretation* (Philadelphia: Fortress, 1987), pp. 79ff., 88.

argued in keeping with an approach which is broadly critical-realist. The cornerstone of Frei's approach is Jesus Christ as 'singular agent enacting the unity of human finitude and divine infinity' who constitutes 'the ground, guarantee, and conveyance of the truth of the depicted enactment, its *historicity* if you will'.[32] In other words, 'in the case of this singular individual, manifestation of his identity involves his actual living presence. Who he was and what he did, and underwent are all inseparable to the authors from the fact *that* he was or is.'[33]

While verisimilitude to historical fact is important to Frei, he takes the Gospel to have a historical component without necessarily being consistent with historical fact in all respects. Frei considers that 'The curious unmarked frontier between history and realistic fiction allows easy transition if one's interest is the rendering and exploration of a temporal framework through their logically similar narrative structure, perhaps most of all in the use of the biblical stories where the question of fact or fiction is so problematical.'[34] Therefore, we must not read the Bible as being all one or the other, this demarcation being quite artificial and unhelpful (as well as practically impossible) because truth transcends factuality; realism is larger than literalism.

Like cantilever structures, however, Frei's biblical narratives have to touch down in historical reference somewhere. The primary touchdown point is the passion and resurrection sequence:

> the development of the gospel story is such that Jesus' identity as the singular, unsubstitutable human individual that he is comes to its sharpest focus in the death-and-resurrection sequence taken as one unbroken sequence. Therefore, no matter what one may believe about the possibility or impossibility, factuality or nonfactuality of his resurrection the story of that resurrection is literally not of the type of a mythological tale. For surely in such tales, unsubstitutable personal identity developed in interaction with equally unsubstitutable transpirings does not constitute a significant theme.[35]

This, then, is the centre of the universe from which all else takes its reference. As the referential centre of the Gospel Jesus story, it is the truth about God and the universe; it is the arbiter of the truth of all stories and all else. It is also the benchmark of what is to be taken as real, the means by which 'realistic' comes to be meaningful, in contrast to the definition

---

32. Frei, *Theology and Narrative*, p. 143.   33. Ibid., pp. 45ff., 84.   34. Ibid., p. 61.
35. Ibid., p. 59.

of 'realistic' as consistent with history as evidenced. If this benchmark is adopted, then it renders disbelief in the resurrection of Jesus not only less credible than the alternative, but also rationally impossible for the Christian.[36] Because the Gospel story is of a piece in a way that makes the accounts of the resurrection inextricable from the rest, it must be taken as of a piece – not certified as all equally factual, but resting unshakeably on the revealed factuality of its centre, a factuality without which the whole thing falls to pieces. As Frei sees it, the meaning and the possible truth of a narrative are two different questions. He suggests that the real meaning of the Gospel narratives is 'the Christology focused by Jesus' death and resurrection . . . rather than a mythological or time-conditioned form of the real meaning of the narrative'. What other alternative is there, he argues, other than having the story mean whatever you want it to mean and thereby 'dying a death of a thousand qualifications'?[37] The Gospels may be an incomplete and ambiguous clue to the rest of Scripture, but nevertheless contain its meaning 'as long as we understand that in the Gospels Jesus *is* nothing other than his story, and that this is both the story of God with him and all mankind, and is *included* in that story – that the Gospels are not simply the story of a being who is to be served by the story for purposes of the metaphysical definition of his being'.[38]

This seems to answer Placher's criticism that Frei, while admitting the legitimacy of questions of historical reference, refuses to offer any theory of reference while implying that the biblical text does not refer beyond itself, thus undercutting its claim on reality.[39] It seems that Frei is advocating an internal realism along Putnamian lines yet with an incarnational reference point, in which the linguisticality of the Gospel is an integral part of the divine reality revealed. If the Gospel, as an inseparable component in that incarnate reality, is our definition of that (both human and divine) reality, it cannot be subject to general theories of narrative, or paradigms, or ethnography. Nor can it be subject to general theories of truth, even critical-realist ones, because it is, itself, the living source of all truth.[40]

Like Lindbeck, Frei sees the normative function of doctrine as being rule-like. Yet Frei's work is distinguished by his understanding – or at

---

36. Ibid., p. 87.
37. Ibid., p. 40. (See also pp. 143, 146 and Hunsinger's Postscript, p. 245.)
38. Ibid., p. 43.   39. Placher, 'Paul Ricoeur and Post Liberal Theology', p. 47.
40. Frei, *Theology and Narrative*, p. 30.

least his exposition – of normativity as centred on the Gospel of Jesus within which the account of certain central events must be taken as factual. As the Jesus story is regulative, it alone is taken to have 'plain meaning' – all else in Scripture is related to it tropologically, analogically or allegorically.[41] Thus, while Christianity necessarily displays an internal logic, this intrasystemic consistency is grounded in the principal Christian truth evidenced in the resurrection, namely the redemptive joint humanity and divinity of Jesus Christ. Apologetics must now become 'essentially a matter of clarifying the meaning rather than demonstrating the truth of a particular claim or set of claims'.[42] Accordingly, Frei dissociates theology from the task of *establishing* truth claims – although his theology relies on those truth claims having been established – rather than, as in Lindbeck's case, questioning theology's capacity to make such claims at all.

Frei (like Lindbeck) advocates a combination 'figural-typological interpretation' which allows for the reciprocity of the reality of Christ as type or pattern (in the Jesus story of the Christian journey) for our own journeys with an understanding of our own journeys or worlds as figurative of the (literal) Jesus story or world.[43] Frei considers that literal reading has been confused with 'true referent' by both historical-critical and fundamentalist interpreters who see the Bible as source or clue, rather than text. However, as he points out, for followers of Wittgenstein understanding the text is not a matter of knowing or establishing its extra-biblical referents so much as a matter of being trained in its use as canon by the Church, or a Christian form of life.[44] If that text, moreover, is inextricably part of the revelation it mediates, then the notion of an extra-biblical referent becomes a category mistake.

Here Frei is adopting a cultural-linguistic approach to preclude the possibility that 'realistic narrative' might be taken to constitute a general theory. This, as George Hunsinger notes, means that 'the *primary* warrant for seeing Jesus as the unsubstitutable ascriptive subject of the gospel narratives is now said to be a matter of "traditional consensus" among Christians regarding the "literal sense" rather than, as before, a matter of formal literary structure'. It is apparent, concludes Hunsinger, 'that a "cultural-linguistic turn", under the influence of George Lindbeck, has

41. H. W. Frei, '"Narrative" in Christian and Modern Reading', in B. D. Marshall, *Theology and Dialogue: Essays in Conversation with George Lindbeck* (Notre Dame: University of Notre Dame Press, 1990), pp. 149ff., p. 151.
42. Frei, *Theology and Narrative*, Hunsinger's Postscript, p. 247.   43. Ibid., p. 64.
44. Frei, '"Narrative" in Christian and Modern Reading', pp. 151–2, 160.

been effected in Frei's thought'.[45] As Hunsinger points out, this move to a pragmatic cultural-linguistic rather than literary-linguistic model requires an explanation of how Scripture and tradition interact, for without the 'objective' component of the Gospel narratives there is a degeneration into a communal authority divorced from its role as bearer of revelation. Accordingly, this unfinished, programmatic aspect of Frei's work in 'conjunction with the eschewal of high-powered theoretical explanatory schemes . . . leads to a new interest in describing how and in what social context the literal reading of the gospel narratives functions within the Christian community'.[46] Such an inevitably co-inherent understanding of the interaction of Scripture and tradition, however, must be inseparable from an incarnational grammar of revelation.

Frei's concerns may be summed up as, first, the need to express a christocentric theistic realism in terms of a critical-realist-oriented cultural-linguistic approach; and, second, a vigilance that the primary Christian reality not be subverted by other perspectives masquerading as general theories. Thus narrativity becomes defined by Gospel narrativity and, one supposes, although this is not spelt out, the grammar of Christian language-games is measured against the normative grammar of the Jesus language-games. The failure to observe this second requirement has, as Frei observes, been a characteristic of Christian theology for the last three hundred years. During this period, following a 'great reversal', interpretation has been 'a matter of fitting the biblical story into another with another story rather than incorporating that world into the biblical story'.[47] We must instead, Frei insists, be committed to the idea of a 'generous orthodoxy' which reverses the habit of three hundred years in fitting the world, theories and all, back into Christianity.[48]

Performing the Gospel

While it seems unanswerable that for Christians a Christ-shaped reality must be primary, if the arbiter of truth about this reality is traditional text-using practices – or a dialectical engagement between text and use of text – such an arbiter would appear unable to explain what was termed in the introduction 'the dynamic and innovative character of a Christianity that is always renewing itself in new and surprising ways'.

45. Frei, *Theology and Narrative*, Hunsinger's Postscript, pp. 258–9.   46. Ibid.
47. Ibid., p. 50.   48. Hunsinger's Postscript, pp. 256–7.

How does a tradition of use explain innovation other than as heresy? Even traditions which have incorporated prophetic self-criticism have tended to throw their prophets into empty wells. By its very nature tradition claims there is nothing truly new under the sun, only old heresies in new dresses. On the other hand, rather than regard new understandings as heresy, theological realists point to an external reference point to the transcendent reality beyond both text and tradition – 'the objective source that gave rise to them' – with reference to which our practices and pronouncements require constant revision and reconstruction if they are to be 'renewed in their original force and rationality'. Yet, as argued in chapter 1, this also does not address the issue of a constructivist element in human language and thought. If the coherence of reality is arguably dependent in part on its human linguistic component, we do more than reach through our images and concepts to grasp worldly reality; we also must help to shape that reality with our descriptions, for all that they are partial and distorted. How are we to balance such an insight about ourselves with the Christian requirement that God's truth is both absolute and Christ-shaped?

Of other theologians who might be given the label 'postliberal', David Ford perhaps addresses these concerns most adequately. He notes how, when combined with his construal of doctrines as grammar, 'Lindbeck's insistence that theology is a reflective, second-order activity plays down its capacity to reach and affirm first-order truth', displacing the 'ontological truth question with a practical question as to "how well [theology] organises the data of Scripture and tradition with a view to their use in Christian worship and life".'[49] Ford considers that if the text is to absorb the world, 'adequate recognition is needed of the dangers of using the Christian story (for all its irreducible particularity and testimony to contingent events) in the interests of a generalizing "grammar"'. For this 'may fail to allow other contingent events their proper particularity because it subsumes them too readily as instantiations of the grammar'.[50]

Ford sees narrative description, or story, as combining realist (descriptive) and idealist (constructive) perspectives which enable us to avoid both stream-of-consciousness and general-theoretic perspectives. In such a perspective there is both a 'finding' and a 'fashioning'. We see

---

49. D. Ford, 'System, Story, Performance', in S. Hauerwas and L. G. Jones (eds.), *Why Narrative? Readings in Narrative Theology* (Grand Rapids: Eerdmans, 1989), pp. 191ff., 212. (See also Lindbeck, *The Nature of Doctrine*, p. 106.)   50. Ibid., p. 213.

this in the 'middle-distance' realistic narratives of the Gospels written 'in the light of the crucifixion and the resurrection of Jesus' in which evaluation is inextricably mixed with description. Attempts to separate the 'Jesus of history' from the 'Christ of faith' break down this admixture and accordingly impose some other model or genre in place of middle-distance literary realism. This does not mean that we cannot infer a model of reality out of the Gospel and other New Testament narratives – the doctrine of the Trinity is a patristic and medieval attempt to do this which manages to preserve this perspective of construction and discovery, finding and fashioning.[51]

For the model we infer is an ethic of love that, when expressed in worship as the central Christian activity, means that this worship is not primarily to do with general truths or mystical experiences (although it contains these) but is fundamentally 'a social meal-and-world-centered communication informed by the key events of the Christian story'. It is this love ethic involving 'the thrust of present speech, action, suffering, and thought' that is able to relate experience to truth and make the 'performance factor' one of the primary players in middle-distance realism. In performance, there is a dialectic of *lexis* and *praxis* which cannot be reduced to propositions and theories, although we infer propositions and theories from it. It is in the performance which is worship that construction and discovery come together.[52]

Ford sees Lindbeck as adopting a middle-distance realism in his rejection of experiential-expressivist and cognitive-propositionalist understandings of religion, but considers that these rejected approaches ought to be interrelated with the cultural-linguistic model to extend its explanatory power. Accordingly, the remedy to Frei's concerns, as Ford sees it, would be to use such a synthetic approach to express the complex reciprocity of the ontological and the epistemological in terms of a perichoretic interwovenness of propositions, narrative and experience. The result would be 'a locus-oriented' Christian theology involving the co-inherence of 'system, story and performance' in which, he concludes, 'there would be no neat distinction of first-order from second-order, and no avoiding the challenge of contingent particularity'.[53]

This approach of Ford's steps back from both propositional and intratextual approaches in the direction of a dialectical Scripture-tradition

51. Ibid., pp. 195–6, 199, 189–90, 200.   52. Ibid., pp. 199–205.   53. Ibid., pp. 214–15.

model of the kind suggested as a development of Frei's work. While Ford regards the postliberal cultural-linguistic model as inadequate by itself, the complex pragmatic realism he proposes is consistent with the post-liberal Wittgensteinian programme which this study will develop further. Also, in its step towards extratextuality in its recognition of the co-inherence of system, story and performance, Ford's approach contains an important revisionist insight. In this interrelation, the objectivity of an inferred ontology counterbalances the subjectivity of experience. The truth inferable from the middle-distance realism of the Gospel narratives must be propositional, coherent and pragmatic, but also constructive, to do justice to this complex reality.

Conclusion

If theological realism has been inclined to sacrifice questions of language and context to preserve what it considers a coherent theory of truth and has therefore failed to deal adequately with the complexity and contingency of human reality, postliberal theology has tended to sidestep or deal inconsistently with Christian truth claims in the interests of questions of language and context. A linguistic-turn framework tends to lead to a coherence theory of truth which, when pragmatized to take language use into account, simply adopts a communal criterion of coherence. With such a theory of truth all is retrieval; the norms determine truth. Some recognition of the inadequacy of this model is suggested by Lindbeck's notion of categorial truth, but this is not developed in a way that is consistent with the christocentric theology he advocates elsewhere.

Yet in Lindbeck's and Frei's dealings with propositional truth there is a programmatic theistic realism. What is lacking, as Ford, Placher and Hunsinger note, is an articulated theory of Christian truth which allows its truth claims to be true. It has been argued here and in chapter 1 that the only coherent realist theory of truth as theistic is the incarnational one 'thickly described' in the Gospel narratives that reveals God's truth in human terms within the framework of human reality.[54] However, this incarnational Gospel model is of greater complexity than any one theory of truth can contain. In being basic to human

---

54. See Need, *Human Language and Knowledge* on this subject, to be taken up again in chapter 5.

reality and therefore inclusive of all aspects of human life including human creativity, it requires Christianity to be realist in a way that allows it also to be contextual and language-ridden, experiential and active. It offers the challenge of incorporating a constructivist, non-retrieved element into what would otherwise be a critical theistic realism. This challenge, here taken up by David Ford, will be pursued further in the next chapter.

3

Interpreting the truth

David Ford has argued that a 'middle-distance realism' that takes a course between realist and idealist perspectives is able to allow both a 'finding' and a 'fashioning' of the Gospel. This is consistent with the suggestion that the incorporation of a postmodern weak thesis within a critical- or internal-realist perspective is not incompatible with a notion of God as the ultimate reality and final judge of truth. One of the questions remaining to be considered is the extent to which human thoughts and words do fashion as well as find a theistic reality.

Reading and commitment

If on a postmodern view people are inseparable from their stories, arguably reading becomes primary. One of the consequences of the linguistic turn in theology is that theological concerns become hermeneutical ones. Revisionist theologian and hermeneut Werner Jeanrond emphasizes the hermeneutical dialectic between the text as witness to revelation and the reading of it as mediating that revelation, between texts themselves and theories of reading texts, and between genres and styles in both. As he points out, such a dialectic renders both the purely objective and the purely subjective impossible. Jeanrond proposes a pragmatic middle way akin to Putnam's internal realism, in which meaning is at least in part determined by use. As a language-using activity, reading 'includes but transcends purely linguistic concerns'.[1]

Where Tony Eagleton, another advocate of a pragmatic approach, contends that *all* language is socially constituted and therefore all

---

1. Jeanrond, *Textual Hermeneutics*, pp. 94–5, 105.

theories political, Jeanrond questions whether this is the only or best way to employ the insight of the social nature of language. Alternatively, reading may be considered as an 'existential activity' on the part of members of a reading community:

> A reader who truly aims at understanding a text must open himself or herself to it. Only then can the text unveil the existential possibilities which it may entail, and only then can the text transform the self of the reader. Reading leads then to a double disclosure, namely the disclosure of the text's sense and at the same time the disclosure of 'new modes of being in the world', the revelation of new modes of self-understanding.[2]

The opening up of oneself to such existential self-transformation is a risky business. If the authority of the text lies in the dialectic between its own self-certification and its use by a tradition or community, is this authority simply a given? To what truth-determining criteria may *this* authority in turn be subject? Also, how is innovation in use authenticated when it is always judged according to a tradition of use that in turn judges and is judged by the traditions built into the text itself? (In such a perspective does truth drop out and meaning take its place?) Is a true reading required to be always simply a retrieval of sense, or may a true reading go beyond that sense? Retrieval of sense tends not to allow room for the prophetic component in reading, the suspicion that the plain sense may not be the whole truth, or the unvarnished truth. As Jeanrond points out, strategies of suspicion reveal in the apparently innocent text a wealth of distortions of structural, cultural, political origin, making it pertinent to ask. 'Should I as a reader allow every text to transform my self-understanding and understanding of the world?' Which leads him to ask: if the reader is at the same time judge of the text and the text's convert, 'at what stage in the process of interpretation should the critique of the text begin?' Jeanrond suggests that to say the text converts us is not to say that we grant biblical texts an immune, privileged status; the text must be viewed as both bearer and subverter of revelation. Thus, interpretation is not only understanding but in its inevitable selectivity also decision-making, there is an ethical dimension – a decision about good and evil – in *every* act of interpretation.[3]

Yet we have to launch our strategy of suspicion from somewhere; there have to be some things immune from our present inquiry if we are

---

2. Ibid., pp. 105–6, 109–11.   3. Ibid., pp. 111, 114.

to make any sense at all of our reading, some things against which we measure others in our quest for the truth. Which means that the question is not simply one of ethical choice, for there is no neutral ground from which we make that choice. More fundamental than choice and judgment is commitment. As Eagleton notes, how one discerns depends on where one stands. Whatever view of reality we commit ourselves to will also determine whether the text *should* so convert us. Critique is, therefore, couched in terms of our allegiance, whatever that is. This does not canonize the view according to that allegiance, but presumes in favour of an interpretation according to that view. Inevitably, then, hermeneutics will be done from some position of commitment to certain beliefs (however 'interpreted' those beliefs are), so that to employ a so-called general hermeneutic will be simply to operate from some faith position other than the one upon which the hermeneutic is being brought to bear. While the Christian hermeneut cannot regard the Bible as one text among others (or the Christian tradition(s) as one use of the biblical text among others) without prioritizing theories of textuality, literature, pragmatics, anthropology or politics over theology, theology is implicit in our commitments to what is for us Ultimately Real and Most Important. Faith comes into everything. Belief is everywhere prior to hermeneutics. We always seek understanding according to a position of faith, whatever that faith is.

This means that to be consistent in our beliefs we must operate only within the premises of our own interpretative base – that is, our avowed primary commitment. Yet to operate entirely within the premises of our own interpretative base is, it seems, to adopt a circular system of justification that reduces truth to a matter of coherence, for what is able to justify the premises themselves? Only if, in the interplay between objective and subjective poles, a theory of truth as revelation is deemed to be more vested in the objective pole, will there be salvation from an endpoint at the subjective pole of 'what is true is what is true for me/us'.

What then are we to take as the objective pole? We may be persuaded that Scripture is consistent with a true interpretation of reality. On what basis do we make that judgment? To what extent do we read our own prior experience, communal and individual, into this Christian description of the world inferred from Scripture? If Scripture enlightens and persuades us, draws us into its world, in the same breath we construe Scripture according to our own reality. Inevitably we find ourselves in the text and fashion the text according to our lights, but where is the warrant for judging our fashioning to be the truth? If truth is always tending to go soft on us in this way, must we then minimize this *eisegesis* by locking ourselves into a hermeneutic of retrieval – if this were to prove possible? And if so, where does the prophetically innovative, the demonstrably constructive element in Christian truth, fit within this model?

Kathryn Tanner contends that the dominance of a modern worldview incorporating certain assumptions about God's nature and God's relation to the world has resulted in misconstruals by theologians of the rules for Christian discourse, so that the classical Christian formulations no longer hang together coherently (although this begs the question whether there might not be some prophetic revelatory aspects to secular culture and some unredeemed aspects to classical doctrine).[4] Indeed, as Wesley Kort observes, while 'it is the function or role of scriptural texts to give persons and groups both a world and a sense of how to carry on in it', it is also true that 'the texts of beliefs and assumptions that enable and constrain the worlds of persons and groups constitute their scriptures'.

> Given the scriptures of our culture, it is powerful rhetorically to refer to the basis of our beliefs, when called to do so, as experience. But it means no more to say that I experience things as I do because of my beliefs than I take things to be as they are because I experience them so to be. My beliefs cannot be separated from my world and that situation is created by the functions my scriptures perform.[5]

As Lindbeck has argued so cogently, religious experience is not able to be somehow neutral and prior to belief.[6] But to say that experience, as always therefore committed – that is 'converted' – experience needs to be 'rightly converted' experience simply brings the argument full circle. Again, how can we be sure we always know a 'rightly converted' perspective when we see one? Can we say that convertedness to Christianity is no more nor less than commitment to a Christian tradition (given that the Kingdom of God is not yet established on earth and the Church not yet sinless)? – in which case it must be asked, how is the tradition itself converted? The question becomes: can Christianity take a God's-eye view

---

4. K. Tanner, *God and Creation in Christian Theology: Tyranny or Empowerment?* (Oxford: Blackwell, 1988), pp. 5, 26.
5. W. Kort, 'Reading a Text as Though it were Scripture', paper presented at the Center of Theological Inquiry, Princeton, March 1994, pp. 7, 2, 9.
6. See Lindbeck, *The Nature of Doctrine*.

of the truth of its own traditions when its theologians, hermeneuts and even prophets must inevitably live within (if on the edge of) such traditions?

As noted, Jeanrond proposes that in the dialectic between the text as revelation and the reading that mediates that revelation, Scripture and Church engage in a mutual critique in which, this inquiry has suggested, more weight may need to be placed on the objective pole – the plain sense of the text – if truth is not to go soft on us. Tanner believes that in the hermeneutical task we need to preserve 'the tension between the obvious sense of a scriptural text and its use in changing circumstances'.[7] Here 'obvious sense' has the connotation of usability, or capacity to make sense of things. Whether a text has the *capacity* to be Scripture – that is, the capacity to make comprehensive truth claims – depends, suggests Jeanrond, on both its genre and its ability and *intention* to create, portray and prescribe a world.[8] If in opting for the objective pole we grant the Bible primacy, we are acknowledging its power to create or reveal a world which internalizes all else according to a certain logic. Is this synonymous with taking it as the benchmark of a truth that transcends the local truths of the tradition that uses it as such? The account of postliberal theology in the previous chapter would suggest a 'perhaps' at best.

Frederick Ferré terms such world-creating systems metaphysical models. In claiming maximal comprehensiveness a metaphysical model must account for everything and be brought down by nothing. Nothing can be used to test it because everything that could test it is already accounted for within it.[9] On this basis, tautologically, to read a text as Scripture is to make that text a 'necessary condition of theological theory', that is, to give it the status of a metaphysical model. And in this sense hermeneutics *is* prior to theology. The function of the model is to lay down guidelines for what may be counted as being real – for an ontology. Conversely, 'anything counted by Christians as real will – must a priori – fall within the scope of this model'.[10] Ferré notes that while the end-point of such an internally watertight explanatory system is not

---

7. K. Tanner, 'Theology and the Plain Sense', in G. Green (ed.), *Scriptural Authority and Narrative Interpretation* (Philadelphia: Fortress, 1987), pp. 59ff., 71.

8. Jeanrond, *Textual Hermeneutics*, p. 117.

9. F. Ferré, 'Mapping the Logic of Models', in D. M. High (ed.), *New Essays on Religious Language* (Oxford: Oxford University Press, 1969), pp. 54–96, 81. See also S. Toulmin, *The Return to Cosmology: Postmodern Science and the Theology of Nature* (Berkeley: University of California Press, 1982), p. 28.   10. Ferré, 'Mapping the Logic of Models', pp. 91, 81.

truth as such but unfalsifiability, paradoxically, this unfalsifiability, in incorporating certain rules as to what is to be taken as factual – rules as to how we are to read the text's own truth claims – cannot be said to rest entirely on coherence. Its unfalsifiability rests on something internal to itself, its own propositions concerning reality – or its ontology – which then, as resting-point, must become external as well. This has the effect of flipping the whole thing inside out. That is, the unfalsifiability or otherwise of a theological model may contribute to its adequacy, but the theology itself makes a truth claim that transcends its model status. Christian models are trusted because of their truth claims, not their unfalsifiability, even when they relate to a divine transcendence beyond human conceiving or evaluating.[11] It is because we believe in Christ, not in the coherence of Christianity, that we claim to know the truth.

It may be said again, then, along with Bruce Marshall, that internalized principles of coherence and comprehensiveness may assist in maintaining the viability of the intrasystemic logic but provide insufficient warrant for taking Christian truth claims seriously. That is, the Bible cannot provide an objective pole to Christian truth if we grant it the power to create a world while suspending belief in the veracity of that world. This is what Marshall concludes. What he terms 'assimilative power' – a system's ability to account for everything within itself – is a necessary but insufficient justifier of that system as a whole. Unfalsifiability alone cannot justify the Christian revelation as 'primary criterion of truth' for coherence and comprehensiveness together do not amount to a sufficient understanding of truth, as Lindbeck acknowledged in his proposal of a 'categorial' (and ultimately theistically, eschatologically verified) truth in addition to the intrasystemic truths of Christianity.[12] David Kelsey suggests that 'Calling a text "Scripture" *means* that it is authoritative for the community that claims it as such' – that is, it is called thus because it is the benchmark of truth for that community and because of that 'it is to be used in certain ways in the common life of the community in order to establish and preserve the community's identity'.[13] We give the text authority by believing it to be true, and believing thus, we use it as a rule of life.

Yet is a theory of truth vested in the dialectic between text and user able to get beyond coherence and the pragmatics of use? Is it able to carry

---

11. Ibid., pp. 91, 78.   12. Lindbeck, *Nature of Doctrine*. See chapter 2.
13. D. H. Kelsey, *The Uses of Scripture in Recent Theology* (Philadelphia: Fortress, 1975), quoted by Murphy, *Theology in the Age of Scientific Reasoning*, pp. 168–71.

the burden demanded of it? Belief that one's Scriptures are authoritative because they are true is no respecter of Christian orthodoxy, even of Christianity. As Wittgenstein has pointed out, belief does not generally require certainty so much as confer it.[14] There is a constructive aspect to our beliefs that turns them into facts, right or wrong. Whether a text's truth is deceptive and the reality it offers is flawed amounts to more than whether or not it is the Scripture that accords with the reader's claimed commitment. Hence Jeanrond's point about the ethical nature of reading. But on what grounds does the reader make an ethical judgment? On the one hand, an emphasis on the objective pole requires a positivism about the truth of the text as if revelation begins and ends there, which seems to deny the role of the Spirit in leading us into new truth. On the other hand, an emphasis on the subjective pole of use, or transformation of the reader's self-understanding, while it takes the lid off revelation, takes away any certainty as to the truth of that revelation. As has been noted, if the reader's experience sets the criteria by which Christian texts are evaluated, a Christianity subject to such an experiential norm must likewise be various and culturally engendered, depending on which tradition has given rise to and provided the necessary prior interpretation of the experience in the first place. As Kort points out,

> people are not free from texts [nor are they] free to be any place on the textual field they choose. People locate themselves or can be located on the textual field ... because people cannot operate within their worlds – indeed, they do not have worlds – without assumptions and beliefs that have been or can be articulated.[15]

In an attempt to save the situation by coming up with some other firm criterion of truth, one might posit a generic core of human experience. When, however, these generic criteria are then brought to bear on the particularity yet open-endedness of the Jesus story, the result is the correlation of this normative particularity and open-endedness with these general principles. As Hans Frei argues,

---

14. See L. Wittgenstein, *On Certainty* (New York: Harper and Row, 1972). Likewise Kort ('Reading a Text', p. 8) sees the role of Scripture as the creation of the 'sense of an unmediated relation between events and entities in the world and their significance and value. A person has a world and can carry on within it because there is no need to question or construct a relation between at least some things or events and their value and meaning.'

15. Ibid., p. 7. For the same reason, on this understanding, a hermeneutic is always employed in a particular context and subject to the worldview of that context, so that a truly general hermeneutic is impossible (see notes 17, 23 and 25 below). It is not a matter of *whether* the hermeneutic is subject to a Scripture, but to *which* 'scripture' it is so subject.

> This move ensures that an independently validated anthropology,
> whatever it may be, will set the terms for the significance of Jesus
> Christ. In one way or another, his significance will simply be that of
> having actualized or confirmed a potentiality that can be discerned
> and validated by reason alone . . . Christology becomes a mere cipher
> for some independent version of anthropology. It is the doctrine of
> human nature, history and existence, not the doctrine of Jesus Christ,
> which serves as 'the integrating, organising, or enabling principle
> around which to gather at least the meaning, and often to evaluate
> the truth of theological assertions'. In short, Christology becomes the
> mere form to which anthropology provides the real content.[16]

If some sort of general or global notion of humanity is criterial,
however much this humanity is seen as contingent on and expressive of
divine reality, then a Christian version of humanity becomes simply a
member of the set {versions of humanity} or alternatively the set {exem-
plars of authentic humanity}. In this way, paradoxically, through the
loss of the particularity of the Gospel narrative, the Gospel is itself lost.
The embodied Christian norm is seen as paradigmatic of a wider general
norm. Whereas a biblical yardstick may seem to lend a tautological
circularity to Christian truth, an alternative anthropological one offers
the further disadvantage of removing any guarantee that the result will
be identifiably Christian.

Personal particularity

If a particular reality is both unique and primary, namely the reality of
Jesus Christ (bracketing for the moment the issue of whether this is
another way of saying a particular text is primary), then the particular
must be prior to the general. The particular must set the boundaries of
the real world. The general may only be abstracted from the particular in
a secondary way.[17] Postliberal theologians suggest a biblical intratextual

---

16. H. Frei, *The Eclipse of Biblical Narrative: A Study of Eighteenth and Nineteenth Century
Hermeneutics* (New Haven, CT: Yale University Press, 1974), p. 28; Frei, *Theology and
Narrative*, Postscript by George Hunsinger, p. 238.

17. It follows that rather than make the Christian particularity subject to general
principles, the reverse must apply. Yet the general principles will continue to inform the
particular hermeneutics, for in so far as hermeneutical methods and tools are
generalizable to situations of use other than the one or ones in which they were
developed, there is also no such thing as an entirely special hermeneutic. Claims
regarding the uniqueness of Christian biblical hermeneutics may be seen to be the result
of an equation of Scripture as such with Christian Scripture, for use in a particular
context does not alter tools beyond recognition. Yet the generic reading of a text as
Scripture is always itself subject to a particular Scripture as well as applied to a particular

hermeneutic along these lines. Frei argues that once the Bible *as Christian Scripture* is selected as arbiter, self-consistency requires us to read it as pertaining to Christ and, reciprocally, to take Christ, as the one to whom the Bible witnesses, who is testified to there as God's own reality and truth come among us, as the key, first, to the whole of Scripture and, second, to the whole of human reality. As Frei suggests, to read the Bible as Scripture in this way is to read it as telling the story of our lives both comprehensively and authoritatively; that is, to understand it as telling the exhaustive truth about ourselves through the story of Jesus which, reciprocally, turns the ordinary 'worldly' details of our life into figures or parables of his life.[18] Thus, a particular human experience, namely Christian human experience as defined by the story of Jesus Christ, must inform human experience at large. As Kenneth Surin states, on this view

> 'Scripture' . . . depicts a real world, temporally structured, which encompasses both the times and stories of the text and those of the reader. Since the world depicted by the Bible is the only real world, the reader must fit his or her own experience into scripture's cumulative narrative, thus becoming a 'figure' of the text. Christian reality claims (mediation) and the formation of the Christian life (application) follow from and are normed by the explicative shape of biblical narrative'. Integral to intratextual theologies, then, are the related principles that it is the 'scriptural' linguistic world which subsumes 'extrascriptural' reality, and that it is this world – the 'true' world – which is decisive for the shaping of Christian 'identity'.[19]

Furthermore,

> a recognizably Christian intratextualism will of necessity take God's action in Jesus Christ for us (the *gratia Christi*) as an irremovable

Scripture, and in Christianity the double contextuality of this reading is instanced and absorbed in the reading of a text as Christian Scripture. The general is always realized within the specific, but the specific cannot be reduced to the general without disappearing, as Colin Gunton points out (*The One, the Three and the Many* (Cambridge: Cambridge University Press, 1993), pp. 2–3). If 'it is the function or role of scriptural texts to give persons and groups both a world and a sense of how to carry on in it' (Kort, 'Reading a Text', p. 7) the world given by Christian Scripture absorbs various hermeneutical theories and methods.

18. 'The world of the Scripture stories is not satisfied with claiming to be a historically true reality – it insists that it is the only real world and is destined for autocracy. All other scenes, issues, and ordinances have no right to appear independently of it, and it is promised that all of them, the history of all mankind, will be given their due place within its frame, will be subordinated to it': Erich Auerbach, *Mimesis: The Representation of Reality in Western Literature*, trans. Wm R. Trask (Princeton: Princeton University Press, 1953), p. 15; quoted in William Placher's introduction to Frei, *Theology and Narrative*, p. 6.

19. Surin, *Turnings*, pp. 203–4. See also Ronald Thiemann, *Revelation and Theology: The Gospel as Narrated Promise* (Indiana: University of Notre Dame Press, 1985), pp. 84–5.

starting-point for doctrinal formulation, and will thus accord its
concomitant – the *solus Christus* – a powerful regulative status, thereby
dispensing with the need for the kind of prolegomenon
commissioned by the extratextualist. A Christian intratextualism is a
discourse whose proper form is necessarily that of an *analogia
Christi*.[20]

Consistent with this suggestion, as mentioned, Marshall suggests
that biblical assimilative power rests on a propositional linchpin, 'Jesus
as *veritas Patris*', which links it to a transcendent reality. It is through
such a statement of equation, or correspondence, that *on faith* we are
able to take its central narratives as 'world-absorbing'.[21] In other words,
faith reads unlimited biblical assimilative power out of the ultimacy of
Christian reality, the *veritas Patris* of Jesus Christ, and not the other way
round (although it should be noted that this proposition represents a
co-inherence between person and story). On this basis Frei suggests a
hermeneutic that takes the central Jesus story of the Gospels as foundational of Christian reality:

> for a beginning let's start with the synoptic Gospels, or at least one of
> them, because their peculiar nature as narratives, or at least partial
> narratives, makes some hermeneutical moves possible that we don't
> have available elsewhere in the New Testament. And having started
> there, I would propose to go on and say, let's see how much more of
> the New Testament can be coordinated by means of this series of
> hermeneutical moves.[22]

New Testament writers such as Paul and other theologians of the early
and later Church relied on a typological, intratextual method of interpretation to establish reciprocal connections between New Testament
and Old, in which the latter supplies types or anti-types of the primary
Christian reality of Jesus Christ. The other, reciprocal side of typology is
contextualization, or figuration; the New absorbs and converts the Old
to its use, while the Old forms as well as prefigures the New. At the same
time we find Christ-types in our own worlds; and when the person or
story of Jesus refigures our own, we and our stories along with all our
understandings of world become indigenous parables, positive or negative, of the Kingdom of God.

Jeanrond is critical of this approach's 'Barthian revelation-hermeneu-
tics' which, he argues, ignores Bultmann's insight that we cannot under-

20. Surin, *Turnings*, p. 172.   21. Marshall, 'Absorbing the World', pp. 80–1, 85.
22. Frei, *Theology and Narrative*, p. 32.

stand biblical texts without first understanding the conditioning effect of the human situation of the interpreter. While for both Barth and Bultmann ultimately the interpreting is done by 'God at work in the human process of interpreting the biblical *kerygma*', for Barth it is always God who interprets us and history, not we who interpret God – 'revelation is not a predicate of history, but history is a predicate of revelation'.[23] At this point it could be argued *tu quoque* by Jeanrond that the postliberal intratextual model is not specific to theology any more than reading a text as Scripture is specific to overtly religious contexts.[24] An intratextual 'thick-description' typology becomes theological only when so used. But wherever it is employed, it has the peculiar characteristic of subsuming everything, as everything may be construed in some part as either type or anti-type of the narrative truth criterion. As will be argued later, far from being confined to religion or mythology, it is endemic in human apperception. Accordingly, this characteristic has a particular affinity with the universalist nature of Christian truth claims. When employed at the service of Christianity, it implements the Christian agenda of making the whole world (hermeneutical methods not excluded) as seen through such a reading of the biblical texts, subject to

23. Barth, *Church Dogmatics* (hereafter *CD*) 1/2, p. 58, quoted by Jeanrond, *Textual Hermeneutics*, p. 129. However, Jeanrond is on less reliable ground when he slates Barth for insisting that 'hermeneutics is not an introductory reflection before actual theology begins' but 'a part of theology proper, and thus part of dogmatics' concerned with 'how to proclaim God's word today so that it is truly talk of God'(ibid., pp. 128–9; *CD* 1/1, pp. 187ff.). Jeanrond regards the intratextual limiting of the interpretation of texts as a similar rejection of the importance of a general or philosophical hermeneutics for theology. Yet, as argued, there can be no prolegomenon to theology that does not operate inevitably from a commitment to another, at least partially antithetical commitment. This, it is suggested, is not only Jeanrond's dilemma but an inconsistency running through the middle of revisionist theology. To be both postmodernly language-ridden *and* general-theory-ridden does not compute. Accordingly, when Jeanrond notes that Lindbeck appears first to utilize general hermeneutical thinking in his cultural-linguistic model and then to abandon it in favour of a special intratextual model, he does not appear to consider that Lindbeck might be aiming for the sort of approach that Jeanrond himself is advocating, namely a dialectic between general and special hermeneutics (ibid., pp. 161–2; Lindbeck, *The Nature of Doctrine*, p. 117). What Lindbeck may have failed to make sufficiently clear is that although ultimately the 'general' must serve the particular (given that we must do our generalizing from one context or another), the models must coinhere. A stand-alone special or general hermeneutic is insufficiently comprehensive to take account of a complex Christian reality. While Jeanrond and Lindbeck may agree about the need for a cultural-linguistic perspective but disagree about whether this entails a special basis for Christian hermeneutics, it is arguable that a cultural-linguistic approach precludes the sort of generality to which Jeanrond appears committed.
24. As Kort again comments, 'While everyone has beliefs and scriptures, not all beliefs and scriptures need be called religious . . . nonreligious people should be disabused of the notion that they operate without beliefs and Scriptures in some mature and level-headed way while religious people are still mired in the texts of their superstitions' (see Kort, 'Reading a text', pp. 5–6).

Christian reality. Typology is quintessentially the hermeneutic of world-absorption. If Christianity absorbs the world, it does so according to a christo-typology which begins as intratextual but immediately involves the reader and the reader's world. But typology is also a two-way street. Refiguring is the obverse of typing.[25]

This is an argument which may turn the intratextual hermeneutic into an extratextual one. Consistent with Jeanrond's suggestion that language-using activity 'includes but transcends purely linguistic concerns',[26] Surin suggests that since the text is inseparable from its use as text, such a model cannot be *either* extratextual *or* intratextual, but must be both. This, Surin considers, may be a corrective to a difficulty inherent in the intratextual approach.

> Intratextualism's firm adherence to the principle of the autonomy of the text conduces to an understanding of the text as a static and homogeneous entity . . . it is not understood as a *process*, as a text-to-be-constructed. The intratextual theologians view the text as a repository of achieved 'meaning'. They fail to see that the text is constituted, as text, in the very act of being understood or received by the reader. This is not to say that the text has no 'objective existence', that it is a mere reflex of the consciousness of the reader . . . What is needed, it would seem, is a truly dialectical understanding of the text, one which takes its 'meaning' to be constituted by the interaction *between* text and reader.

As he puts it, we 'have to begin, not at the point where the narrative is, as it were, already doing its work, but at the earlier point where the subject is about to enter into it, i.e. the point where she is "baptised" into the Christian semiotic system'.[27] We step back as well as forward from the static entity of the text into its converting use. Yet in this dialectic of conversion, the converter does not escape unscathed. For, as Surin concludes (consistent with Jeanrond), the process is also a prophetic one aimed at redeeming the Church as well as the individual.

25. What this amounts to is that the postliberal intratextual hermeneutic thus recast as a 'conversion' model may be employed as a general hermeneutic to explain what it means to read a text as Scripture in distinction to other ways of reading. At the same time, reading a text as Scripture allows it to absorb, or convert the reader's world to its reality-description while in turn the text is itself absorbed in being presented through the figure(s) of the reader's world. As the world so absorbed includes the absorption model itself, that model itself becomes subject to evaluation in terms of its consistency with the scriptural absorber. For typology to be an acceptable hermeneutic, world-absorption must be what Christianity does and must do, according to Christianity's own self-understanding. In this way the general hermeneutic can only be so because it is also the special hermeneutic.   26. Jeanrond, *Textual Hermeneutics*, pp. 105–6.
27. Surin, *Turnings*, pp. 215–16.

> The church is the gospel-shaped 'narrative space' where Christians learn to 'sacrifice' themselves, over and over again, to the community's narrative texts, to the 'new' language. This they do by consenting to be interrogated by those texts in such a way that they learn, slowly, laboriously and sometimes painfully, to live the way of Jesus. This interrogation – which is fundamental to the church's 'pedagogy of discipleship' – may, depending on historical circumstances, have the consequence of actually decomposing, as opposed to reinforcing, certain already existing patterns of Christian 'identity'. These alternative 'identities' will be articulated in a language which gives speech to all that is denominated by the category of the 'other'. It will be a language capable of undermining the filiative and affiliative bonds which sustain the unredeemed order.[28]

Thus the Church, as user of the biblical text, and the text, as repository of the rules for its own use, together (dialectically) constitute a prophetically self-critical yardstick of truth in which we see the mutual discernment of Word and Spirit.

If the Christian converting and redeeming of our primordial connection-makings superimposes a new framework of reference on all that we did, felt and believed before, at the same time the converting text is always experienced in the light of what the Christian tradition takes the subject of that text to be, the person of Jesus Christ. Our text-using practices express a christological relation to reality that both arises from and in turn shapes our beliefs about and experiences of that reality. Accordingly, the process of converting encounter is instigated and effected incarnationally. Necessarily so, as Surin points out, because on both scriptural and logical grounds it is the divine entry into human suffering and death that converts our lives to God's saving pattern. Without this redemptive action that identifies with the human condition, we could not be lifted out of a situation beyond our own salvific means.[29] That is, the soteriological grammar central to Christianity requires in turn a revelational grammar that is incarnational.[30] It is as we participate in the meeting point of divinity and humanity in Jesus Christ, a participation in which all our human words and concepts are caught up, that formulations and practices are judged according to God's truth.

In this way 'acceptance of the primacy of the scriptural world can and does go hand in hand with acquiescence in the principle that the

---

28. Ibid., pp. 217–18.   29. For an extended discussion on this point, see chapter 7.
30. Ibid., pp. 136ff.

response of the reader/disciple(?) plays a crucial role in its interpretation'.[31] And the upshot of this is that if Scripture is the ground of hermeneutics, conversion is its beginning. Yet conversion involves more than a text; it is preeminently a matter of grace. The incarnational grammar rules both an intratextual and extratextual context through the presence of the risen Lord in the Church and the Spirit's drawing and conviction. The role of the Spirit in the conversion of our minds to God's truth may, as Surin suggests, involve undermining or 'actually decomposing, as opposed to reinforcing, certain already existing patterns of Christian "identity"' insofar as these are unredeemed – the 'filiative and affiliative bonds which sustain the unredeemed order'. For, as Marshall has argued, absorbing the world does not leave Christianity unaffected; Christianity's absorption of world is at the same time reciprocally *Christianity*'s refiguring or 'indigenization'. God is not a monopoly of tradition and text. As the text converts its readers, the readers convert the text by figuring it in the stories, experiences and concerns of their own lives. Christianity internalizes rather than rejects and in this internalizing it discovers new things about God's presence in the text and the world as it is refigured in new and surprising ways.[32]

Surin's argument may then be considered to support Jeanrond's points about intratextual hermeneutics but from the point of view of reforming rather than throwing out what he sees as an essential component in a rather more complex hermeneutics. And in line with Surin, it may be suggested that a hermeneutic of conversion, as dialectically involving text and subject of text, text and user/reader of text, is more than an intratextual hermeneutic. It is also hinted that this may amount to more than a dialectic between the text and its using tradition.

The question, however, is still: how are we able to be prophetically innovative in our reading? When the criterion of what is good is worked out between the text itself and the text-interpreting community, an incarnational model may still amount to an exercise in retrieval if it is understood only in terms of the intra-Gospel dialectic between the person of Christ and its textual witnesses. But there again, Christianity's attempts to assimilate alien truths is not always successful and never complete. Not only does the world to be assimilated keep changing in the face of our imperfect comprehension of it; there is also inevitably some mutual modification. If this may be seen as undermining the

31. Ibid., p. 212.   32. Marshall, 'Absorbing the World', p. 85.

objective pole of truth, it also forces the net of truth wider than that of retrieval. If there is more to reading than retrieval, then we cannot regard our reading of the Christian Gospel as fixed.[33] So we must allow for an eisegetic aspect to our reading, however difficult it might be to come up with a coherent model of Christian truth that is able to incorporate this, not simply because we have to regard imperfect retrieval as a necessary evil but because, somewhat paradoxically, the very commitment to comprehensive truth requires it.

Marshall employs the example of Aquinas' use of Aristotle as a non-controversial instance of what he calls assimilation and (mutual) modification. Aquinas uses the best available (Aristotelian) physics, cosmology and metaphysics of the day to supplement the biblical creation stories in a way consistent with that text. While Aquinas takes some of Aristotle's formulations as consistent with the plain sense of the text, inevitably the Aristotelian annotation changes that sense.[34] While these changes must not contradict the plain sense, at the same time they must be able to hold their own in the intellectual world outside Christianity. In effect, to take the plain sense of Scripture as primary is to undertake not to presume it false, even though our construals of its sense may be limited and distorted. So goes Aquinas' Principle of Charity: 'Every truth which can be adapted (*aparti*) to divine Scripture, while agreeing with the way the words go, is the sense of Scripture.'[35] Our partial and perverse interpretations make it imperative for us to take account of the message provided if we find ourselves needing to reject a large number of apparently reasonable extra-biblical truths. Without abandoning Aquinas' axiom that Scripture is not to be presumed false, we need to abstain from asserting positivistically that the reading which seems presently to make the best sense of the text is the only and perfect sense – or, we might add, that the best sense of the text is our only recourse to truth.

Jeanrond suggests that we may be able to account for innovation within a model of critical plurality. As he puts it,

> We should test any . . . claim over against our best and most sincere
> appropriations of the salvific initiatives of God in Jesus Christ as
> experienced and textualized by the different biblical communities. In
> this task of locating the primary material focus of Christian identity,
> our christological interpretation of the biblical canon functions as a

33. Ibid., pp. 82, 85.   34. Ibid., p. 94.
35. Aquinas, *De Potestas*, 4,1,r, quoted by Marshall, ibid.

critical tool for our interpretation of the biblical models of authentic
Christian praxis in the Christian tradition until today. Yet even this
christological interpretation which Martin Luther had proposed as
the critical aim of all biblical interpretation . . . can only claim a
preliminary authority, for it too will always need revision.[36]

There is the need always to reinterpret again and again the 'originating
event' of the tradition in the same way that Jesus himself reformulated
the Jewish faith. The self-criticism – or criticism of tradition – which is
integral to Christianity and requires

> a continuous assessment of all its manifestations and doctrinal
> symbols may be achieved through the mutual review and criticism of
> different traditions of use. This assessment may well lead to a
> thorough rethinking of ecclesial authenticity and to an always
> renewed search for the most adequate understanding of and response
> to Jesus Christ's call on us to participate in God's creative and
> redemptive project.[37]

The use of a text means the addition of a gloss. The notion of an
'essential' or true reading of the text lures us like a mirage, for we do not
have the option of not glossing the text, of being context free. But at
least there is still the possibility of comparing glosses, both those built
into variant or parallel texts and those of subsequent interpretations. In
this way, as every biblical scholar knows, the self-critical process is aided
and abetted by the very plurality that may appear to hinder it.[38] Correc-
tives come through dialogue between traditions and individuals, as
Lindbeck maintains, a return to reading the Bible together, a reading
which is informed by the Spirit as well as historical-critical method and
takes seriously the normativity of Scripture. In saying this Lindbeck is
suggesting that the use of a typological hermeneutic, which is quintessentially a hermeneutic of retrieval, does not preclude the employment
concomitantly of a dialectical model in which the normative text does
not become such until used as such, where that use is more than one tradition and so transcends any local norms. Accordingly, questions such
as: has the community then and now interpreted its norm correctly?
How much have cultural factors skewed the original account as well as
the present interpretation? Has the text on the whole converted us to a
Christian worldview or, on the contrary, have we instead skewed it
according to our own particular prejudices and baptized that bias with a

---

36. Jeanrond, *Textual Hermeneutics*, pp. 165–6, 176–7.   37. Ibid., p. 180.
38. See chapter 7.

Christian name? – do not cease to be valid or answerable with the use of a typological interpretation, but simply point to the need for that typology to be worked out in a wider, prophetic *perichoresis* of church, world and text. The world as it truly is may be Christ-shaped, but that Christ-shape is ever more than is dreamt of in our philosophies. God's truth by definition must be wider and deeper than our best interpretation of the plain sense of the text.

Story and person

To return to Frei, and this time to Frei's Christology: for Frei, personal identity is equated with storied particularity in a way that is consistent with both Christianity's 'scandal of particularity' and the world's language-riddenness. If the whole truth of the Bible and hence of the world is summed up in the 'who' of Jesus Christ, this 'who', Frei considers, is identical with his story. Therefore Frei's (and Lindbeck's) typology is a 'thick description', one in which the whole narrative is taken as representing the character to be typed. If we encounter the person of Jesus Christ within the biblical witness, the events, actions and the propositions inferable from the story are embedded in and are an inseparable part of the revelation they mediate; the person is inextricable from the vehicle. Frei asserts that

> The strong link between a person's continuing centeredness in himself on the one hand and his person qualities, changing bodily structure, and overt activity in both physical and social contexts on the other is so tough and organic that it is perfectly proper to describe what a person *is* by what he *does* and *who* he is by what he is and does.[39]

This serves to point up that the actuality of the crucifixion and resurrection is necessary to the Gospel's internal logic. 'If Jesus was not raised from the dead, then he was not who this story claims he is, and the narrative coherence of the story considered as a unity radically collapses.' The personal identity of Jesus 'involves his actual living presence. Who he was and what he did, and underwent are all inseparable to the authors from the fact *that* he was or is.'[40] It also serves to underline that personhood is indelibly particular. Characters are not exemplars; they are themselves; their story is their own and as such it is who they are. Thus:

---

39. Frei, *Theology and Narrative*, p. 62.   40. Ibid., pp. 242 (Hunsinger's Postscript), 45, 84.

> the pattern of redemptive action exhibited in Jesus is so identical with his personal story that he preempts the pattern. It is *his* story and cannot be reiterated in full by the story of anybody else – just as any particular person's story, whether fictional or real, is exclusively his own and not also that of somebody else.[41]

And it means that the appropriate method of interpretation is simply 'to observe the story itself' as its sense is internally given and does not lie in its significance for the reader (although the reader's experience must be a filter for that sense). Hunsinger remarks that this is the essential difference between postliberal and liberal theology – that for all that meaning is embedded in the narrative and accessed through a traditioned use of that narrative by a community, for post-liberal theology the locus of sense is objective rather than subjective.[42]

Yet what is the significance of saying that Jesus Christ is no more nor less than his story? While the thick description of narrative certainly offers a more comprehensive way of constituting personal identity than mere facts or inferred self-understandings, one cannot help but feel that there is still something reductionist about this model. Vital as Jesus' particularity is, and necessarily dependent as it is on the Gospel narratives, it does not follow that this particularity is a monopoly of the text. The text's being a necessary condition of access to the particularity of Jesus' identity does not mean that it is a sufficient condition. The inseparability of person and story is not the same thing as their identity. Here it seems apparent that the linguistic turn, even the pragmatically nuanced linguistic turn of postliberal theology, while helpful in reinforcing the need for us to take the Gospel narratives as a whole rather than setting ourselves up as judge of which propositions ought to be extracted from them, is also acting as an ontological strait-jacket.

If, to hark back to Surin, the context for the reciprocal absorption of text and reader is to be incarnational, perhaps more precisely the relation of character or person to depicting narrative could be described as one of co-inherence. The story constitutes the character whereas the character is the source of the story; while the person is accessed through the story which recounts his actions, words and adventures, at the same time the story is formed around the actions of a person who could well have other stories apart from these ones. If we do not simply conflate person and story, this means that the starting point could just as reasonably have been person instead of text, external as well as internal, but nevertheless

---

41. Ibid., p. 46.   42. Ibid., p. 242 (Hunsinger's Postscript).

it could not have been one *or* the other because they are inextricable. To take this approach allows for differences in emphasis. It allows that anthropological considerations may legitimately have a higher profile in focusing on the human person's or community's absorption by and refiguring of Christ's person within an incarnational model while still recognizing that such absorption and refiguring cannot be cut adrift from the Jesus of the Gospel. It means that theology and conversion cannot be reduced to hermeneutics. It also allows that truth may be more than static, that the Spirit's disclosure of the dynamic truth of the risen Christ, while co-inherent with the stories of the Jesus of the Gospels, is also eschatological in its direction, reaching back to us from the future to draw us forward into the truth of all things and to make all things new.

The central Christian grammar of transcendence is expressed in terms of an interpersonal encounter in which the initiator and questioner is always God and the transformation and obedience is always ours. But this transformation which takes place in Christ, in which we are involved in Christ's creative remaking of ourselves and our stories, involves the incorporation of this remaking within the truth in a way that we can only attribute to the work of the Spirit, but which also changes that truth. It is as if, as we are caught up into God's truth, there is a 'gain to actuality'[43] that is a gain to God's creation and therefore to God's truth about the world. As Daniel Hardy puts it, our seeking of 'the intellectual conditions for truth-telling about God's presence in our interweaving . . . is an activity in which the trinitarian God participates'. Within the song of creation 'sung by the divine Spirit which in its polyphony interweaves all in an inextricable relation', our Christian texts, doctrines and practices – 'the "fixities" which we habitually prefer' – resemble still pictures taken of a dance as an attempt to capture 'the rhythms of movement in static forms' which we then mistake for 'the primary characteristic of the "nature" and interrelation of God, human beings and nature'. In the fabric of God's truth there is enough open texture left by the interweaving 'song of the Spirit' which is God's creative relation to the world for the arrangement of its factors not to be fixed, to allow us to develop creatively our own ways of living in the world.[44]

At this point it is apparent that the dialectical model is trinitarian rather than simply christological as the Holy Spirit reveals to us a risen

---

43. See E. Jüngel, *Theological Essays* (Edinburgh: T. & T. Clark, 1989), pp. 104–10.
44. Hardy, 'The Spirit of God', pp. 239–43. This idea will be developed further in the following chapters.

Christ who transcends not only our previous readings but all readings, revealing them to be a series of '"fixities" which we habitually prefer', the still pictures taken of a dance. The co-inherence of person and text takes place within the larger *perichoresis* of the Economic Trinity in which there is enough open texture created in the interweaving 'song of the Spirit' for the arrangement of creation's factors not to be fixed, to allow us to have a role in shaping worldly contingence.[45]

Conclusion

The question posed at the beginning of this chapter concerned the extent to which a Christian theistic realism allows human words to participate in creating worldly reality. The programmatic conclusion reached is that if there is to be room, then a model is needed that is not only extratextual as well as intratextual, but is also able to transcend the local certainties of traditions and communities. (Again, as with postliberal theology, the boundaries traced by our awareness of our human language-riddenness cannot be allowed to dictate an ontology.)

It has been suggested, first, that this model is incarnational; second, that it is trinitarian. This programme sets two tasks for the following chapters: first, there is the need to work out more precisely the place and role of language in both incarnational and trinitarian models. It is not enough to say that we can solve these problems merely by going 'higher', although that may be an essential part of the answer and the 'vertical' solution will be developed further in chapters 5 and 6. Obviously, the question of innovative 'truth-making' concerns the relation of human to divine creativity and therefore involves the doctrines of God and creation as well as Christology and Christian anthropology.

It also involves on the 'horizontal' plane the etymology of language use and the relation of epistemology to ontology within the economic trinitarian and christological models. In what way Christianly speaking does our language come to be able both to invent and to discover? And how does this relate to revelation and conversion? The exploration of these issues requires the importation of another paradigm and organizing model that will flesh out the process as well as annotate the content, and may then inform the theological endeavour. This will be the project of the next chapter.

---

45. Ibid., pp. 239–43.

4

The anatomy of language-riddenness

It has been noted that while theological realism and liberal revisionism are both able to account for new truths, they differ on whether
this new truth is something we discover as our concepts are brought into
line with it and are able to grasp it, or whether this is at least in part
something that human concepts participate in and have a role in creating. Although these positions may seem implacably opposed in coming
from quite different metaphysical stances, this opposition might be construed as simply reflecting these different premises rather than ruling
out one or the other as false. In other words, the clash of premises may
itself be seen as indicating the need for a more comprehensive integrative model that is able to accommodate both realist and postmodern
elements. What has emerged so far in the search for such a higher organizing model is a sketch of a theistic realism whose logic has been
identified as both incarnational and trinitarian and its dynamic accordingly as co-inherent, or perichoretic.

It has been suggested that it will be necessary to supplement the horizontal 'how' dimension with some input from another paradigm before
beginning to work out the 'vertical' aspects of such a model. If this
imported paradigm is able to supply more infrastructure, it will be possible to describe more adequately the process as well as the content of the
theological endeavour in a way that is still consistent with *its* structure.
The proposal to be tested here is that a Wittgensteinian paradigm will
serve this purpose, but a Wittgensteinian paradigm that goes beyond the
postliberal use of Wittgenstein and is more comprehensive than the postmodern weak thesis although essentially consistent with it.[1]

---

1. The legitimacy of employing a Wittgensteinian 'secondary explainer' within Christian
theology is confirmed by Wittgenstein himself, who saw the task of philosophy not as the

The paradigm

As postliberal theology bears witness, Wittgenstein's linguistic philosophy provides a means of integrating linguistic and non-linguistic aspects of human reality by taking practices – or activities involving the use of language – as the bedrock of human living in the world. Necessarily, according to Wittgenstein, language use subsumes language as such because it is *use* that mixes up language and world, and *users* that refer, rendering the object of the reference not simply something 'out there' but instead the thing-plus-its-use-in-*this*-context. Hilary Putnam's observations have expressed this same theory, but in Wittgenstein it is possible to trace the logical lineage of this position and expand its scope in a way that provides more useful material for theology. Wittgenstein's later philosophy is based on the premise (now claimed as postmodern) that inescapably, when we think or talk about language, we must do this thinking or talking in language. If particular uses of language are presupposed in all examinations or explanations of language, then language itself cannot give an explanation of how it links up with the world, for 'one cannot transcend language in language or transcend one's thoughts in thinking'.[2] In other words, it is impossible to *explain* the linking-up of language with the non-linguistic aspects of reality. The linking may only be demonstrated. This means that it is necessary to deal in irreducible language–world cross-sections rather than with language and world as separate layers of reality. These sign–world links are

Footnote 1 (*cont.*)
imposition of an external metaphysic but as clarification within a particular discourse or form of life. As such it need not be uncritical. Torrance condemns linguistic philosophy as having 'a superstitious veneration for ordinary language in [its] insistence that nothing is valid which is not describable within its compass', which renders it unable to account for the creation and refinement of the linguistic tools needed to express new truths. As he observes correctly, 'We must translate what we learn into our ordinary language if it is to be understandable and communicable; but we learn nothing new unless we break out of the grooves in which our thought has already been directed to run through our ordinary language. This is where an alert theology has an all-important role to play, in constructive as well as critical activity, in demanding and carrying through a significant shift in the meaning of ordinary terms to cope with the new insights and in creating new forms of expression apposite to new truth where the adaptation of old forms of speech and thought does not prove adequate.' What is *incorrect* here, it is suggested, is the narrowness of Torrance's view of linguistic philosophy – at least as represented by Wittgenstein – for there is arguably room within a Wittgensteinian model to allow for 'a rational element in dissatisfaction with existing language' and to suggest that 'the breaking away from the norm' means not only the discovery but also the creation of a new aspect of a linguistically interwoven reality (see Torrance, *God and Rationality*, p. 19).
2. M. B. Hintikka and J. Hintikka, *Investigating Wittgenstein* (Oxford: Blackwell, 1986), p. 3.

made by activities involving the use of language, by what Wittgenstein calls 'language-games'.[3]

Wittgenstein makes it clear that 'the term "language-game" is meant to bring into prominence the fact that the speaking of language is part of an activity, or of a form of life'.[4] Language-games are activities involving language, or 'micro-practices',[5] occurring within forms of life, whereas, orthogonally, forms of life are the institutions, belief systems, or ways of life constituted by complexes of particular 'moves' in various language-games – particular ways in which language-games are played in a particular context. A form of life is in effect a community of consensual activities ruled and shaped by certain beliefs. This is not necessarily a geographical community, although it may be, and it is not to be confused with larger systems such as whole religions, disciplines or cultures, because these, as Christianity demonstrates, may contain many sub-groupings supplying many local perspectives and many variations in the way practices are carried out.[6] To put this another way, whereas a given language-game is not usually confined to a particular form of life but the same types of language-using practice may occur in various forms of life, in any given situation a language-game will contain particular content or 'moves' that will either identify it as belonging to that situation of use, or will at least be consistent with its so belonging.

If, then, with a change in use, the meanings of words and actions change, there must come a point where the difference in use is such that it is questionable if the game is still the same game. If, for example, some of the content of Christian liturgical practice is changed in line with political sensitivities, at what point does it cease to be Christian and become some other religious expression? If the language is all caught up with the form of life, when the language changes so does the form of life. Some language-games are utterly ubiquitous, for example the practice of fact-stating, although their moves will differ from situation to situation – even the meaning of 'fact' may differ from one context to another, as the difference between scientific and religious facts demonstrates. Others are peculiar to certain contexts: for instance, the peculiarly religious language-game of praying and more narrowly the peculiarly Christian one of Holy Communion which, unique as it is to Christianity,

3. Wittgenstein, *Philosophical Investigations*, § 23. See also § 421 and *The Blue Book, Blue and Brown Books* (Oxford: Blackwell, 1958), p. 4.   4. Ibid., §§ 12, 23.
5. See N. Lash, 'How Large is a Language Game?', *Theology*, 87 (1984), 19–28.
6. Wittgenstein, *Philosophical Investigations*, § 24.

will have 'moves' that vary from congregation to congregation, a fortiori from denomination to denomination.

Thus language-game 'moves' express the content peculiar to a particular context just as the moves of chess are specific to chess and do not apply to checkers – or more subtly, as one chess game's moves chosen from a large number of possible moves are specific to that particular game of chess. When employed in the Christian context, generically religious language-games such as praying, meditating and fasting will have a specifically Christian – indeed local Christian – form and content encapsulating Christian experience and belief. One may infer rules or 'grammar' governing these moves – infer rather than identify – as language-games must be considered prior to the rules for the use of language extrapolable from them (although the rules will then reciprocally determine what counts as part of that game). This is because the only criterion for the use of a word (or gesture, or other non-verbal form of communication) is in the last analysis the entire language-game in which it plays a role.

Within this general premise that language-games and forms of life – rather than things and individuals which we then describe in words – form the basic units of human reality, Wittgenstein develops four ideas that will be seen to be of particular help in developing the horizontal infrastructure sought. These four ideas both intersect and are cumulative. The first of these is the concept of training.

According to Wittgenstein, the only way of learning the use of words is by observing or engaging in the practice of a language-game. We are trained in the use of language and learn its meaning this way rather than through the learning of propositional rules. To learn a language-game is to be trained by a community in the practice of a skill.[7] Training is ordinarily understood to be 'any activity designed systematically to improve job knowledge skills and/or abilities of individuals'.[8]

The concept of knowledge as primarily and fundamentally 'knowing how', or training, is also found in Michael Polanyi's work. Polanyi uses the term 'subception' to mean 'having the structure of a skill'.[9] He distinguishes two kinds of knowing – specifiable and non-specifiable. The non-specifiable part of knowing is the unreflective use of words and other forms of language as a part of activities, the intertwining of lan-

7. Ibid., §§ 146, 31, 6.
8. See R. Harre and R. Lamb (eds.) ,*The Encyclopaedia Dictionary of Psychology* (Cambridge, MA: MIT Press, 1983).
9. Polanyi, *The Tacit Dimension*, p. 8. See also S. Patterson, '*Word*, Words and World', *Colloquium*, 23/2 (1991), 71–84.

guage with the rest of the world. What Polanyi terms 'non-specifiable' is consistent with what Wittgenstein terms 'ineffable'. The role of words in practice constitutes a first-order use of words. 'When we use a tool we are attending to the meaning of its impact on our hands in terms of its effect on the things to which we are applying it. We may call this the semantic aspect of tacit knowing. All meaning tends to be displaced away from ourselves.'[10] To specify this use (that is, to articulate what we mean by our practices which involve the first-order use of words) is to translate actions or experiences into concepts.

As the notion of training is traditionally narrower than that of learning and more specific and practical and social in scope, Wittgenstein's use of the term to describe the learning of a language-game is appropriate in view of his emphasis on the acquiring of specific practices. Yet the primacy Wittgenstein accords to language-games has the effect of making training in language-using activities an integral component in all acquisition of knowledge.[11] In the same or similar way that everyday or first-order language-games are learnt in the first instance by training, so subsequent new applications of language may be learnt by a transfer or generalizing of that training.[12] These are then themselves inculcated by means of training.

Wittgenstein's understanding of training in effect expands what was originally a narrow concept applied initially to a narrow and special range of learning, but later called transfer of learning and applied more widely in educational psychology. While Wittgenstein does not himself talk of training in terms of transfer – not explicitly at any rate – the idea is implicit in what he has to say about training as such as well as in other aspects of his thinking described below.

To state the psychological theory Wittgensteinianly: what we learn in one place we are able to employ in another by bringing one language-game under the grammar of another similar language-game[13] – similar

10. Ibid., p. 13. Wittgenstein also refers to language as a tool.
11. Wittgenstein, *Philosophical Investigations*, §§ 5, 7, 25; *Blue Book*, pp. 17, 81.
12. This theory first appeared in a classic paper by E. L. Thorndike and R. S. Woodworth, 'The Influence of Improvement in One Mental Function Upon the Efficiency of Other Functions (I); II The Estimation of Magnitudes; III Functions Involving Attention, Observation and Discrimination', *Psychological Review*, 8 (1901), 247–61, 384–95, 553–64; cited by C. E. Osgood, *Method and Theory in Experimental Psychology* (Oxford: Oxford University Press, 1953), p. 524.
13. There is a 'solid base of experimental support' for the hypothesis that similarity between situations facilitates transfer. See A. P. Goldstein, 'Transfer and Maintenance', *The Prepare Curriculum: Teaching Prosocial Competence* (Champaign, IL: Research Press, 1988), p. 531.

enough for us to imagine that what we know about one practice will apply to another, except that in the most basic instances of this phenomenon (the sort that first-year psychology students are familiar with) we do not 'imagine' it at all in the sense that we do not creatively construe the transfer. These instances cannot be upper-cortically instigated because the same phenomenon is observable in rats and possibly even in lower species. Yet for all that, the primitive transfer of training at rat-in-a-maze level seems not only of a piece with the transfer that has happened when our dog 'thinks' that her wrapping an ice-cream in a paper napkin is an appropriate storage technique because covering bones with leaves is an acceptable substitute for burying them, but also at the bottom of (although not a sufficient explanation of) what happens when we see a piece of our own life-situation in terms of a piece of biblical narrative. The transfer upon which we build our creative construals is not somehow less creative because it has preconceptual, or subceptual, roots.[14] This notion of transfer is inherent in two other notions of Wittgenstein's to be discussed later.

While the subceptual aspect of transfer of training exemplifies Polanyi's dictum, 'we know more than we can tell',[15] for human beings there is a linguistic component to this training transfer. When we learn to understand things in certain ways, the training we receive is not so much a training in understanding as such as a training in *activities* involving certain world–word links. The transfer of that training is the transfer of ways of doing things that rely on a particular linking up of words with world to a new context of use. As Grant Gillett puts it,

> Although most of the time what I perceive is what is there (this is entailed by my grasp of the meanings of words), at times I can perceive an aspect of something which involves assimilating that object, in an imaginative way, to other (equally public) objects of experience. By so doing, I forge an internal relation (based on the practices in which a term is used) between the x I am seeing and y. The assimilation essentially involves the application of a term with meaning, marking the concept ‹y›, to x so that we see it as y. When I see an aspect, I locate what I am seeing in a conceptual practice the specifications of which involve concrete situations and what people say and do in them. To see an aspect is thus to draw upon a technique

14. Arguably this does not undermine the revelatory nature of this generalizing activity so much as draw attention to a common creatureliness. As such it begs the question of animal creativity in relation to what is normally classified as adaptive behaviour.
15. See Polanyi, *The Tacit Dimension*.

(or rule-governed habit or custom) which ties sensory contact to action and discourse.[16]

The notion of 'seeing as', or aspect-seeing, mentioned here will be picked up later. It is enough to say at this point that if a primitive, subceptual process of transfer is at the bottom of our more sophisticated hermeneutical construals, likewise 'seeing as', or aspect-seeing, is the root initiator of transfer. As indicated, these ideas of Wittgenstein's are at least implicitly interwoven or co-inherent, yet understanding them singly is necessary as they relate to different facets of human activity and comprehension.

The second Wittgensteinian notion to be examined, his understanding of reference, provides a description of the relation of propositions and experience to a language-ridden world. Wittgenstein eschews any attempt to describe the link between language and world *as such* not because he believes such a link does not exist, but because logically any description of a language–world link, as in itself a use of language, will already be a language-game that assumes certain language-world links. For this reason Wittgenstein came to regard his earlier *Tractatus* propositional picture and mirroring theories as models of an 'internal' reference within a wider, more complex theory; picturing and mirroring do not so much disappear as cease to be regarded as primary language–world connectors. Instead they model internal correspondences.[17] A general theory of simple isomorphic naming or picturing relations will no longer do, for it is apparent that the situation is far more complicated than simple theories of correspondence can accommodate. Linguistic 'pictures', in so far as they can still be said to be pictures, are pictures projected by particular rules governing how reality is to be read; they operate within a reality defined by language-games. Yet at the same time the language-games themselves, as the 'projective links with reality', have to be incorporated in the 'picture' if the picture is to serve its purpose of depiction.[18]

---

16. G. Gillett, *Representation, Meaning and Thought* (Oxford: Clarendon Press, 1992), p. 191.
17. As Putnam argues also.
18. A prevalent view of Wittgenstein confuses the unsayability of the sign–world link with the inaccessibility of world or the impossibility of reference, taking language-games (thus shorn of their world-connecting function) as essentially equivalent to language usages and the playing of language-games as accordingly equivalent to participation in a discourse. On this view, to understand language is to 'understand the role in our lives played by different kinds of utterance in different circumstances'. Truth comes down to a matter of assertability or justifiability – 'sayability' in a particular context (Hintikka and

Putnam explains all this succinctly: 'There is a commonsense way of clearing up the puzzle about how many objects there are in the room, and that is to say, "It depends on what you mean by 'object'". This commonsense remark is perfectly right, but deeper than may appear to the commonsense mind itself.' The thing and its description, and the description and its use, are inseparable in such a way that it is questionable whether we could perceive or comprehend anything at all without language, for to 'talk of "facts" without specifying the language to be used is to talk of nothing; the word "fact" no more has its use fixed by the word itself than does the word "exist" or the word "object"'. The rules for the use of a word that fix a concept (for example, the concept of 'egg' commonly means to us something oval, hard, fragile, smooth, edible, produced by a bird) have been laid down by consensual practice. That this context may be both large and invisible to us through its very humdrum familiarity does not render it universal ('egg' means something rather different to an entymologist or marine zoologist), but merely points to this particular 'grammar' having ruled our use of the word over many years and in many places. Nor does the deceptively straightforward verifiability or falsifiability of the proposition render it immune to an origin in the rule-governed language-using practices of a community. As Putnam puts it, 'Meanings are not objects in a museum, to which words somehow get attached . . . But sophisticated interpretative practice presupposes a sophisticated understanding of the way words are used by the community whose words one is interpreting.'[19]

The upshot of this theory of reference is that any notion that we can check up on our descriptions of things according to an extra-linguistic 'how they really are' is illusory; for us there is no 'behind' to language.[20] Yet this is not to say that we have no input at all from 'out there'. As Putnam remarks,

> Denying that it makes sense to ask whether our concepts 'match' something totally uncontaminated by conceptualization is one thing; but to hold that every conceptual system is therefore just as good as

Footnote 18 (cont.)
Hintikka, *Investigating Wittgenstein*, pp. 226–7, 230–1). Yet this is a serious misunderstanding of what Wittgenstein is about. 'Ironically, the impossibility (for Wittgenstein) of saying anything about language-games in language stems from this very semantical function they perform' (Hintikka and Hintikka, *Investigating Wittgenstein*, 216).
19. Putnam, *Representation and Reality*, pp. 113–14, 119.
20. 'Would it be correct to say that our concepts reflect our life? They stand in the middle of it.' Wittgenstein, *Remarks on Colour*, ed. and trans. G. E. M. Anscombe (Oxford: Blackwell, 1977), 3, § 302.

every other would be something else. If anyone really believed that, and if they were foolish enough to pick a conceptual system that told them they could fly and to act upon it by jumping out of a window, they would, if they were lucky enough to survive, see the weakness of the latter view at once. . . . The very inputs upon which our knowledge is based are conceptually contaminated; but contaminated inputs are better than none. If contaminated inputs are all we have, still all we have has proved to be quite a bit.[21]

A corollary of all this is that if our reference to 'the thing out there' is always to 'the thing plus its description' (where the description is a product of the use that defines its meaning) – which indicates a constructivist component in our propositions – likewise our reference to an experience is to 'the experience-plus-its-interpretation'. If the proposition or fact is a picture of a non-linguistic entity or event which relies on the way that entity or event has already been comprehended linguistically, in the same way the interpretation of an experience is a linguistic picture of the experience, where that picture is a product of antecedent uses of that linguistic picture in terms of similar experiences. This means that the experience comes packed with an implicit proposition about the experience which renders that experience intelligible. Without the comprehension afforded by at least a fuzzy concept of what the nature of the experience is, it could not register *as* an experience. Without such a key, we would have 'had the experience but missed the meaning'.[22] As Lindbeck points out, this means that religious symbols construed under a phenomenological approach as prethematic or prelinguistic universals may be traced instead to social origins. Therefore it is 'conceptually confused to talk of symbolizations (and therefore of experiences) that are purely private' – that is, prior to communal linguistic conventions.[23] And Putnam agrees that 'even our description of our own sensations, so dear as a starting point for knowledge to generations of epistemologists, is heavily affected (as are the sensations themselves, for that matter) by a host of conceptual choices'.[24]

These implications of Wittgenstein's theory of reference – the constructive aspect of both propositions and experience – may be related back to the training aspect of Wittgenstein's thinking and at the same time to a third aspect. To play a language-game in a particular context is

21. Putnam, *Reason, Truth and History*, p. 54.
22. T. S. Eliot, 'Four Quartets', *Collected Poems: 1909–1962* (London: Faber & Faber, 1963).
23. Lindbeck, *The Nature of Doctrine*, p. 35.   24. Putnam, *Reason, Truth and History*, p. 54.

to play certain moves which depend on certain perceptions, on 'seeing something as something'; but for that 'seeing something as something' to happen requires our having been trained in certain language-using activities.[25] Although there has to be something there to perceive in the first place, we are nevertheless trained to perceive.[26] Aspect seeing may enable the transfer of our training, but at the same time training lies behind the seeing. At some point a new way of understanding or experiencing the world will dawn upon us, but the dawning has involved learning a new activity involving a new use of words. Again, these models are reciprocal, or co-inherent: training underlies perceiving; perceiving underlies the transfer of training.

Gillett observes that 'When Wittgenstein discusses perception he spends a great deal of time on "seeing as" or "aspect-seeing" . . . The fact that we see some things now as this and now as that suggests that we do so by means of representations which are distinct from those things.'[27] Likewise, Stephen Mulhall suggests that

> Aspect-dawning is characterized by the observer's felt need to employ a representation which might otherwise refer to subjective visual experience – to one way of seeing the figure – as if it were the report of a new perception. It must be so characterized because it is precisely this combination of felt need and the implication of a perceptual change that creates the paradoxical air definitive of aspect-dawning experiences – the paradox manifest in our saying of a figure we know to be unchanged: 'Before I saw something else, but now I see a cube.'[28]

Gillett argues that while it may depend on an innate potential, aspect-seeing, like perception in general, is learned. If language-using activities connect signs with the world within a given context, then the contextual consensus regarding 'what means what' must be prior to our comprehension of our environment. Comprehension depends on some prior knowledge of 'what means what' which is integral not only to interpretation but also to perception. It follows that while a particular experience may be private (i.e. solitary) this privacy is only partial. If we are to be able to comprehend a novel experience we must have the means to interpret it. That same experience, or something similar enough to be

25. Hintikka and Hintikka, *Investigating Wittgenstein*, pp. 193–208.
26. See Gillett, *Representation, Meaning and Thought*.
27. Ibid., p. 189 (see also his chapter 1, 'Concepts and Generality', pp. 6–31).
28. S. Mulhall, *On Being in the World: Wittgenstein and Heidegger on Seeing Aspects* (London/New York: Routledge, 1990), p. 11. Wittgenstein, *Last Writings in the Psychology of Philosophy*, vol. 1, ed. G. H. von Wright and H. Nyman, trans. C. G. Luckhardt and M. A. E. Aue (Oxford: Blackwell, 1992), § 493.

relatable to it, must have been undergone and described in some way by someone else, so that it acquires a 'grammar tag' that enables us to read it. The interpretation of the aspect we see, which enables us to know and say what we see, is inseparable from the perceptual process itself.[29]

Nevertheless, as Mulhall points out, not all perception is aspect-seeing. Aspect-seeing occurs when we are aware that there is more than one available option, when we are faced with an ambiguous picture. It is 'an orientation which provides the framework within which [the seer] might go on to make certain hypotheses.' In aspect-seeing we consciously attach a certain description to the picture in preference to another. We tag it as readable according to a certain rule for its use. Normally we are unaware that we attach any description at all, simply because one description is the clear choice. The value of such ambiguous situations or figures for Wittgenstein is that they make the descriptive attachment obvious, for 'When an aspect of a picture dawns, we recognize that a new kind of description of the perceived figure might be given, and we see it in those terms; when we continuously perceive that aspect, we take the status of the figure as a particular kind of thing (viz. a picture) for granted.' Mulhall argues that seeing aspects of pictures is essentially the same as understanding the meanings of words; linguistic meanings too are subject to aspect-perception. Wittgenstein himself was concerned to press an analogy between the experience of meaning and experiences of aspect-dawning in general. Here aspect-dawning is expressed in the language-game of determining or discovering the meaning of a word, and continuous aspect-perception in the various language-games which employ or exemplify that use thereafter.[30]

To relate the concepts covered so far: when everything to which we refer comes already language- and context-wrapped, the result is a complex circle of reciprocity. The language-games that are all mixed up with the realities we experience and hold beliefs about are also all mixed up with the experiences and the beliefs themselves. Each has a part in the other's existence; each indwells the other. An experience, then, may, be understood as irreducibly experience-plus-interpretation (propositional picture of the experience) while, as the merry-go-round turns, that propositional picture (belief or fact) is seen to be itself dependent upon the experience that confirms or justifies it. The egg is experienced

29. Gillett, *Representation, Meaning and Thought*, p. 189.
30. Mulhall, *On Being in the World*, pp. 18, 20, 27–8, 35, 38 (see also Wittgenstein, *Philosophical Investigations*, §§ 195a–d, 214d).

as an egg because it *is*, in fact, an egg; on the other hand, it is confirmed to be an egg because it is experienced *as* an egg! There is no getting behind the mutual interdependence of what we believe and experience as real. Their co-inherence as expressed in language-using activities must therefore be treated as primitive, a given. 'What has to be accepted, the given, is – so one could say – *forms of life*.'[31]

But forms of life change, and we leave some forms of life and enter new ones. Or at some point we comprehend an aspect of a form of life that we had not seen before. Furthermore, in coming to comprehend something new, we transfer previous training from one situation to another. In everything new there is something old, and in everything old the facts of which we are sure are facts internal to a form of life which rules them to be facts. It is important to consider one more Wittgensteinian notion before getting down to the theological implications of all this, however. Wittgenstein does not consider language to be a flat and featureless verbal plane. While the meaning of words is in many cases established by the uses to which they are put, if every new use of a particular term constituted a new semantical connection there would be a hopeless plethora of equivocality in which any stability of meaning would be lost. In this situation identity must go soft.[32] Obviously some uses rely on other, more basic ones; for example, the language-game of making a mistake will be parasitic on concepts incorporated in basic perceptual practices. If primary language-games are the basic activities of human living carried out in the context of various forms of life, there is in secondary or second-order language-games, such as believing, or doubting, or verifying, or theologizing, the addition of an extra layer of meaning in that the reference of the secondary game is in the first instance to the primary one (which in turn effects the basic, first-order, sign–world connection). I believe my father is gardening. I verify it by phoning him. Both the believing and the verifying language-games refer to the primary one of gardening. Wittgenstein describes the relation of secondary to primary games as that of superimposition.[33]

Metaphoric or parabolic secondary language-games take primary connections between words and things and through them express further meanings, tell further truths and express further realities without jettisoning the primary truth and reality through which they

31. Wittgenstein, *Philosophical Investigations*, p. 226.
32. Putnam, *Mind, Language and Reality*, p. 179.
33. Hintikka and Hintikka, *Investigating Wittgenstein*, p. 219.

refer. The parable or metaphor, as a second-order theological proposition ('the Kingdom of God is like . . .') is not deprived of reference (as Lindbeck asserts) but refers through other references; we see some things through other things.

This is a species of training transfer. Transfer explains the superimposition, but the reverse is not the case. Not all transfers involve the superimposition of secondary upon primary language-games, but all conversions of primary by secondary involve transfer, just as all transfers involve perceptual decisions that enable us to relate things by reading the whole in terms of a part. And as usual with Wittgenstein, this is not a one-way street but a reciprocal process. As the secondary game converts a primary game to its own use, it is contextualized by that which it converts – the primary game – so that each informs the other and inevitably each is modified. The term 'conversion' is a deliberate choice to point up the theological significance of this dynamic. In his parables Jesus takes up the data of what is humanly primary and converts its import and meaning so that it may reveal what is truly primary, the fundamental truth about reality. The connection of this theory with the hermeneutical models described in the previous chapter is obvious and will be developed further later on.

Meanwhile this understanding of primary and secondary uses of language may be extended, finally and briefly but significantly, by Roger White's analysis of primary and secondary predications in which predications made of God assume ontological primacy over the same predications made of a creature or aspect of world. Where philosophical, or metaphysical, and religious ways of understanding the world overlap, the difference in perspectives means that uses of terms held in common will be different, yet sufficiently similar to prevent 'a clear-cut answer to the question whether the word is used in the same sense or not, and where different considerations pull us in different directions over this question'. At this point it is a matter of which sense we are going to adopt as primary in the sense of fundamental. In this respect, as White observes,

> A primary sense is neither . . . necessarily the sense most frequently encountered, nor an etymologically prior sense. When we say one sense is primary and another secondary, we are saying that to explain the secondary sense one must necessarily bring into account the notion signified by the word in the primary sense.[34]

---

34. R. White, 'Notes on Analogical Predication and Speaking about God', in Brian Hebblethwaite and Stewart Sutherland (eds.), *The Philosophical Frontiers of Christian Theology* (Cambridge: Cambridge University Press, 1982), pp. 197–226, 200–2, 210.

Of course, when the 'God-sense' is primary, Wittgenstein's secondary sense has become ontologically primary and the reverse.

The application

It is now possible to begin to relate all the interrelated aspects of Wittgenstein's thinking so far discussed: training and transfer of training, the referents of propositions and experiences, aspect-seeing, and the relation of primary to secondary language-games, within an organizing theological model. On the horizontal human plane the theological concept which arguably integrates and makes sense of them all humanly yet theologically is conversion. Conversion may act as a common-denominator connecting link between human language-using and learning processes and God's incarnation into this language-riddenness. Here it is suggested not only that these various Wittgensteinian descriptions of human perceiving, learning and knowing processes are descriptions of kinds of conversion, but also that the interaction of these perceiving, learning and knowing processes is the means by which our conversion to a christological reality occurs. Therefore the description of how language is involved in these processes may be drawn up into a christological and trinitarian framework. Furthermore, these descriptions which delineate both received and innovative aspects of making new moves in language-games – Ford's 'finding and fashioning' – lend structure to the description of a creaturely givenness which is still in the process of being given, in which the recipients are also in part the givers.

First, within this organizing model as a first step in the integration of its various aspects, Wittgenstein's notion of 'seeing as', or aspect-perception (which has been noted to relate reciprocally to training and underpin transfer of training), may be related to the hermeneutical tool of typology to provide a description of the typological process.[35] On this argument, the roots of typology as a device which converts characters and narrative to a new use lie in the apperceptive process of aspect-seeing. In playing a typological language-game we see someone or something as someone or something else, or in the more extended narrative intratextual typology, we see someone's story in terms of someone else's, a narrative in terms of another, the master narrative of Jesus Christ. To do this we must see aspects in common in the midst of

---

35. See G. Green, '"The Bible As . . ."'; also his *Imagining God* (San Francisco: Harper & Row, 1989).

the differences and be able to relate them in such a way that the aspect in common frames the whole within which the differences are able to extend and colour each other. In the world outside the text, in relating people, stories and events through typology, we transfer the knowledge that is the product of training in one context to the other context. If typology is understood thus in terms of the focusing on an aspect of a person, story or happening which then when transferred provides a key to the interpretation of another then, so far from being simply the revival of a premodern biblical hermeneutic, it may be recognized as being built into the way we organize and understand the world. Yet biblical typology is an extended and deliberate 'seeing as' which is to aspect-seeing as analogy and parable are to metaphor. As it were, the language-game of 'seeing as' provides the initial link upon which exegesis rests, a discernment that is spontaneous as much as deliberate, subceptual as much as conceptual. It involves a training transfer through the superimposition of itself as secondary language-game upon the primary language-games whose grammars determine our seeing options.

Garrett Green has employed Wittgenstein's notion of 'seeing as' in a theology of revelation as imagination. Where the 'experiments of the gestalt psychologists . . . showed that we perceive not by the cumulative association of atomistic sense data but rather by grasping a whole pattern',[36] Wittgenstein's employment of ambiguous figures such as the 'duck-rabbit' shows us that

> everything we perceive or know depends on our grasping a particular pattern by which diverse parts present themselves as a whole. We do not construe the world piecemeal by assembling discrete elements into organized wholes; rather, having a world means seeing according to a pattern, having a vision of how things hang together as the precondition for recognising the parts as parts in the first place.[37]

Imagination is the agent of this vision, for, as Mulhall notes, the use of 'as' signals awareness of another option, the beginnings of a move away from the 'rigid and exclusive paradigm' of the ordinary. The options are enormously more varied than our blinkered habits allow us to comprehend. There are many possible descriptions of what is seen, if we do not fixate upon an 'exclusive and rigid paradigm'.[38] Thus perception, when

---

36. Green, *Imagining God*, p. 65.   37. Green, '"The Bible As . . ."', p. 85.
38. Here Wittgenstein is trying to make us see the 'elasticity of the concept of "what is seen"'. Mulhall, *On Being in the World*, pp. 13–15 (cf. Wittgenstein, *Philosophical Investigations*, p. 198).

it involves aspect-seeing, necessarily involves imagination; 'seeing as' is the 'copula of imagination'.[39] Imagination can involve using something as a paradigm to display 'a pattern, a coherent nexus of relations, in a simple and obvious way' that envisages a world. Green argues that in religion a normative text may be paradigmatic in this way. For instance, 'Christians have imagined the world according to the paradigm exemplified by the [Apostles'] creed.' Green contends that access to the transcendent is entirely by means of these paradigms which point analogically to the reality described. If 'imagination is the human ability to perceive and represent likenesses (the paradigmatic faculty), religions employ that ability in the service of cosmic orientation, rendering the world accessible to the imagination of their adherents in such a way that its ultimate nature, value and destiny are made manifest'.[40]

The analogy of the paradigm to what it paradigms is construed on faith. Our taking of what is revealed to be the truth means the reading of 'as' as 'is'. Accordingly, for Green, Christian hermeneutics is imagination in the service of faith in which 'Commitment in faith and assent by the mind constrained by the imagination are one and the same.'

> The point of contact for divine revelation is materially the paradigmatic image of God embodied in Jesus Christ; formally it is the human imagination – that ability of human beings to take elements of their 'middle-sized' world as paradigmatic images of reality to which they would otherwise have no access . . . Christian revelation so [formally] conceived remains an utterly human phenomenon, comparable with other uses of imagination.[41]

On Green's account, then, the formal or horizontal/human aspect of revelation involves an act of faithful imagination. Imagination is 'the instrument of revelation, the means by which God makes himself known in the present life of believers', by which the 'human likeness to God, worn away by sin' becomes 'newly minted in the humanity of Christ'. It is the medium through which the material (incarnational) revelation is appropriated, the point at which our own realities encounter the converting Christian reality. At this point of conversion our imaginations become '"faithful", "Christomorphic", *Gottförmig*, constituting a newly created analogy between God and humanity' in construing our own story in terms of God's.[42] Imagination, as here

39. Green, '"The Bible As . . ."', pp. 88–9.   40. Green, *Imagining God*, pp. 67–9, 79–80.
41. Green, '"The Bible as . . ."', pp. 88, 92.
42. Green, *Imagining God*, pp. 104, 106–8, 105–6.

understood in terms of aspect-seeing, is thus the medium through which God acts to reveal to us the true story of both God's and our own lives. Thus the true function of imagining language-games emerges only when they are seen through the God-revealing language-game of incarnation.

As observed, Green has linked imagination with aspect-dawning in describing the process of revelation, a process in which the imaginer contributes to the revealing process but in a way that conforms to Christ. As already suggested, a further development of Wittgenstein's notion of aspect-dawning in relation to typology and conversion is possible if conversion is understood as occurring through a transfer of the training we receive in linking words up with non-linguistic aspects of reality, where training transfer is understood as an integral part of the subsumption (conversion) of primary language-games by secondary ones. What we acquire in one context is transferred to another situation where it comes under a new interpretative gloss, a new grammar or rule. Here the familiar world–word connecting activities are played out again, but in a new context of meaning; the novel activity acquires meaning through application of the familiar, but at the same time the familiar has superimposed on it a secondary grammar; it is understood through something else. The primary 'imagining' language-games become revelatory through a superimposition of a christological grammar which provides the secondary (yet fundamental) reference for their moves; at the same time revelation is 'seen through' imagination. As mentioned, the generalizing is reciprocal in that what is generalized and the new context of use become referents for each other and, as each is seen through the other, both are modified. While our understanding of revelation may be changed by seeing it in terms of imagination – that is, we may discover a humanly creative component to it – at the same time we may learn more about the true nature of imagination by experiencing it as revelatory. The situations are now inseparably linked. Each informs and indwells the other. As the training becomes new-context-shaped, so the context expands to include a new use, practice or description. Cognitively we are turned in a new direction.[43] Our understanding of world comes under a new, theological, description by means of a transfer of our previous learning of how to go on in the world to a new

---

43. Cognition is here taken in the contemporary psychological sense to embrace behavioural as well as mental processes.

situation of use – that is, through the conversion of our primary human language-games.

Arguably, then, this training/aspect-seeing/superimposition mechanism is the human-cognitive root of *metanoia*. If 'seeing as' may be understood as the precipitating event in this process of transfer, the double reciprocal reference of primary and secondary language-games is the process through which these more basic cognitive processes become conceptual. Here the relationship between transfer of training and the superimposition of secondary upon primary language-games might be seen as the relationship between the cognitive restructuring that takes place at subceptual level and that higher-cortical re-cognition which is at least partly conceptual, where the former is a part of the latter process but not the reverse. Patently not all aspect-dawnings and training transfers are personally transformative and/or converting even though, arguably, our coming into a fuller knowledge of and participation in God's creation is a part of our conversion (but which has to be brought inside an incarnational grammar to become such). On this view the discovery and appropriation of what is being revealed is at the same time an act of creation. It may be argued that novel metaphors are created with the re-grammaring transfer of our training in aspect-seeing[44] and, as implied, this metaphor-making is basic to the extended and deliberate 'seeing as' of biblical typology.[45] Here the imperative of *metanoia* demands that the transfer between the use in the old situation and the use in the new, which both discovers and invents, creates a tension between the transferred terms and their new situation which may be expressed metaphorically or parabolically. As Surin puts it, 'At this juncture the human subject is suspended between two narratives, one "pre-Christian" and the other "Christian".'[46] Here the horizontal grammar of conversion comes under, co-inheres with the vertical grammar of incarnation. The point where the two worldviews meet is the person of Christ. We are

44. While transfer of training is intimately related to the formation of metaphors, Gillett's comments nevertheless are pertinent to metaphor conceived more broadly, where 'seeing' becomes itself a metaphor for the various types of metaphorical construal and description. Thus a Wittgensteinian view of metaphor-making language-games reasonably begins with 'seeing as' but goes beyond perceiving of aspects. Metaphor-making is discussed further in chapter 5 in connection with the doctrine of creation.
45. This is not to imply that all training transfer is expressed metaphorically, although it is arguably the case that transfer of training (or learning) is integral to the metaphorical process (see S. Patterson, 'The Theological Implications of the Relationship between a Wittgensteinian Understanding of the Relationship of Language to World and the Role of Metaphor as an Agent of Revelation', unpublished Ph.D. thesis, University of Otago, Dunedin, New Zealand, 1991).   46. Surin, *Turnings*, pp. 216–17.

addressed and commanded by the reality of Jesus Christ in an encounter in which the horizontal human grammar of conversion comes under the vertical divine grammar of incarnation. Our assent to this challenge is our active participation in the re-grammaring of our pre-Christian narrative, or forms of life. What were previously for us the primary facts about reality now receive a new figurative meaning as Christ's reality trains us in a new use of old words in which all primary references are to God. When our way of thinking has been thus converted, our human, creaturely forms of life with all their richly creative metaphoric and parabolic resources are taken to be God-given, gratuitous in the sense of being a product of grace, bestowed freely and unmeritedly. As Jüngel has said, the 'absolute' metaphor is the entry of God's being to speech in the person of Christ.[47] If in our encounter with Christ we are transformed through the converting of our minds, God's incarnation is into a human reality which is both world and language, being and knowing.

Conclusion

The aim of this chapter has been to develop a more precise 'horizontal' theory of truth as both discovery and innovation before going on to consider the 'vertical' divine dimension in such a theory. As suggested in the previous chapter, it is too simplistically 'God of the gaps' merely to assert that innovative 'truth-making' is the work of the Spirit. While that may indeed be the case, it is imperative upon us to pursue the 'how' of this in human terms as far as possible, but within the Christian assumption of creaturely contingence.

In this chapter the aim has been first to identify and describe some Wittgensteinian models of language and knowledge in relation to the world which, taken in conjunction, may serve to flesh out our understanding of these relations, and then to begin to fit these notions into an integrating theological model for which they then may provide the infrastructure. At this stage, as a first step from the human psycho-sociolinguistic to the theological, the integrating model is that of conversion. As the Wittgensteinian models themselves interweave and coinhere, this has not simply been a matter of mapping out a surface by adding pieces together but more an exercise in caving. Within the overall exercise, contributing or reciprocal theological models have served a mediating

47. Jüngel, *Theological Essays*, pp. 56–7.

function in gathering together the Wittgensteinian material under their headings. Garrett Green's work on the revelatory role of imagination is one of these, as is the Frei/Lindbeck typological hermeneutic. This gathering which is in turn itself gathered into the conversion model is an instance of Polanyian integration in which each level serves as a higher organizing principle for the lower one(s) and at each level the whole is more than the sum of its parts.[48] The parts articulate the detail that is gathered – without such detail conversion and imagination are opaque notions – but conversion is more than the sum of human psycho-social processes just as revelation is more than human imagining.

Yet is this view of conversion really the beginnings of a case for 'truth-making'? Is not our conversion to the community norms of our trainers, the biblical hermeneuts, the inculcators of doctrine and shapers of cognition – which is what the postliberal theologians (with the exception of Ford and Green, if they may be termed that) have been saying all along? That would arguably be the case were it not for the enigma of the transfer process that lies at the heart of perception and conversion. While we are trained to a degree in the subceptual 'seeings as' that precipitate the transfer, training is not the whole thing. In the hidden ineffable interface between words and world novel connections are made that break with tradition. There are those retrieved practices, terms, rules, facts, interpretations and beliefs which are transferred, and there is a juxtaposition which is new. While not all transfers result in innovative combinations, there are as many possibilities of novelty as there are individuals. To be human is to be innovative, to be born into and to continue life-long in the creative relation with words and things through which we participate in the making of both world and truth. This is the creaturely humanity which God has both made and embraced incarnationally; this, therefore, is the creaturely incarnation in which we participate in Christ.

The effect of employing this supplementary perspective, then, is not, as might have been thought, to reduce conversion or revelation to psycho-social human processes or to account for innovative truth solely in these terms. As indicated, the transfer of training at the heart of this cognitive process cannot explain itself as a self-steering mechanism, for it appears that the cognitive restructuring that expands our actuality is an interweaving of training *and* transfer, of tradition and something else

48. See Polanyi, *The Tacit Dimension*, chapter 3.

that cannot be accounted for by what has gone before, that cannot be explained within the paradigm or on the horizontal plane of human psycho-social processes. There is a need for something more than the horizontal dimension to make sense of the innovative aspects of imagination and metaphor-making as agents of revelation. Conversion as a human process cannot explain itself. Here the Spirit works in our inner parts as 'among the inner parts something open, something wild, a long rumour of wisdom [which] keeps winding into each tune' to reorganize us cognitively.[49] It remains now to bring the complexities of the horizontal into play with the vertical, divine dimension of innovative truth.

49. Hardy, 'The Spirit of God', p. 250.

5

The nature of theistic realism

It has been suggested that the innovative capacity of human thought and language cannot be explained without a 'vertical' (theistic) dimension.[1] Having drawn human cognitive and linguistic re-grammaring and refiguring processes inside the 'horizontal' process of conversion, we may describe more adequately the 'how' of the conversion of old realities into new ones but we cannot explain conversion itself without drawing it inside Christology as a whole, just as we cannot explain Christology itself except in relation to the doctrine of God. In the same way, neither can Christology alone make sense of divine involvement in human language-using and cognitive processes in revelation and conversion.[2] If these processes help articulate the way God works in the world, they articulate an Economic Trinity which includes the pneumatological operation within creation.

The giant proposition

On a Wittgensteinian and Putnamian view the distinction between reality and truth is an internal one as it relies on a correspondence that in turn relies on certain premises. These premises lay down a distinction and correlation between language and world, which lies so deep in our concepts that much of our language and thinking cannot make sense

---

1. The co-inherent nature of Christian doctrine means that it is impossible to examine the God–human relation without traversing several doctrinal areas, notably the doctrine of God including trinitarian doctrine, Christology and pneumatology, as well as the doctrines of creation, Christian anthropology, sin, salvation and ecclesiology. This traverse, while inevitably sketchy and incomplete, will take the rest of the book.
2. In each case, in a Polanyian (and Gödelian) way, the whole is bigger than the sum of its parts and can only be explained in terms of a greater whole.

without it.[3] According to Fergus Kerr, behind the realist notion that we have access to 'objective' reality lies the illusion that our context is the only reality. That this context is apparently divisible into mind and matter tempts us into a choice between things and thoughts as the primary reality, a choice which overlooks what Wittgenstein has called *das Leben,* the stream of life.[4] From this splitting up of our primary reality comes the idea that meaning-making is a business of designating objects and that therefore meaning is a function of reference. As this assumption disregards the evidence that in many cases words receive their meaning from their use, there is then the need for 'a theory to explain how mere sentences manage to represent reality'.

> The hardest thing, philosophically, is to free reflection from the bewitching power of the devices of our language ... The very signs that enable us to act rationally, and, among much else, to reason and reflect, in the first place, raise fantasies that alienate us from ourselves. Our signs are so natural that we come to imagine that we could communicate without them: meaning becomes a purely mental activity.

Thus we have to say with Wittgenstein, 'Would it be correct to say that our concepts reflect our life? They stand in the middle of it.'[5]

As Putnam reminds us, the distinctions and correlations we hold are based on contaminated inputs – we take these propositions to be a true picture of a world that is in turn a picture of other pictures, determined by certain other propositions that we take to be true. The rules (or grammar) governing what is to be taken as real are inferred from the connection-makings that these rules regulate. Thus the language-game of pointing out colours relies on the rule: 'red is a colour', but the rule itself, that *this* is a colour, has arisen out of the game itself, from the question arising out of the pointing, 'What are these?' This may be an artificial way of analysing what goes on, but it serves to make us aware

---

3. 'One thinks that one is tracing the outline of the thing's nature over and over again, and one is merely tracing round the frame through which we look at it.' 'A picture held us captive and we could not get outside it, for it lay in our language and language seemed to repeat it to us inexorably' (see Wittgenstein, *Philosophical Investigations,* §§ 114, 115).

4. Kerr, *Theology After Wittgenstein,* pp. 133–5. Wittgenstein, *Philosophical Investigations* §§ 196, 428, 435; *Remarks on the Philosophy of Psychology,* vol. 2, ed. G. H. von Wright and H. Nyman, trans. C. G. Luckhardt and M. A. E. Aue (Oxford: Blackwell, 1980), § 687. 'We have been tempted into the habit of thinking that either *die Dinge* or *unsere Vorstellungen* must be the primary thing, but the choice between realism and idealism overlooks *das Leben:* that is Wittgenstein's suggestion' (p. 133).

5. Ibid., pp. 134, 136 (Wittgenstein, *Philosophical Investigations,* §§ 209, 693; *Remarks on Colour,* 3, § 302).

that the descriptions and definitions are part of the things and events themselves, because the *knowing-how* of our practices has inculcated the *knowing-that* of our facts, and these *knowings-that* now underlie our *know-how*.

Yet the very postmodern recognition that these circularities constitute various human local realities turns truth into mere assertibility unless it is accompanied by the recognition that this reality is in turn subject to a further judgment. New truths are on these terms provisional gains to actuality which cannot be verified in terms of a correspondence with an external reality but seem inadequately warranted by their internal endorsement, however right this seems. As Lindbeck puts it, the human forms of life in which this circular process goes on resemble giant propositions in that they beg verification as a whole, but may only be verified from outside, from correspondence or otherwise to a transcendent reality.[6] If at human level we seem caught in the postmodern flux between language-riddenness (a critical realism that allows a noetic component in being) and reality-riddenness (an idealism that allows a reality-riddenness in our knowing) that flux begs to be judged according to a higher truth, in terms of a higher reality.

> For the realist view to prevail, the existence of a supratemporal perspective on the world is covertly admitted. A realist approach to the truth-value of assertions in certain specifiable classes apparently trades on the presence of a higher being. From a theological point of view, then, the anti-realist project amounts to an attempt to bring out the theistic element in realist philosophy.[7]

As previously noted, here Kerr is following up a suggestion of Michael Dummett's that 'statements cannot be true or false unless it is in principle possible for us to know whether they are'. Kerr suggests that if the only alternative to realism, anti-realism, may be seen to be incompatible with Christianity it is because it makes meaning subject to human verification, entailing a 'pervasive anthropocentrism' and 'the temporalization of rationality'. On the other hand the grammar of realism requires that 'the truth of a statement [of an appropriate class] involves the possibility in principle that it should be, or should have been, recognized as true by a being – not necessarily a human being – appropriately situated and with sufficient perceptual and intellectual powers'. A statement must be either true or false, 'even if God alone knows'.[8]

---

6. Lindbeck, *The Nature of Doctrine*, p. 49.   7. Kerr, *Theology After Wittgenstein*, pp. 128, 137.
8. Ibid., pp. 127–30. 'It may be noted in passing that, in an unpublished paper which is

This then is theistic realism as distinct from critical realism.[9] Theistic realism keeps the grammar of realism intact in that it requires a correspondence between proposition and reality, but at the same time avoids the impossible requirement of a separation of language and world, for it is a realism according to which all human attempts at truth, innovative or otherwise, cannot be verified other than 'vertically'. And it is also a realism that on the human 'horizontal' level is able to be more generous, more inclusive and tolerant of the postmodern flux in not insisting on a human verification. The judgment of all our 'giant propositions', including Christian forms of life, *is*, however, provided theistically on the horizontal human level by the God we 'read' in terms of Christ. The coherence of realism relies on incarnation, a point that is ironically underlined by postmodern thinking.

Arguably, then, to advance a theistic realism is to think God, language and world into correct relation to one another. All that is claimed to be real and true humanly speaking is accountable to what is real and true divinely speaking, but this does not render questions of truth transcendently, inaccessibly external to this world awaiting some future Judgment Day. There is an incarnational framework for the whole of human reality that in converting that reality to its own transcendently encompassing reality draws it into participation in God's reality. The 'then, now, and not yet-ness' of Jesus Christ is significant to our inquiry. First, however, the previous drawing of human re-grammaring and refiguring processes into a conversion model must now in turn be drawn into this incarnational framework.

As has been mentioned, primary or first-order language-games are basic activities of human living whereas secondary ones involve second-order uses of language. There is in a secondary language-game, such as analogy-making or metaphor-making, the addition of an extra, or double, reference in that the reference of the secondary game is to the primary one which provides it with its subject matter and which in turn makes its primary sign–world connection. When a primary language-

apparently in effect a reconstruction of Bishop Berkeley's argument for the existence of God, Dummett has suggested that 'anti-realism is ultimately incoherent but that realism is tenable only on a theistic basis' (Dummett, *Truth and Other Enigmas*, xxxix). The theological ramifications of Dummett's reformulation of the controversy between realism and anti-realism may thus turn out to be of immense importance (cf. Kerr, *Theology After Wittgenstein*, p. 128).

9. Yet we should avoid the species of Platonism that simply conflates reality and truth, in which the false becomes simply the unreal. Rather the truth co-inheres with the reality it proclaims.

game is converted to the use of a secondary, theological one, the secondary language-game takes up the primary sign–world link and through it expresses a further meaning. In this transfer process the primary meaning is changed rather than obliterated through the superimposition of the secondary. Secondary uses of language extend but do not substitute for primary uses: 'It is only if a word has a primary sense for the speaker that he can use it in the secondary one.'[10] Therefore, each use is prior to the other as each depends upon the other.

Secondary language-games and their second-order propositional moves, therefore, refer not to an extra-linguistic world *as such,* but to first-order everyday human language-games as the primary links we make with the world. Conversely and reciprocally, from within the convertedness of what Christoph Schwöbel has termed an 'ontology of faith',[11] everyday language-using activities, whether explicitly Christian or not, refer back to secondary language-games whose moves are second-order theological propositions. Thus the language-game of praying when practised in a Christian context is subject to the 'Jesus-as-mediator' grammar of the Christian secondary language-games which now assume ontological primacy. Petitions are typically offered 'through Jesus Christ', the premise (or grammar) being the simultaneous divinity and humanity of a Saviour who can represent humanity to God and God to humanity. And as mentioned, ordinary world-describing or fact-stating language-games also assume a secondary theological grammar when the world is understood as having primary reality as God's creation and its inhabitants as God's creatures radically contingent upon the Creator. 'World' carries a new and primary meaning as God's creation, both good and fallen, context of divine incarnation and redemption, but remains world in every other respect as well, the difference being that all these other respects are now viewed through the new primary meaning. Our understanding of the full and true implications of 'world' has changed as we have become aware of our contingence as creatures 'hooked into' God.

The fundamental meaning of what we do and say is now given in these secondary-become-primary uses and the meaning and import of the data of what is humanly primary are given their ultimate reckoning which is the truth of God. As Roger White has suggested, Aquinas' general point concerning predications of things to God means that

10. Stephen Mulhall, *On Being in the World*, p. 68.
11. See Christoph Schwöbel, *God, Action and Revelation* (Kampen: Pharos, 1992).

within Christianity predications of something to God must assume ontological primacy over predications of the same thing to a creature or aspect of world. For this reason, in a given form of life, 'A primary sense is neither . . . necessarily the sense most frequently encountered, nor an etymologically prior sense',[12] but the sense according to those language-using practices which provide the scaffold or hook for that form of life.

Second-order language-games may also be conscripted by the theological grammar (as with the making of theological metaphors). In Wittgenstein's language-game of doing linguistic philosophy, there is a move which states: 'what is given are forms of life', whereas in the language-game of doing Christian theology there is an equivalent 'move' which states: 'what is given is the radical God-givenness of forms of life'. In the first, 'horizontal' instance, human forms of life are primary, but this primacy is no longer primary in the second instance because this givenness is contingent upon God's giving for its origins and continued existence and future perfection. Consequently, in doing theology the theological use of 'given' taken as synonymous with 'gratuitous', as pertaining to grace ('given or received without charge or obligation') must take precedence over the non-theological uses of 'given', here especially the philosophical sense of 'without cause or justification'.[13]

From this position it is possible to describe the relation of theological language-games to Christian Scripture. As suggested earlier, biblical material provides 'moves' or content for theological language-games (such as preaching, teaching, reflecting and testifying). Under a Christo-typology such as Lindbeck's and Frei's, this biblical content is brought under the primary incarnational grammar that Jesus Christ is God's redemptive, salvific reality stated in human terms. In Christian theological language-games, this primary grammar rules the use of, first, other theological propositions or doctrines (which might be viewed as exegetical commentaries on it) and, second, the content of Scripture and experience, so that while the Bible read as Christian Scripture is the source of Christian truth, as such it is also subject to how that truth is understood and interpreted in theological language-games.

It could be argued, therefore, that conversion occurs at two levels: on one level the experiences and practices of everyday human living in the world are understood in their true light through the biblical absorption in which, to hark back to Frei, the story of our life is seen in terms of God's

---

12. White, 'Notes on Analogical Predication', p. 210.   13. Ibid.

story and our story as figuring that of God. On another level the theological language-games which infer propositions about God, creation and creatures from the biblical norm are themselves established and judged continually by the incarnational and redemptive grammar of the Gospel. Again, this is a complex co-inherence of rules and moves in which the whole must be taken as a given whose ultimate truth is subject to divine judgment. As language-games are not reducible to their rules and moves, what is normative to Christianity is not merely a merry-go-round of doctrinal and biblical circularity but also primarily and inseparably the Jesus language-games from which the primary incarnational grammar was and is inferred. The player of those language-games, Jesus of Nazareth, is not reducible to that grammar any more than a game is reducible to its rules.

An important corollary of the co-inherence of language-games with their rules is that in the economy of conversion the grammar of incarnation is necessarily soteriologically expressed. There is a co-inherence at the heart of Christology between its incarnational grammar and its soteriological language-games, a language-ridden flux of being and doing. The language-games of Jesus' birth, life, death and resurrection operate according to the grammar, 'Jesus is the Christ, the Son of God, God Incarnate.' The incarnateness of God cannot be separated from the saving language-games through which divine incarnation is revealed just as those saving activities cannot be separated from the incarnation through which God makes the contact with humanity necessary to our salvation. In the economy of conversion the connection between incarnational grammar and soteriological practice – what Stephen Need describes as the 'inner workings of the unity between the rational and the empirical'[14] – is expressed in the refiguring, re-grammaring transfers that introduce new moves into old language-games and re-create an old life as a new form of life in Christ. This creative component to Christology logically requires a doctrine of God that includes a cosmic Christ as God's creative Word whose agency integrates creating and redeeming. It also demands the enabling of the Spirit in this christological agency.

Contingence

A necessary consequence of a transcendent divinity is that everything creaturely is dependent on its creator for its origin and continuing exis-

---

14. Need, *Human Language and Knowledge*, p. 190. The issue of language and rationality is being largely sidestepped here as it is the subject of a subsequent book in progress.

tence. Incarnation brings the meeting point of this transcendence and contingence into (in patristic parlance) the dialectic between the two natures (φνοςσιυ) in one person ('νποοτασις).[15] With incarnation, humanity is caught up into and participates in this dialectic. As a result, the anatomy of conversion, physically and mentally rooted in human perceptual, cognitive, learning and knowing processes and woven into the links between language and world, is a process that operates within this dialectic. Yet the brute reality of contingence remains, for all that our participation in Christ is a participation in a dialectic between contingence and transcendence.

Colin Gunton's neo-Irenaean trinitarian model of God suggests the structure of this contingence. 'On an Irenaean account', he points out, 'what holds the creation together – its *inscape* . . . are the Son and the Spirit, by whom the world is held in continuing relation to God the Father.' In the first place, God's being is constituted in the perichoretic relationality of 'Father', 'Son' and 'Spirit'; in the second, God's relation to the universe is perichoretic. All things, sustained in being by the Spirit, dwell in Christ who is their coherence and who as God's intelligibility in worldly terms indwells a world also constituted in relationality.[16] Whereas without Christ there is no coherence, a theology of the Spirit gives due weight to the particular, for the 'Spirit's peculiar office is to realize the true being of each created thing by bringing it, through Christ, into saving relation with God the Father'.

This office, which Irenaeus and Gunton see as 'the work of perfecting the creation', might be inferred to include the perfecting of the particularities of a language-ridden human creativity that participates in the process of a continuing creation and re-creation realized in Christ through the work of the Spirit.[17] A christologically mediated creation, Gunton considers, is essential to a Christian understanding of creation in itself as well as in relation to God's creative activity.[18] While a christological doctrine of creation is creedally ensconced, the mainstream Western

---

15. See ibid., pp. 58–67, 212–13.
16. As Gunton notes (*The One, the Three and the Many*, pp. 55, 178–9), 'It is to Paul and other New Testament writers that we owe the confession that all things cohere in Christ. . . . God comes into relation with that which is not himself through his Son, the mediator between himself and the creation, and the Son is rightly conceived as *Logos*, not only the Word spoken to time from eternity, but the immanent dynamic of meaning which holds time and space together.' This is Torrance's point: 'the theological view of the world is read off the self-revelation of God in Jesus Christ and the Christian understanding of the interrelation of the incarnation to the creation' (see Torrance, *Divine and Contingent Order*, p. 70).   17. Gunton, *The One, the Three and the Many*, pp. 181, 189–90.
18. C. E. Gunton, *A Brief Theology of Revelation* (Edinburgh: T. & T. Clark, 1995), p. 44.

traditions have tended to opt for a natural theology in which the doctrine of creation is worked out prior to its consideration in Christian terms. As a result, the terms of what is possible in creation and divine creativity have been decided ex-Christianly and then imposed on a subsequent Christian interpretation. In the trinitarian doctrine developed by Irenaeus, however, Christology links and grounds creation and redemption.[19]

Gunton's development of Irenaeus' christological doctrine of creation is consistent with White's Wittgensteinian reversal of ontological primacy. The everyday human experience of world comes under the divine interpretation of world as christologically created and redeemed. It follows that the relation of natural and social science to Christology is that of an empirically based natural cosmology to a prior trinitarian theological cosmology. Scientific theories then carry over into theology the credibility they have acquired through empirical testing, although these data are not there employed as verificatory of things theological but inform theology through their theological reinterpretation. In this context the whole empirical sphere of observation is read as creation and the descriptive and investigative work of science becomes the exploration and elucidation of the internal logic and structure of that creation *as* creation, as the universe created and redeemed by God through Christ. As noted, Torrance refers to this exploration within an acknowledged contingency as natural theology.[20]

While we may grasp the depths of creation's reality in this way the question remains of whether we may have a hand in making it – whether the grammar of contingency will allow this. Are our inspirations and innovations only truly so in so far as they are already determined by God – already God's creations – that is, already subject to judgment as either true or false – or might they *become* God's creations? That is, to what extent are human beings able themselves to make the sort of contributions to an ongoing creation that seem indicated by a critical-realist or postmodern view of reality as language-ridden?

According to Kathryn Tanner, human creativity may be seen as part of God's continuing creative agency without being swallowed up deterministically by it, because God's agency and ours are related orthogonally, so that the entire 'horizontal' plane of human agency is upheld by God's 'vertical' agency which serves to enable rather than suppress it.

19. Gunton, *The One, the Three and the Many*, p. 41.
20. See Torrance, *Space, Time and Incarnation*, pp. 69–70; *Reality and Scientific Theology*, p. 45.

As she puts it, 'Two different orders of efficacy become evident: along a "horizontal" plane, an order of created causes and effects; along a "vertical" plane, the order whereby God founds the former.' In this way contingence is preserved without restricting human freedom.

> Predicates applied to created beings may concern what happens within the created order; they can be understood to hold simply within the horizontal plane of relations among created beings. Predicates of that sort say nothing about the vertical relation of a creature's dependence upon God. Ascribing them to created beings cannot run contrary, then, to our rules for talk of God's agency and the creature.[21]

Yet does this really, as it stands, state anything other than the bald fact of divine transcendence and human contingence?

The personal framework

In the case of late modern or postmodern science, the discipline itself no longer claims a capacity to get at the facts about reality in a straightforwardly objective way. Its theories and models are construed as paradigms or components of paradigms with their own internal logic, resting on certain premises about The Way Things Are which are reciprocally related to observation and analysis. As Thomas Kuhn and others have persuasively argued, the observations are theory-laden and the facts value-laden.[22] Yet as Nicholas Wolterstorff argues, if scientific theories are, as Kuhn suggests, underdetermined by data, this has the great advantage of allowing Christian scholars to 'choose from among the class of empirically adequate theories those that are most consistent with Christian convictions'.[23] Provided the criteria are clearly maintained, arguably a postmodern scientific perspective is better able to serve a Christian doctrine of creation than its modern alternative, not simply because it is less deterministic but also because it is more complex and holistic. In taking into account the integral role of language and society in the scientific theories and models through which we both discover and shape reality, postmodern scientific thought demonstrates that science is not the only supplementary explainer to be

---

21. Tanner, *God and Creation*, pp. 85, 89–90.
22. T. S. Kuhn, *The Structure of Scientific Revolutions*, 2nd edn (Chicago: University of Chicago Press, 1970).
23. N. Wolterstorff, *Reason within the Bounds of Religion*, 2nd edn (Grand Rapids: Eerdmans, 1984), p. 84.

annexed by theology in a theology of creation. Science provides a necessary but insufficient explanation of the internal structure of creation (what Torrance calls its natural theology) which needs to be reciprocally related to other explanations in the interests of comprehensiveness.

So, postmodern science allows for an anthropic component in observation and measurement which seems not incompatible with an internal-realist as well as a christological perspective. As Torrance has pointed out, since the universe includes humanity, its reality includes human knowledge of that reality, and it is through this knowing – through the universe's being known – 'that the structure of the universe manifests itself'.

> Theologically understood man and the universe belong together and together form what we mean by *world* in its relation to God. Man is an essential constituent of the creation, its 'crown', as traditionally theology has spoken of him, the priest of nature through whose scientific activity under God the inherent intelligibility of the universe comes to expression and articulation. Just as God made life to reproduce itself, so he has made the universe to express itself, to bring forth its own structure and order in ever richer forms, and in that way to find its fulfilment as the creation of God. This is what takes place through man, for man is that unique element in the creation through which the universe knows itself and unfolds its inner rationality.[24]

This may be related to Polanyi's suggestion that 'knowing and being are . . . unified in a single act' so that we 'indwell' what we know and that knowing, when it is true knowing, 'has a significant bearing upon reality'.[25] It is also consistent with Gunton's suggestion that 'creation's non-personality means that it is unable to realise its destiny, the praise of its creator, apart from persons. It is not personal, but requires persons in order to be itself.' He goes on to remark more radically that the anthropic principle in its suggestion of 'a necessary relatedness of the cosmos to human intelligence' might enable theologians to 'conceive a positive relation between human rationality and the structure of the universe'.[26]

Although Gunton has not specifically addressed the place of lan-

24. Torrance, *Reality and Scientific Theology*, pp. 2, 68.
25. Need, *Human Language and Knowledge*, pp. 190–1, 194.
26. C. E. Gunton, 'Trinity, Ontology and Anthropology: Towards a Renewal of the Doctrine of the *Imago Dei*', in C. Schwöbel and C. E. Gunton (eds.), *Persons, Divine and Human* (Edinburgh: T. & T. Clark, 1991), pp. 47ff., pp. 56–7.

guage in a perichoretic creation, his references to coherence, intelligibility and meaning may be seen as preludes to such a discussion. In a more
recent book he suggests that creation's intrinsic rationality 'might be
called a semiotic system . . . a system whose intrinsic, not extrinsic,
rationality, is a sign of its createdness'. Such a system does not amount
simply to a divine speech-act according to 'the oft-remarked speech-act
conception of creation: God speaks and things happen', for this would
entail that words alone create the world, 'encouraging the view that we
create our world through speech'. For this reason, he suggests, a semiotic
model must be supplemented with 'models of divine construction and
earthly mediation'.[27] Need develops this viewpoint epistemologically.
Knowledge, as personal knowledge that involves an indwelling of the
knower in the known and thereby entails an inclusion of knowing in
being, is an active knowledge. As Torrance suggests, 'the inner relation
between *logos* and being, or the concept of the truth of being, does not
reduce to a vanishing point the place or function of the human knower,
but on the contrary provides the ground upon which the inseparable
relation of knower and known in human understanding can be
upheld'.[28] It follows from this, Need argues, that the mind 'shapes as it
knows'.

> The unity between the knowing mind and the known object is crucial
> and is grounded in both sides of the process. It is essentially personal
> in that the one who knows engages with that which is known by
> contributing to it. As for Coleridge, knowing is a making or a doing
> as well as a discovering of what is actually objectively real.[29]

Accordingly Need sees this sort of knowledge as being inherently imaginative in its revelatory function, as being 'heuristic conversation' rooted
in 'imaginative rationality'.

As mentioned, Need's Polanyian understanding of knowledge as primarily and fundamentally personal – as the lived knowledge of persons,
places and things (rather than facts) that has the nature of a skill – subsumes knowing as factual and propositional.[30] The knowing-how sort
of knowledge may be regarded as consistent with the sort of knowledge
of practices that is the knowing how to play language-games. This is the
sort of knowing that is accessed in the doing. Thus the propositional

27. Gunton, *A Brief Theology of Revelation*, pp. 61, 69–70.
28. Torrance, *Reality and Scientific Theology*, pp. 7–8.
29. Need, *Human Language and Knowledge*, pp. 185, 194, 203.
30. See Polanyi, *The Tacit Dimension* and M. Polanyi, *Personal Knowledge* (London: Routledge, 1958).

knowledge subsumed by personal knowledge may be inferred to be equivalent to the grammar inferable from language-games.[31] We might be said to 'indwell' our language-games – or our practices – in the way we indwell the people, things and places we know. And again, that indwelling has a part in constructing the reality in which it participates. It might be said that in knowing one another we help to construct one another's reality.

Need argues that this dialectical model is consistent with Chalcedonian formulations. He suggests that the 'unity of the two [divine and human] elements in Christ is the root of an epistemological unity between the knower and the known ... [and] the difference between the two elements in Christ [is] the root of an epistemological distinction between knower and known'.[32] Following this lead, it may be possible to construct a theology that builds on Torrance's view of humanity as creation's mediator, expression and fulfilment, but also takes in what Gunton implies and Need infers: that human language has a creative role in this process.

Underdeterminedness

In the trinitarian doctrine developed by Irenaeus, Christology links and grounds creation and redemption.[33] Hardy observes that this is an implication of 'the congruence with the world by which God is himself'.[34] This study would add that it is in the incarnational meeting of divinity and humanity in Christ that, as Torrance puts it, the truth of reality is revealed both 'in terms of the grasping power of the active intellect' and 'also in terms of the intelligible self-evidence of the divine reality and the intuitive apprehension and intellectual consent which it compels in us'.[35] Yet, as Need (in agreement with Coleridge) has interpreted Polanyi, this grasping is not only a discovery and a consent; it is also an active constructing. This is in tune with Hardy's insight that while creativity is always God's wherever it occurs, 'the interweaving of these factors in contextuality is not fixed, and human beings creatively develop their own contextuality'.[36]

As mentioned, Hardy likens creation to a song sung by the divine

31. See Patterson, '*Word*, Words and World'.
32. Need, *Human Language and Knowledge*, p. 203.
33. Gunton, *The One, the Three and the Many*, p. 41.   34. Hardy, 'Spirit of God', p. 252.
35. Torrance, *God and Rationality*, pp. 20–1.   36. Hardy, 'Spirit of God', p. 243.

Spirit which in its polyphony interweaves all in an inextricable relation. From this relational perspective, as noted, 'the "fixities" which we habitually prefer . . . are to be seen more like the capturing of the rhythms of movement in static forms than as the primary characteristic of the "nature" and interrelation of God, human beings and nature. A suitable analogy is the position of individuals in the interwovenness of human beings.' The contextuality we actively develop is not something external to us but something which is intrinsic to human biology and sociality. Nor is it something external to God. Here perhaps a strong and rich tradition of divine transcendence has been emphasized at the expense of divine immanence. Hardy contends that indeed God is only knowable in relation to human contextuality. Through the trinitarian economy God is the context of the world's 'rich interweaving of all the social and natural factors'. In the world's ecology, between living being and environment, 'there is a structured relation, a structural congruence'. This congruence permits room for 'undetermined interactions' or 'perturbations' which initiate both preservative and destructive changes to that organization and therefore to the identity of both living being and context, providing 'possibilities for constructive change'. God's presence may be discerned both in the vitality that brings about the change which in its perturbative rippling outward underlines the inextricable relationality of all things and in 'something open, something wild' among the inner parts of creation: 'a long rumour of wisdom [which] keeps winding into each tune' as a '"fierce vigil of contingency"'.[37]

When a trinitarian economy is worked out in creation, neither Christ nor Spirit may be identified with divine activity in the world. Instead, 'the operation of the Holy Spirit achieves its consistency by following the initial conditions which we conventionally identify as the "Father" and the congruence with the world which we identify as the "Son"'. Hardy suggests that 'What occurs in the life of the Trinitarian God is an outpouring of energy through which the initial conditions of God are fulfilled, and this fulfillment is in God, but occurs also through the congruence of God with the world by which God is himself.' Consistent with God's active self-ordering, the trinitarian divine agency within creation supports a complex interweaving of particularities within a contextuality in which they retain their own integrity relative to others.[38]

37. Ibid., pp. 241–6, 249–50. 38. Ibid., p. 252.

Through the invention of new language–world links in an under-determined creation, human contextuality contributes to and extends creation's structure and order. Yet the world's christological congruence with God entails that this human participation in its shaping is not a bootstraps endeavour but takes place contingently within a reality that is both incarnational and eschatological, that has its beginning and its end in Christ. If as Need suggests, 'the Incarnation of the Word of God is the basis upon which human language is linked with Christology',[39] it is the meeting point of divine transcendence and creaturely contingence[40] in the person of Jesus Christ that is the locus of this underdetermined-ness, the 'open structure among the inner parts', the space within the congruence. As Need also suggests, metaphor has a key role in this dialectic, and this points to the role of the Spirit.

Metaphor and creation

In the previous chapter it was suggested that the *metanoia* which enables us to see the world in Christian terms is mediated through a transfer of the training we receive in linking words up with the world. What we acquire in one communal context under one reality description is trans-ferred to another situation where it comes under a new context of inter-pretation; with emigration language-games take on new moves and new meanings. A new construal, or 'seeing as', depends upon the creative transfer of our previous training in language-games so that the moves of one become interpretative filters, and in effect referents, for the moves of another.

It was also suggested that transfer of training may be linked to an un-derstanding of metaphor in terms of the activity of metaphor-making. Metaphor-making is an activity involving the use of language in an un-familiar or new way, a speaking 'of one thing in terms which are seen to be suggestive of another',[41] which is a creative act resulting in a new

---

39. Need, *Human Language and Knowledge*, pp. 201, 212.
40. The divine as contingent must define all contingence and express transcendence within what is contingent. Ray Anderson suggests that 'there are two strands to the inner logic of historical transcendence: first of all, the transcendence of God is God's *placing* of himself into concrete historical relation to man as the limiting reality of man's authentic existence. . . . When man comes up against this limit of transcendence, his existence is qualified by the "God who is for man". Second, the transcendence of God acts as the "covenant response" which is made possible by the transcendent limit itself': see R. S. Anderson, *Historical Transcendence and the Reality of God* (Grand Rapids: Eerdmans, 1975), p. 151.   41. Soskice, *Metaphor and Religious Language*, p. 15.

linking of words and world. If the aspect-dawning characteristic of a new metaphor is not only revelatory but also creative, it is not only a human creation but may be seen as part of God's continuing creative agency. For, as Tanner suggests, 'Talk of the creature's power and efficacy is compatible with talk about God's universal and immediate agency if the theologian follows a rule according to which divinity is said to exercise its power in founding rather than suppressing created being, and created being is said to maintain and fulfil itself, not independently of such agency, but in essential dependence upon it.'[42]

To argue back in the other direction, it is consistent with this to suggest that creaturely power and efficacy, including the power and capacity to create new uses of language, are created as potential (and therefore also divine potential), so that the finished product of creation is left open or underdetermined with its contextual interweavings unfixed, as Hardy points out, to allow room for the exercise of a free human creativity. These loose ends, so to speak, in the interweavings of language and world permit the possibility of metaphoric 'perturbations' which initiate changes to the identity of both.[43]

There are, Samuel Levin points out, two logics of metaphoric construal. There is the standard one in which the metaphoric utterance is seen as deviant, construed as another (literal) utterance, and then mapped on to the actual world. And there is the converse approach in which the metaphoric utterance is taken literally and mapped on to a possible world. The possible world is then construed in terms of the actual world. 'The result of the construal process, in both cases, is an interpretation – of the language in the first case, of a world in the second.' If the second logic is followed, 'the poet is a creator and the poem a world'.[44] In a related way Ricoeur sees metaphor as both organizer and organizee of reality: 'What it creates it discovers; and what it

---

42. Tanner, *God and Creation*, pp. 85, 89–90: 'The theologian talks of an ordered nexus of created causes and effects in a relation of total and immediate dependence upon divine agency. Two different orders of efficacy become evident: along a 'horizontal' plane, an order of created causes and effects; along a 'vertical' plane, the order whereby God founds the former. Predicates applied to created beings may concern what happens within the created order; they can be understood to hold simply within the horizontal plane of relations among created beings. Predicates of that sort say nothing about the vertical relation of a creature's dependence upon God. Ascribing them to created beings cannot run contrary, then, to our rules for talk of God's agency and the creature.'
43. Hardy, 'Spirit of God', p. 246.
44. S. Levin, 'Standard Approaches to Metaphor and a Proposal for Literary Metaphor', in A. Ortony (ed.), *Metaphor and Thought* (Cambridge: Cambridge University Press, 1979), pp. 124–35, 131–3.

finds it invents.' As we must operate within an existing language order, metaphor's creation or discovery of a new order must be by way of creating rifts ('perturbations') in the old order which was itself created in the very same way. Ricoeur talks about an 'initial polysemy' in which a word has several common uses. These established uses in the language-games in which they feature are a 'sea anchor' which is 'dragged' by metaphor. Metaphor makes an assertion which confounds those uses and violates existing categories. 'Order itself proceeds from the metaphorical constitution of semantic fields' and is in turn transgressed by the constitution of a new field.[45]

In this way metaphor can be seen to break the circularity of verification between proposition and language-game through the revelation of a use which has not hitherto been recognized as a move in any existing language-game. But how is the use now recognized? Whether or not the hypothetical possibility presented by a novel metaphor is accepted as in some sense real or true depends on the context of understanding within a particular milieu, but this is an understanding that must break with both traditional and normative use – with both case law and statute. How do we arrive at communal decisions regarding the success of a metaphor? Theories of metaphor cannot answer these questions. They can only point to the mystery.

If new aspects dawn, or new possibilities arise out of novel language–world linking activities, these are both initially transcendent of existing concepts and accordingly transcendent of antecedent actuality. They are, as Jüngel suggests, a 'gain to actuality'. The Aristotelian conception of actuality does not allow that the world may contain nothingness. It equates possibility with the 'not-yet of an actuality to come' and therefore only distinguishes between the actual and the not-yet-actual. Any possibility beyond this has no substance.[46] Jüngel sees it as important that we 'dismantle the primacy of actuality' for theological (christological) reasons. Yet the unseating of actuality from pride of place exposes a paradox, the metaphorical paradox. While possibility

---

45. Ricoeur, *The Rule of Metaphor*, pp. 121–2, 124, 131. Ricoeur notes that traditional theories of reference can be only speculative as they require a standpoint outside of language if the language-world relation is to be known. But his answer to this problem (p. 304) seems to be the positing of a metalanguage: 'Speculative discourse is possible, because language possesses the reflective capacity to place itself at a distance and to consider itself, as such and in its entirety, as related to the totality of what is. Language designates itself and its other.' This is undoubtedly convenient, but is it coherent? Of course, speculative discourse is possible but can it be other than heuristic? How can language alone express the language–world link?   46. Jüngel, *Theological Essays*, pp. 104–10.

is shown by metaphorizing to subsume actuality, possibility can only be asserted (and thereafter conceived) within actuality. This assertion (or the judging of the truth of the assertion) requires that the possible be accurately distinguished from the impossible, a distinction which, as has been noted, is unverifiable from within actuality without resorting to a sort of conceptual positivism. Nevertheless, the claim which this assertion constitutes is a claim of a possible (albeit unrecognized as such) state of affairs to be actual, the granting of which extends the borders of actuality: 'a space for freedom is made in actuality in which that which is possible can arise'.[47]

Thus actuality is continually expanding as it incorporates unknown possibilities by means of metaphor. Metaphor demonstrates empirically that what is actual at one time is not the same as what is actual at another (and, moreover, that not all knowledge is conceptual knowledge). As Hardy comments, we are in the habit of thinking in 'fixities' which freeze the dynamic reality into static forms. If metaphors succeed it is because they 'really bring to speech that which is'. Yet 'that which is' is more than actuality at any given time and thus expands actuality (expands the 'horizon of being'), constitutes 'a gain to being' and a 'gain to knowledge'.[48] This underlines the diachronic, dynamic nature of language-games in *das Leben*, the stream of life. Metaphor's violation of actuality is at the same time an extending of actuality – or the sign of the extending of actuality – to incorporate more of actuality than can presently be comprehended.

At any one time, the signs of actuality's incompleteness are visible in the incongruence of new metaphors. On a Wittgensteinian view, it must be emphasized, such gains to actuality are not gains to either world or language, but to both: to a language-ridden world. According to Jüngel, metaphor is not simply a use of words but lets that-which-is (language-world) come to speech. When a metaphor is made or encountered, the impression it gives initially is that here is a word, or combination of words, or structure, which is not a bona fide move in the language-game purportedly being played. There is then the further realization that the language-game which appears to obtain does not obtain – or at least the moves have changed and the game with them. Between these two perceptions, we may experience metaphor as a kind of schizoid entity which inhabits two possible worlds simultaneously: the

47. Ibid., pp. 119–20.   48. Ibid., p. 41.

current actuality within which the metaphor and its language-game do not fit (but seem to be claiming to fit) and the seemingly impossible but dawningly possible actuality within which they do fit in a manner still to be determined. This dilemma must be resolved in favour of one world or the other; either the metaphorical product is accepted as expressing a true proposition (dawningly conceivable) in the actual world, or it is rejected as expressing nonsense. Its acceptance as true in the actual world means that the actual world has changed; it has expanded to incorporate a previous mere possibility (or even impossibility) as actual.

Once reality is reckoned to include language, the way is open for possible worlds to be a component of that reality. Imagination becomes a creative discovery of a new rationality – as Coleridge puts it, 'a repetition in the finite mind of the eternal act of creation in the infinite I AM'.[49] When related back to the christological nexus of both contingency and underdeterminedness, metaphor-making may be seen as part and parcel of the continuing creation of the world, the unfixed, underdetermined interweaving of factors in contextuality which human beings are free creatively to develop. As Jüngel puts it, 'the language of faith does not allow actuality to dictate what it has to say to us about actuality . . . This does not mean that actuality is passed over or missed. Rather, it is enhanced. But this has consequences for actuality.' Possibility, and hence a wider-than-present actuality, enters our world, and confronts it with 'the possibility of its non-being, from which alone new being can arise'.[50] We invent metaphors, models, hypotheses and theories within the 'slack in the system' provided for the exercise of creaturely efficacy, but that invention is at the same time, the Spirit's 'song' of creation. We know, in the eureka moment that the inspiration is ours but not ours, within but also without.

Conclusion

Just as any explanation of the 'horizontal' process of conversion requires the 'vertical' component of Christology, so it might be concluded that the coherence of realism relies on incarnation, but a 'now, and not yetness' of incarnation that leaves room for the continuing unfolding and perfection of creation and redemption. Integral to this process are

---

49. S. T. Coleridge, *Biographia Literaria*, ed. J. Shawcross (Oxford: Clarendon Press, 1907), 1, 13, p. 202, quoted in Need, *Human Language and Knowledge*, p. 148.
50. Jüngel, *Theological Essays*, pp. 66–7.

both human creativity in itself and its redemptive re-creation through the conversion of our percepts and concepts. Within this incarnational framework – 'the congruence of God with the world by which God is himself' – our participation in our own and the world's creation and re-creation is a participation that operates subtly in the depths of human cognition where 'the grasping power of the active intellect' not only discovers that which is, but effects 'gains to actuality' to bring about new and surprising moves in human language-games.[51]

In a continuing creation which is at the same time a redemptive recreation at the heart of Christology, at the cutting edge of contingency through the Spirit's enabling, new language (as novel metaphors or new moves in language-games) emerges as an inextricable part of that which it describes and therefore as creative discoverer, or inventor.

A remaining question is whether the role of language at the heart of Christology means that language transcends human creatureliness. There are also implications arising from the discussion on human creatureliness that must be explored in the light of a Christian anthropology.

---

51. Torrance, *God and Rationality*, p. 21.

6

Becoming persons

Colin Gunton has suggested that the concept of 'person' is ontologically and logically primitive – the 'idea' in terms of which other concepts are understood, an idea which can only be grasped (like language-games) in respect to particular instances. The task of this chapter is to examine the nature and relation of divine and human personhood. This will be done by first constructing a 'language-ridden' Christian anthropology from below – that is, in its horizontal aspects – with a view to drawing this anthropology inside its vertical component. Second, the nature of divine personhood will be explored in relation to human personhood. It will be suggested that incarnation is the linchpin between immanent and economic trinitarian realities that draws human personhood into participation with divine personhood and enables us to know what God is like.

The intention is to provide a programmatic sketch of a series of burgeoning implications of a 'language-ridden' theistic (and incarnational) realism for the doctrine of God and Christian anthropology (including the doctrine of sin and ethics) which will beg a great deal of further development in terms of both delving deeper into the areas already covered and generalizing sideways into other areas of Christian doctrine.

Language and relation

Gunton argues that a relational model best describes the complex pluriformity of contemporary reality. Personal distinctness is constituted in relation. Everything is constituted as what it uniquely is in relation to everything else. It follows that 'persons also are constituted in their particularity both by their being created such by God and by the network of human and cosmic relatedness in which they find their being'.[1] Thus,

> All particulars are formed by their relationship to God the creator and redeemer and to each other. Their particular being is a being in relation, each distinct and unique and yet each inseparably bound up with other, and ultimately all, particulars. Their reality consists, therefore . . . not in the universals they instantiate, but in the shape of their relatedness with God and with other created hypostases.[2]

It is possible to arrive at this conclusion that all being is relational in character 'from below' in identifying *perichoresis*, or perichoretic relationality, as the key principle of personal existence.[3] If we exist as persons through and for each other, this is not simply according to a superimposed theological principle but as a (divinely instigated) pragmatic fact of human existence. What is central for us is the communicative activity in which we are trained in a form of life. The personal is inherently communal and social (and as such, when truly expressed, ecclesial).[4] What we take a person to be – the very notion of person and experience of being a person in this or that context – depends on a social consensus: 'the "I" is not hidden in the head: it is the world viewed'.[5]

Putting aside an old controversy in its tradition, contemporary psychology has moved away from modernist notions of an inner 'essential self' towards regarding human personhood as the product both of nature and nurture. As one recent writer puts it, we are 'hardware overlaid with cultural software', where the 'hardware' is our animal, natural component which is enriched and complicated by language learned in a social setting.[6] Rather than envisage the mind as a place where language happens, instead we must recognize that it is language in the form of self-talk that drives the mind along. Whereas the animal mind is locked into the present, driven by its environment, words give us access to our past by triggering our memory banks. From its development first as a tool for communication and group activity, language becomes the

1. Gunton, *The One, the Three and the Many*, pp. 172–5, 203.

2. Ibid., p. 207. Therefore 'Barth is right in holding against Descartes and others that we can believe in the existence of the material world because we believe in God' (p. 204).

3. Ibid., p. 53.

4. The significant point that true personhood is doxological (and thus ecclesial) is made by Alan Torrance. See A. J. Torrance, *Persons in Communion: Trinitarian Description and Human Participation* (Edinburgh: T. & T. Clark, 1996), pp. 307ff., also this inquiry's discussion in chapter 7.

5. Kerr, *Theology After Wittgenstein*, p. 105.

6. See J. McCrone, *The Myth of Irrationality: the Science of the Mind from Plato to Star Trek* (London: Macmillan, 1993).

means of organizing our own pattern of thoughts. When children chatter to themselves, imitating adult commands, they are talking themselves through what they are doing. From an initial description of what is happening comes prescription of what is going to happen, hence the ability to plan is born. Long before adulthood this has become an internalized process.

What is being suggested here too is that it is the use of language that makes us human and distinguishes us from the non-human; the self-consciousness that seems to be the thing that sets us apart and makes us unique is a product of our language-riddenness rather than the reverse.[7] We become persons through training in the language-using conventions of a form, or forms, of life. First, training in language-using activities and, second, the transfer of that training in a way that generalizes it to new situations, is the process that enables us to become human. Robert Cathey argues that

> The anthropological alternative to mental individualism is the rediscovery of human agency and the agent's perspective on what it means to be a self. For we cannot speak of agency apart from the embodiment of mind, meaning, emotion, intention, and will in the field of human practice, shared language, gesture, ritual, traditions, and community ... To speak of myself as a unique individual, as an 'I', is to already presuppose a cultural-linguistic setting in which my actions, words, gestures, and participation in shared customs, institutions, stories, and rituals can shape, form, and manifest my identity to others. Human selfhood is always already embedded in communally shared concepts of identity.[8]

Cathey argues that the 'background of Wittgenstein's anthropology of the embodied, "traditioned" agent who means and refers is summed up in his concepts of "language-game" and "forms of life"'. Thus, to 'understand language as ... a multiplicity of forms ... of expressive activity, as Wittgenstein encourages us to do, is to rehabilitate the self as a responsive agent in vital connection with others of the same kind'.[9]

In a similar way to Cathey's use of Wittgenstein, Frei uses the work of another linguistic philosopher, Gilbert Ryle, to counter the 'myth of the essential self'. According to Ryle, 'the human self is not some unknowable inner entity, whose nature may or may not be revealed by the words

---

7. This is also Jüngel's view. See Jüngel, *Theological Essays*, p. 145, and the discussion below.
8. Robert Andrew Cathey, *Foundations with Faces: A Prolegomenon to a Postliberal Doctrine of God* (Ann Arbor, MI: UMI, 1990), p. 317.
9. Ibid. pp. 317–8, 325; Kerr, *Theology After Wittgenstein*, pp. 110, 134.

and bodily actions so mysteriously related to it. Rather, my words and actions constitute my identity.' The modern individualistic view of the self as a disembodied and subjectively self-certain entity in relation to which 'language is merely a medium of apparatus that remains outside the minds that (deign to) employ it'[10] contains a reflexive paradox in that the self we perceive can never include that aspect of the self that is doing the perceiving. Therefore self-awareness is never self-contained but requires others to complete it.[11] Human personhood itself must be regarded as a 'language-ridden' affair because its description is always part of the reality described. Linguisticality is inherent to humanness not only as an aspect of human life in the world but as essential and integral to human self-awareness. Frei, following Ryle, maintains, 'it is the development of intention into action that constitutes the self. The true self does not remain within, manifested with greater or lesser authenticity; one is the person one has come to be through one's enacted intentions.'[12]

Linguistic communication is an inherent factor in human personhood, for without language – even sign language or gestures – our ability to relate to one another is impaired. (In the case of those unable to communicate in this way, there is a reliance even more on the linguistic capacity of others if these individuals are to be included as persons.)[13] As might be expected, a Wittgensteinian model maintains a reciprocal relationship between personal being and human activities. While on the one hand it is as persons that we play language-games, on the other hand the language-game-playing which enables us to relate to one another, to God and to the world constitutes who and what we are as human persons. Thus an integral part of being human persons – that is, of being relational beings – is communication and our paramount communicative and world-comprehending tool is language. Although the use of language implies users who manipulate something other than themselves, at the same time, as earlier discussions have suggested, these

---

10. Ibid., pp. 76, 105.
11. See I. Ramsey, 'The Systematic Elusiveness of "I"', *Philosophical Quarterly*, 5 (1955), 193–204.
12. Frei, *Theology and Narrative* , pp. 10–12. G. Ryle, *The Concept of Mind* (New York: Barnes & Noble, 1962). See especially pp. 11–13.
13. The obvious implication of this – that other creatures, such as higher mammals might be considered to participate in human personhood through our relationships with them – has been suggested by C. S. Lewis. This might also be read into Gunton's thesis of the radical relationality of all creatures and his endorsement of the Pauline suggestion that the rest of creation awaits its redemption in participation with humanity, although he resists extending the personal factor in creation beyond humanity (see below).

users may be seen as inextricably wrapped up in their language-using practices rather than as physical and/or mental beings with certain properties who may or may not use language in the course of performing certain actions. The concept of selfhood therefore comes to include the self as player of language-games.

There are several implications in all this for Christian anthropology. First, the language factor carries with it a powerful anthropocentric aspect because language has a creative role in reality. If we are able in part to construct our world(s) with our words or our word–world connecting activities, then in effect the world gets drawn inside our concepts and practices in a way that might be seen as reciprocal with their going on in the world. Parallel with this observation, Gunton suggests that 'creation's non-personality means that it is unable to realise its destiny, the praise of its creator, apart from persons. It is not personal, but requires persons in order to be itself.' He goes on to remark more radically that the anthropic principle in its suggestion of 'a necessary relatedness of the cosmos to human intelligence' might enable theologians to 'conceive a positive relation between human rationality and the structure of the universe'.[14]

A consequence of this principle, as Gunton notes, is that science becomes personal.[15] Not only has it to contend with a subjective component through its indwelling of and being indwelt by human theories and models, but the whole nature of its reality is altered. For reality has been recognized to be fundamentally personal in that the cosmos which science describes and measures is in part created through its being known by human beings.[16] This is not to claim along with postmodern nihilists that reality is no more than 'signs playing out their patterns against the void'.[17] It is merely to recognize that the inextricability of the human element from the cosmos means that our human relation to it is not only physical but also linguistic and conceptual.[18] It might be suggested that linguistic and non-linguistic aspects of reality mutually indwell each

14. Gunton, 'Trinity, Ontology and Anthropology', pp. 56–7.
15. Gunton, The One, the Three and the Many, p. 55.
16. See also Need, Human Language and Knowledge, p. 194, on the constructive aspect of personal knowledge.
17. See Loughlin, Telling God's Story.
18. As Putnam notes, 'Recently psychologists have stressed just how much theory construction is involved in even the simplest cases of perception. Not only is this true at the neurophysiological level, but it is also true at the cultural level' (see Reason, Truth and History, pp. 137–8). But postmodern science does not let go of realism, even though reality has become multifaceted. It does not commit the ultimate silliness of considering the whole universe, including perhaps some immanent God, to be our creation simply because we must conceive of it in language.

other, which allows that if human conceiving and knowing activity takes place within the physical universe in which human minds have evolved, at the same time the universe is drawn inside the human mind in order to be for us, and be known by us.[19] Person and world become co-inherent. If the postmodern cosmological view of creation is that of a self-observing, self-describing, self-evaluating 'personal' universe,[20] in annexing this theory for theology we make it an aspect of natural theology. According to this view, if human intelligence is doing the observing, describing and evaluating, it may only truly do this within the christological locus of its contingent relation to its creator. A christological Christian anthropology subsumes an anthropic cosmology.

A second, related implication is that as possibility becomes a component of reality, we not only think and hypothesize but also imagine our world and ourselves. Just as our personhood includes our ability to think and imagine, so also our selves as persons are in part thought and imagined by ourselves and the others with whom we relate. Then the projections of our individual and collective imaginations – stories, fantasies, games – all come to inhabit and condition our individual and collective being as we indwell them. As Polanyi and Need emphasize, knowing is a component of our being, and knowing is more comprehensive than factual, propositional knowledge.

Here, of course, not only does present actuality become kaleidoscopic but with the incorporation of possibility the distinction between actuality and possibility blurs.[21] With the incorporation of the possible, hypothetical or fantastic in ourselves, we include a hypothetical or metaphorical aspect in our factuality. If we hypothesize aliens in outer space and construct them in cyberspace, these hypotheses and constructions become a component of our reality. (And given that so much of science rests on hypotheses, this should not surprise us.)[22] Likewise, a novel

---

19. This implies a working of the conceptual, linguistic aspect of reality into our understanding of the trinitarian structure of God's encounter with the world in an extension of the Economic Trinity. See chapter 5.

20. Of course, this view may be criticized according to postmodernity's own criteria as the sort of 'master narrative' which it claims is not possible – as advancing a general theory when no general theory is possible! But as suggested, it is compatible with a species of critical realism.

21. See the discussion in relation to metaphor in chapter 5. (See also Sue Patterson, 'Creation and Postmodernity', in V. Pfitzner and H. Regan (eds.), *The Task of Theology Today: Doctrines and Dogmas* (Adelaide: Australian Theological Forum, 1988).

22. As Karl Popper has argued, empirical evidence can only falsify a hypothesis, never prove it. No amount of evidence consistent with a hypothesis can confirm it as true; it can only render it more probable than other hypotheses not supported by that amount of evidence.

metaphor constitutes a 'gain' to being and knowledge in which the gain is to our own being as well as to that of creation as a whole.[23]

A third and again related implication is that personhood is both local and multifaceted. Persons as beings-in-relation are persons under a certain description, constituted in relation to context, so that a person is not simply one and the same person in all of their contexts and relationships but as many different persons (or nuances of person) as other persons and contexts indwelt. In this way the multifarious aspects of human reality amount to more than a pluriform humanity as the pluriformity is intra- as well as inter-personal. If the one is in the many, the many are in the one.

Yet, as Surin notes, the one thing mandatory to Christian faith is the impossibility of telling the world's stories apart from the story of Jesus of Nazareth.[24] It is possible to imagine a plurality of human forms of life on a personal and a wider scale or level, all of which 'indigenize' Christ. Yet from a Christian anthropological point of view, if we are to have a plurality of persons according to contexts, this plurality of personal and communal worlds requires not only a mutual coinherence between the personal and the communal but also a mutual indwelling of the communities themselves. For an incommensurability of personal as well as communal worlds or stories is antithetical to the relational understanding of personhood and community central to the Christian doctrines of God and humanity.[25]

> It might therefore be concluded that an incommensurability of human worlds (out of which a Christology from below might read a corresponding many-Christs model) is a fallen state, a latter-day Tower of Babel, awaiting its eschatological redemption. Here again we bump up against the deeply fissured nature of human reality. The postmodern pictures are fallen as well as christological. The Christ who encompasses all human realities and brings them into participation with one divine reality is the Christ who heals the fissure and breaks down the walls of incommensurability.[26]

A fourth implication is that if we are persons under certain descriptions, we are also inseparably persons under certain evaluations. Consider, for instance, the evaluative import of a factual statement such as 'Jim has spilt his dinner on his tie.' Another layer of grammar, an evaluative one, is built into the rules which determine what is meant by

23. Jüngel, *Theological Essays*, p. 41.   24. Surin, *Turnings*, p. 177.   25. Ibid., pp. 174–5.
26. Patterson, 'Creation and Postmodernity', p. 13.

'dinner', 'tie' and 'Jim' (as presumably adult male). Within or superimposed on the factual description identifying Jim as a male with dinner
spilt on his tie is the more enduring moral evaluation of Jim as careless,
messy, inadequately socialized or perhaps drunk. (What sort of person
is Jim? Careless, messy, lacking in manners, fond of the bottle!) Our
language-games contain moves that both assume and foster certain
personal evaluations. Evaluations, of course, are not only moral. The
relevance, competence, usefulness, stylishness and interestingness of
our various activities also get attached to us as evaluations of our personhood. Thus in human relationships there is an inherent evaluative component carried by the language-games we share or observe in one
another. Persons incorporate their own values and others' evaluations.
As Hilary Putnam puts it,

> every fact is value loaded and every one of our values loads some fact
> . . . *fact* (or truth) and *rationality* are interdependent notions. A fact is
> something that it is rational to believe, or, more precisely, the notion
> of a fact (or a true statement) is an idealization of the notion of a
> statement that it is rational to believe. 'Rationally acceptable' and
> 'true' are notions that take in each other's wash . . . being rational
> involves having criteria of *relevance* as well as criteria of rational
> acceptability, and . . . all our values are involved in our criteria of
> relevance. The decision that a picture of the world is true (or true by
> our present lights, or 'as true as anything is') and *answers the relevant*
> *questions* (as well as we are able to answer them) rests on and reveals
> our total system of value commitments. A being with no values would
> have no facts either.[27]

A world that is not only language-ridden but also value-ridden must
consist of a plethora of linguistic and evaluative aspects of creaturely
existence that are as various as are species of human and varieties of
human context. The pragmatic (what Putnam terms) 'human flourish-
ing' is likely to be our only trans-contextual criterion of good or adequate, as opposed to bad or dysfunctional, personhood. This is the
postmodern jungle. Any form of life may claim to be more authentically
human than the others and there is no God's-eye viewpoint from which
we are able to confirm or refute this claim. Of course, there is thus no
reason why Christianity should not advance itself in this respect and
claim Jesus Christ as definitive of true human personhood. And, as suggested, arguably this position is consistent with the weak postmodern

---

27. Putnam, *Reason, Truth and History*, p. 201. See also pp. 134–5.

thesis that allows metanarratives but insists that they are always contextually nuanced and which allows us to argue that Christianity without a master-story, a metanarrative, ceases to be Christianity.[28]

A fifth implication is ethical. If the late modern view of the person is utilitarian or instrumental, so too is the language and context-ridden postmodern one, if in a different way. The postmodern view of persons as multifaceted is a fragmented one. If we become many different persons as we inhabit many different realities, so that our contextuality – our being-for-this-place and purpose – becomes constitutive of our being, then good becomes purely utilitarian: a good for this place or that place, for this thing or that, or this person or that. The inherentness of good in the person is lost. But as we always knew, people are good or otherwise in a way that is indefinably more than the sum of their beliefs and actions or the consistency between these. Personhood as a co-inherence of being and doing is more than our various beings and doings. We can no longer separate being and doing, intention and action in morality and ethics, as the language-riddenly relational understanding of personhood has removed these divisions. As Alistair Macintyre and Stanley Hauerwas have argued in their rehabilitation of virtue or communitarian ethics,[29] the modern and postmodern reductionist notions of good as utilitarian/teleological *or* deontological *or* principled *or* behavioural need to become subsumed within a more wholesale notion of good as reposing in personal character, or virtue, where these constitute not only a co-inherence of personal being and doing but at the same time, as a result, a co-inherence of the many persons we are in our various contexts – the many virtues we may display in connection with utilitarian goods – with the one person who is the repository of character or virue, or goodness in itself. It follows that personal integrity and character will require a transcontextual consistency of being and doing if we are to be able to predict the sort of moral decisions and actions the person is likely to adopt across all their contexts.

These implications suggest that the underdeterminedness in an

28. As noted in the introduction, Louglin argues that this position is postmodern – and that it views Christianity itself as postmodern – because it sees Christianity as 'not founded on anything other than the performance of its story. It cannot be established against nihilism by reason, but only presented as a radical alternative, as something else altogether. It is also postmodern because its story – God's story – imagines a world "out of nothing", a world of becoming, in which people are not fixed essences but life-narratives with a future' (cf. Loughlin, *Telling God's Story*, p. 21).

29. See A. Macintyre, *After Virtue*, 2nd edn (London: Duckworth, 1997), and (for instance) S. Hauerwas, *Vision and Virtue* (Indiana: University of Notre Dame Press, 1981).

unfolding creation that allows human creatures the space to construct their own contextuality – the 'slack' in the christological seam between transcendence and contingence that constitutes human freedom and as such is inherently linguistic – is the locus of both personal making and unmaking. If it is constructive of us as persons in that creativity is inherent to our being, it is destructive of personhood in that, apart from being contingently partial, the reality we hypothesize or metaphorize may be a fallen reality in being distorted or deceptive.[30] The negative moral cash value of a recognition of the language-riddenness of human personhood is that as well as the capacity of utterances to harm others which has long been recognized in ethics and law, there is also the recognition of the capacity of thoughts and imaginings to create false and distorted worlds that are diminishing and destructive of the relationality on which our personhood depends. As Green notes, imagination co-opted by sin becomes destructive, producing false images and appropriation of parts to misrepresent the whole, where the primary 'beneficiary' of this destruction is the imaginer.[31]

Persons, sin and language-games

In a sense a Wittgensteinian model must locate a relational, agential and linguistic doctrine of humanity within ethics because it takes communal rule-governed language-using *practices* as primary and constitutive of human being. Taken *en naturelle*, as has been noted, this approach bottoms-out in the pragmatic local bedrock of 'this is simply what I do'. If our facts are value-laden just as our values ride on what we take to be facts, in the end we run out of justifications and can only assert the validity of a way of life on faith, as it were. This bootstraps circularity of our forms of life might escape our notice were it not for our encounter with evil. As Kenneth Surin points out, the brute reality of evil forces us to recognize the language-and-context-ridden deceptiveness of natural criteria and to seek a measure of good beyond the human interpretations subject to relational bias and will-to-power.[32]

---

30. See Patterson, 'Creation and Postmodernity'.   31. Green, *Imagining God*, p. 90.
32. This, as Kerr has observed, means that if our beliefs, experiences and practices form an interwoven reciprocity, any possibility of verification (or justification) of these beliefs, experiences and/or practices according to any absolute scale of reality and truth must entail a verification or justification of the whole complex plethora of belief-practice-experience from some transcendent viewpoint (Kerr, *Theology After Wittgenstein*, pp. 127–30). See also chapter 5.

A Christian ethic-from-below must inevitably be naturalist if it takes as its criterion of good and evil what is so according to human experience. We may never fail to be aware of the presence of 'the deadliest and most horrible evil ... inherent in the very fabric of the universe ... seemingly unaccountable in its origins, often violently capricious, [that] threatens the very intactness of our lives, and in the end testifies overwhelmingly to the frailty of our human moral powers'.[33] Yet in taking this universal and insistent human experience of evil as definitive we may fail to be aware of a more subtle level or category of human evil, that of the 'normal everyday' which may go unnoticed because, as Alistair McFadyen notes,

> one of the primary disorientations of sin is the production of the belief that the category of sin is restricted to the exceptional, the abnormal; in which case, sin refers outwards from normal life to exceptional behaviour or circumstances in a way which excuses the normal and everyday from its accusation. One of the principal distortions of sin lies in its inhibiting of the possibilities of its own recognition.[34]

In the sense that 'bad' language-games are avoidances or perversions of the communication which is fundamental to being persons-in-relation, they express a distortion or antithesis of the primary divine grammar of creation. They are in this sense destructive, denying or misrepresentative of reality. Bad language-games as the dynamic of sin are woven 'into the fabric of the everyday, defining and confining it, presenting itself precisely in the guise of everyday normality, the unexceptional, as the rational, that which cannot be avoided or which is positively required'.[35] In human forms of life characterized by fallenness, 'sin refers outwards from normal life to exceptional behaviour or circumstances in a way which excuses the normal and everyday from its accusation'.[36] Thus we may overlook fobbing off and buck-passing even if we feel uncomfortable about lying and stealing. Yet all these normal practices, in being overlooked as bad, are employed according to a self-

---

33. K. Surin, 'Atonement and Christology', *Neue Zeitschrift für Systematische Theologie und Religionsphilosophie*, 24 (1982), 131–49, 140.

34. A. McFadyen, 'The Doctrine of Sin and the Sexual Abuse of Children', paper presented at the Center of Theological Inquiry, Princeton, Summer 1993, p. 2 (draft ms).

35. Even to the point of including what may seem exceptional as, for example, in Lewis's story of Mr A's and Mrs B's desertion of their respective spouses in which Mr A says that he had to take his chance of happiness when it came – what else could he do? C. S. Lewis, 'We Have No Right to Happiness', in *God in the Dock: Essays on Theology* (Glasgow: Collins, 1979), pp. 102–8.   36. Ibid.

deceptive grammar which assures us that this is merely rational or required behaviour if we are to survive in the 'real world'.

Behind such grammar lies the modern 'root-grammar' or worldview that we are 'in a position to decide how to take the world'.[37] As Gunton has observed, this amounts to self-idolizing, where the purported universal, the 'infallible self-certain consciousness' cannot perform its role because it cannot 'encompass the realities of human relations and of our placing in the world, and so operates deceptively or oppressively'. Through the displacement of God effected by human self-divinization, 'the exclusion of God opens the way for the demonic'.[38] By contrast, pragmatic postmodern models when they are also relational ones may be reinforcers of Christian ethics in demonstrating that individual self-consciousness is no longer the criterion of personal reality. Our minds are not our own unique, private centre of being: 'the "I" is not hidden in the head: it is the world viewed'.[39] With the inseparability of action from attitude and belief comes the realization not only that we are not our own but the world's, but also the entailed realization that sin cannot be self-contained in any sense as something (for example, pornographic or violent fantasies that might be confined to our own heads or lives).

In avoiding or distorting relationships or withholding reality from others, bad language-games diminish others as persons; in being self-deceptive, they diminish us as persons.[40] Postmodernly we are aware that we construct a world in thinking, imagining and speaking it. If we construct (or 'destruct') ourselves as persons according to our wishes and desires (or those of the entertainment industry), we also construct or

---

37. Kerr, *Theology After Wittgenstein*, p. 105. Frei and Kerr point out that attempts at a reformulation of this individualist model make poor headway in the face of the great attractiveness of the notion of an infallible self-certain consciousness and the pervasiveness of the traditional metaphysical view that language (and also language-games) 'is merely a medium of apparatus that remains outside the minds that (deign to) employ it'. (See also Frei, *Theology and Narrative*, pp. 45ff.)

38. Gunton, *The One, the Three and the Many*, pp. 31, 72.

39. Kerr, *Theology After Wittgenstein*, p. 105.

40. To the extent that bad language-games do not work, or are dysfunctional, and therefore are meaningless, they are not language-games at all – although it is hard to imagine a completely dysfunctional language-game, as even the seemingly senseless head-banging or rocking of autistic or severely brain-damaged people has some intelligibility as self-comforting or frustration-venting activity, even if their grammar must be inferred by others in relation to the context of the activity – which only serves to underline the irrreducibly social nature of language and personhood. (Language-games may express a certain rationality but do not in themselves necessarily meet certain standards of rationality.) Theoretically a polar extreme of non-communication would lie outside of personhood altogether and therefore outside of human forms of life and the world they embrace and indwell, in 'outer darkness'.

'destruct' others according to our delusions or self-protective self-deceptions about them. And in turn other people's perceptions, imaginings and delusions of us are conveyed to us, in our relationships with them, as the persons we are in their eyes.

Again, the deceptive virtual reality of television and computer screens becomes more than virtual in creating us as persons according to their grammars and root-grammars. And here again the awareness of sin is obscured by the evaluative grammar we and they attach to mass media – the normality and everydayness of it all, the very utilitarian requiredness of late modern technology in a late modern world. And where this technology is interactive, the very value-ladenness of the term 'creativity' carries the assumption of goodness in such a way that we cannot talk of an *evil* creativity without it seeming a contradiction in terms, even in a post-Frankensteinian age in which science itself does not hold that all human creativity is good or at least morally neutral regardless of its consequences. Arguably it is impossible to work out theologically how a human creativity contingent on divine creativity – a creativity vested in us as an aspect of our creation in God's image, a creativity which is good in itself – could be bad in its consequences apart from some formulation of a doctrine of the fall.

If a doctrine of sin is to take account of the unavoidable bias and myopia of an anthropocentric ethic, it cannot be naturalist. Reckoning good and evil cannot be done according to humanitarian principles alone. At the same time, this reckoning must take into account that 'evil and suffering, and human responses to these occurrences' occur in 'quite specific historical and material configurations'. Given the need for both transcendence and historical particularity in ethical considerations, an anthropologically oriented Christian ethic will seek redemption or transcendence of its anthropocentrism in some sort of christological solution; that is, it will recognize that in the Christian context at least 'the cross of Christ is theologically normative for any discussion of the "problem of evil"'.[41]

This account may have tended to suggest that sin and evil are to be equated platonically with unreality, or ignorance because, according to an *ex nihilo* doctrine of creation in which our radical dependence upon God constitutes our reality as contingent reality, sin becomes a denial of contingency which amounts to a refusal of reality, a denial of our own

---

41. K. Surin, *Theology and the Problem of Evil* (Oxford: Basil Blackwell, 1986), p. 48.

being. Yet the platonic element is shed if we place the entire doctrine of sin inside a christological framework. If we accept that the reality of sin is no more because Christ has redeemed us, then sin itself becomes yet another self-deception, but one in which all the others are vested – a deep delusion about ourselves that we are and can be outside of a relation to Jesus Christ which has terrible consequences because it is a denial of our personhood – our very being.[42] Yet it is only half self-deception. To say that we have been redeemed is to state the objective 'is' of Christology; the 'is not' that expresses Christology's eschatological aspect expresses our yet-to-be-redeemed-ness. We are redeemed in that Christ's *alpha* and *omega* embraces the whole of human history, from beginning to end; we are becoming redeemed in that we have yet to travel the whole course of that journey within Christ.

To say that the cross is normative for a Christian understanding of evil is to say that propositions about the nature of evil are inseparable from the salvific activity that overcomes evil. Rather than driving us to seek discernment or platonic enlightenment, the suffering occasioned by evil forces us to seek salvation from it. Where our language-games of suffering and triumphing over evil become enfolded in those of Jesus Christ, there we may not only gain relief from evil but also begin to know it for what it is.[43]

At this juncture, as Surin points out, it is not possible to advance a coherent soteriology without implying an incarnational Christology. Invoking a theology of the cross as a 'putative "answer" to the "problem of evil"' will require that we refrain from dismissing 'as patently absurd the suggestion that the "grammar" of God incorporates a "rule" to the effect that, as a consequence of the life, death and resurrection of Jesus of Nazareth, speech about human suffering is in some sense speech about divinity's very own history'. We know God through what God does, in the '"speaking-out" of the event of revelation, a revelation with a texture to be articulated in terms of a *theologia crucis*'. That is, what God does in Jesus Christ, the saving action that re-creates us as truly human is all caught up with the meaning of who Jesus Christ is, a meaning necessarily couched in incarnational grammar if salvation is to occur.[44] 'We attain to our true

---

42. D. Kelsey, 'Whatever Happened to the Doctrine of Sin?', in Robin Gill (ed.), *Readings in Modern Theology* (London: SPCK, 1995), pp. 236ff.

43. Surin, *Theology and the Problem of Evil*, pp. 61–2.

44. Ibid., pp. 154, 143, 159–60. 'To put it starkly: without incarnational propositions we could not even say that it is *false* that God brought salvation to mankind, because the question of salvation cannot arise unless the depth of evil that confronts us is rendered

humanity because God identifies with the utmost depths of evil and suffering in our lives, he interrupts our continuity-in-evil in and through Christ.'[45] 'The salvation of human beings is enacted by God in the realm of humanity', as Irenaeus has argued. 'Jesus Christ is the re-creator of a humanity whose relationship with God has been distorted by sin.'[46]

Relating divinity and humanity

Taken by itself, as has been seen, the Wittgensteinian model tends to universalize into a relativist metaphysic, but it does not universalize well. Its nature precludes the making of coherent metaphysical claims and it is arguably self-consistent only when subject to other criteria such as a theistic realism. However, it has shown itself to be consistent enough with a Christian anthropology of relationality to be imported into it as a supplementary 'natural theology'. There the anthropological is converted by the theological, and the anthropic principle that contains the non-personal and non-linguistic within a personal language-ridden reality is in turn subsumed within a theistic principle. The anthropocentrism of the language-game model enables it to cohere readily with incarnational christological formulations.

If linguistic communication is the connecting point between a Wittgensteinian perspective and a relational Christian anthropology, it is also fundamental to the way human personhood is related to God's. Jüngel suggests that

> Two basic characteristics define our linguistic being. We are both those who are addressed and those who state. We are both at one and the same time. However, theological anthropology makes an ontological distinction between these two basic characteristics in their very togetherness. It must be clarified anthropologically not only that one of these two characteristics is the condition of the possibility of the other, but also that that characteristic makes it possible ... for us to be or to become again *human* persons.[47]

Footnote 44 (*cont.*)
explicit, and this, as our typical salvation-scheme indicates, can only be done by God's direct and personal engagement with the depths of this evil. I would say that every proposition involved in the articulation of this salvation-scheme presupposes the truth of incarnational propositions where the Incarnation is understood in ontological terms, i.e. as the personal presence of God in the life, death and resurrection of Jesus Christ' (Surin, 'Atonement and Christology', p. 148).   45. Surin, *Theology and the Problem of Evil*, p. 149.
46. Ibid., p. 161.
47. Jüngel, *Theological Essays*, p. 145. Quoted in Torrance, *Persons in Communion*, pp. 325–6.

Alan Torrance suggests that we may understand the linguistic aspect of both divine and human persons in terms of an 'analogy of being' – as a '"hinge" of communication between the divine and the human' which constitutes 'a real and given event of communication beween the divine and human orders'. As such, this 'analogy of being' is a one-way street: 'created reality requires to be interpreted in the light of this communion – and not the other way round'.[48] Theologically there are classically two interconnecting one-way bridges: *imago Dei* and Christology.

According to Gunton, human personhood is created by God as relational in God's image. We are truly persons in so far as we are in relation with one another (and with the rest of creation[49]) and participate in God's personhood in this way. If '*person* means primarily what it means when it is used of God', and if 'God is a communion of persons inseparably related, then surely Barth is thus far correct in saying that it is in our relatedness to others that our being human consists'. We may infer from this that if language is part of personhood it is part of a personhood-in-relation divinely defined.[50] Thus, human personhood may be understood as

> taking shape in a double orientation. In the first place, we are persons insofar as we are in right relationship to God. Under the conditions of sin, that means, of course, insofar as the image is reshaped, realised in Christ . . . To be in the image of God is to be created through the Son, who is the archetypal bearer of the image. To be in the image of God therefore means to be conformed on the person of Christ. The agent of this conformity is God the Holy Spirit, the creator of community . . . The second orientation is the 'horizontal' one, and is the outcome of the work of the first . . . The human person is one who is created to find his or her being in relation, first with other like persons but second, as a function of the first, with the rest of the creation. This means, first, that we are in the image of God when, like God but in dependence on his giving, we find our reality in what we give to and receive from others in human community.[51]

As suggested, language may be seen as integral to this image because the use of language enables relation as well as being the agent of its comprehension and evaluation. In so far as our being-in-relation constitutes

48. Ibid., p. 356.
49. There is insufficient space here to go into the implications for this study of the stewarding and priestly aspects of human personhood-in-relation-to-creation that Gunton and T. F. Torrance describe.
50. Gunton, 'Trinity, Ontology and Anthropology', p. 55. (Barth, CD/2/1, p. 272.)
51. Ibid., p. 59.

us as persons in the image of God, it is through language-using activity that we relate to each other and to the world, where that activity relies on particular agreements as to how words link up with the world.

For Green, human imagination is a central aspect of this personhood. It acts as 'the instrument of revelation, the means by which God makes himself known in the present life of believers' and is thus the locus of divine and human contact. It is the 'faithful imagination' that construes our own story in terms of the scriptural one, in which God acts to reveal to us the true story of our lives.[52] In suggesting that 'faithful imagination' is central to the relationship between God and the human creature, Green relates his concept of 'paradigmatic imagination' (image as pattern, paradigm) to the *imago Dei*. 'The theological importance of the *imago Dei* is . . . the original relationship that it posits, and the point of the relationship lies in its function [as communication]. Human beings are like God in their ability to imagine but are limited in that ability by the material at hand – that is, by the available images.'[53]

Moltmann's dictum that the *imago Dei* is the *imago Christi* [54] provides the possibility of a more comprehensive 'top-down' account of a human creativity that may include imagination. Human personhood-in-relation both participates in and anticipates its fulfilment in Christ, in whom, as created image, it is radically contingent upon the One whom it images; '*person* is an eschatological concept', to be fully realized 'when God is all in all'.[55]

This makes the second bridge logically an incarnational Christology. It is in the person of Jesus Christ that human personhood is conformed to divine personhood. According to Gunton 'all things cohere in Christ . . . rightly conceived as *Logos*, not only the Word spoken to time from eternity, but the immanent dynamic of meaning which holds time and space together'.[56] Incarnation, as T. F. Torrance points out, is 'the place in all space and time where God meets with man in the actualities of his human existence, and man meets with God and knows Him in His own divine being'.

52. Green, *Imagining God*, pp. 106–8.   53. Ibid., pp. 84–9.

54. 'The restoration or new creation of the likeness to God comes about in the fellowship of believers with Christ: since he is the messianic *imago Dei*, believers become *imago Christi*, and through this enter upon the path which will make them *gloria Dei* on earth. According to Romans 8.29 they will become "conformed to the image of the Son" and, through their discipleship, grow into the messianic form of Jesus': see J. Moltmann, *God in Creation: An Ecological Doctrine of Creation* (London: SCM, 1985), pp. 225ff.

55. Gunton, 'Trinity, Ontology and Anthropology', pp. 60–1.

56. Gunton, *The One, the Three and the Many*, pp. 178–9.

Jesus Christ is the place of contact and communication between God and man in a real movement within physical existence, involving interaction between God and nature, divine and human agency ... It is place that is filled with the energy of divine being and life, but place that is also filled with the energy of human being and life. Hence we have to think it out in a kinetic way in accordance with the nature and activity of God who locates Himself in our space and time as one with us, and in accordance with the nature and activity of the earthly and temporal existence in which He has become incarnate.[57]

As noted, it is in the incarnational meeting of divinity and humanity in Christ ('the Incarnation of the Word of God which links human language with Christology')[58] that the co-inherent relation of knower to known is not only a discovery and a consent but also an active constructing. This knowing as relational is a dynamic 'becoming' which, as such, is inherently underdetermined. As it is the meeting point of divine transcendence and creaturely contingence in the person of Jesus Christ that is the locus of this underdeterminedness, and as our personhood is subsumed in the personhood of Christ within which this dialectic occurs, then the creativity inherent to human personhood also takes place within this christological knowing. That is, there is an underdeterminedness within the incarnate person of Christ which subsumes the underdetermined 'is–is not' metaphoricity of human personhood which, as Moltmann and Gunton point out, is also a diachronic and eschatological 'not-yetness'.

The boundaries of the cosmos, but at the same time its very heart, are where its personal element – its humanity – is realized in meeting its personal creator. This encounter, described by Torrance as 'kinetic' – one of dynamic movement – has also been described as divinely kenotic, a self-emptying on God's part in order to make room for that which is other than God, but a self-emptying that occurs in the context of personal relationship and therefore takes the form of sacrificial love. As Surin puts it,

we see 'kenosis' in terms of God 'making room' within the mystery of the divinity for the order of finite things. In creation we are, as it were, summoned to think of all things in their proper relation to God. In so doing, we see ourselves as creatures, as terminating a relation of radical dependence on that from which we have our being. By seeing the matter thus – that is, by seeing all things as themselves standing in a transcendent relation to God – we see our own relation to the world and its Creator in a different light. To have a sense of the

57. Torrance, *Space, Time and Incarnation*, pp. 75, 78.
58. Need, *Human Language and Knowledge*, pp. 201, 212.

'logic' of creation is therefore to perceive the 'need' to change our thinking, speaking and doing. It is to engage with the world and its Creator in a new and different way. To seek to do this in a Christ-shaped world, to acknowledge that the world has this shape, is to begin to grasp the 'logic' of the divine kenosis. It is a 'logic' which invites us to embark on or to recognize that we are already embarked on, the Church's pedagogy of discipleship.[59]

If it is in Jesus Christ that we become fully persons in the image of God, then in turn it is in human personhood in Christ that all creatureliness receives its completion and salvation (the *imago Dei* is the *imago Christi*). In this personhood 'even more anthropologically primitive than language is human agency which takes up language and puts it into play in the give-and-take of daily living and dying'.[60] We become truly human through absorption into God's story, and this is a 'work-in-progress' which begins

not at the point where the narrative is, as it were, already doing its work, but at the earlier point where the subject is about to enter into it, i.e. the point where she is 'baptised' into the Christian semiotic system. At this juncture the human subject is suspended between two narratives, one 'pre-Christian' and the other 'Christian', poised to undergo . . . 'the shock of entry into narrative'.[61]

With that converting entry which is the human subject's entry into Christ the self receives an incarnational grammar that re-creates it, and yet this is a creative unfolding of a potential new person – a 'now-but-not-yet' – in which the role of the subject's imagination has a place. In human personhood the underdeterminedness of creaturely contingency may be understood to be expressed in the freedom granted to us to have a hand in creating ourselves. Yet, as Surin goes on to say crucially, the end of this re-creation which will bring the sum of our human activities and relationships within our relationship with God in Christ is vocation or discipleship.

Language-ridden divinity?

As mentioned in the previous chapter, Gunton suggests that creation's intrinsic rationality might be understood as a semiotic system which

---

59. K. Surin, 'Some Aspects of the "Grammar" of "Incarnation" and "Kenosis"', in K. Surin (ed.), *Christ, Ethics and Tragedy* (Cambridge: Cambridge University Press, 1989), p. 106.
60. Cathey, *Foundations with Faces*, pp. 328–9.   61. Surin, *Turnings*, pp. 216–17.

while grounded in God amounts more than simply to a divine speech-act as it requires supplementation with 'models of divine construction and earthly mediation'.[62] Communication implies agency. Following Barth in working 'backward' from God's self-revelation in Christ, Jüngel argues that this revelation – God's becoming manifest – 'means that God's being is relational being'. Yet if God is to be God, this cannot be a relationality in which God is dependent upon some other for being. Instead, this relationality must be understood as first and foremost a self-relatedness. And as such

> God's self-relatedness must rather be understood as a *becoming peculiar* to his *own* being, a becoming which allows us to comprehend God's own being as a 'being in act'. Only when God's self-relatedness is understood as a becoming peculiar to his own being is God's being-for-us also adequately considered. God's self-relatedness, his power to be in relation to himself (ειναι προς εαυτον), would then be the power of his being in relation to another (προς 'ετερνος).[63]

Jüngel observes that the fact of revelation entails that God is eternally capable of self-interpretation – 'interpreting himself through himself'. God has 'the ability to possess predicates' because of 'the *event of the Word* which is there before all predication and which makes all predications possible. In this sense it will have to be true that God's being, which has been formulated from the event of revelation, is in himself *verbal* (*wörtlich*) . . .' Jüngel sees God's being-as-verbal as being expressed in God's self-relation, in God's saying 'yes' to being triune persons in relation.[64]

God's verbal agency as an integral aspect of both self-communication and world creation may be seen as the source of all human activities involving language. Again, Jüngel proposes that 'human speech about God . . . owes its being to revelation in which God himself – and that means his being! – manifested himself in human language. The historical predicate by which God manifested his being in human language is called Jesus of Nazareth.'[65] God 'speaks' or 'utters' the Word who is Christ, the Word by whom all human words are created and judged. In this way human language use is grounded in divine language use.

This attributing of 'language-riddenness' to God, then, is not a matter

62. Gunton, *A Brief Theology of Revelation*, pp. 61, 69–70.
63. E. Jüngel, *The Doctrine of the Trinity: God's Being is in Becoming*, trans. H. Harris (Edinburgh: Scottish Academic Press, 1976), pp. 99–100.   64. Ibid., pp. 95–6.
65. Ibid., p. 97.

of naive anthropomorphism. It is to recognize that a trinitarian doctrine of God entails that communication is inherent to God's being and that the reality of God's immanent and incarnate self-communication is prior to and definitive of our own. (This line of reasoning connects Christology to the doctrine of the *imago Dei*.) Moreover, if we express a relational view of reality in terms of language-games while at the same time maintaining the primacy of a divinity in whom communication is inherent, this double requirement ('God's being as essentially *double* relational being')[66] may prevent both a modern exclusion of language from reality and a post-modern or new hermeneutical reduction of God to either God-language or divine speech-acts. Instead, we may recognize divine language and divine truth as inherent in God's immanent reality and revealed in Christ as the source and renewal of all human language-games. According to the central Christian grammar of incarnation, in Christ divine communication is 'indigenized' as the transformation of human communication. In participating in divine intelligibility, human language becomes what it truly is. Rather than a transcendent divinity's being the entirely extra-linguistic subject of predicated attributes, instead an incarnate divinity defines the predicates. The predications become the divine self-interpretation included in the revelation of that divinity.[67]

Divine linguisticality does not have to conflict with the Christian understanding of divine transcendence and creaturely contingency. The assumptions, first, that divine transcendence is above and beyond language and, second, that language is a human (mental) monopoly, owe their origin to the way the modern world has objectified reality as extra-linguistic and then projected this extra-linguisticality on to God. To maintain this premise of extra-linguisticality as a necessary part of the doctrine of God is, as Tanner would put it, to allow this imported metaphysic to skew what is central to Christian belief. Jüngel's theory of trinitarian agency suggests that we might read the Economic Trinity as *becoming* the Immanent Trinity, and vice versa, in a sort of diachronic coinherence summed up in the reciprocal processions of *kenosis* and *theosis*, sending forth and receiving back. God's self-communicating 'language-games' become human language-games when 'uttered' in Christ. On the other hand, in the receiving back of the 'Son', human language-games are theotically drawn into and participate in God's language-games. God is eternally uttering the Word which creates the world and the incarnate,

66. Ibid., p. 99.   67. Ibid., pp. 95–8.

kenotic, crucified God is eternally being resurrected and restored to the Godhead.

Conclusion

The argument of this chapter – an argument that has proceeded from both top and bottom – has been that a theistic realism entails that both divine and contingently human reality is inherently personal. Consequently as well as antecedently, this personal reality is both communicative and dynamic in its nature. What are the implications of divine language-riddenness for a theistic realism? First, that it is essentially a critical realism. In divine personhood as self-relational agency,[68] the co-inherence of being and doing is also the co-inherence of being and knowing, of reality and truth. The 'objectivity' of God as ultimate reality is at the same time an immanent intersubjectivity of knower and known.[69] Within the eternal divine coming-into-being which is the eternal co-inherence of coming-to-know of the self-communication that is love, there is arguably an underdeterminedness in God's immanent reality. This underdeterminedness at the heart of God in the reality that is the coming-into-being of reality, implies both an immanently divine source of new realities and truths and a provisionality to present divine actuality. This allows us to infer a continuing revelation without going outside of a trinitarian, incarnational Christology and all that implies, but in the same breath suggests (in that provisionality and becoming) a Rortian '*cloudy* windows all the way up'. On this basis, true knowledge is eternally as well as temporally knowledge in the discovery and the making, a knowledge that is grasped in its coming into being.[70] Hence the proposition that a theistic realism is inherently a critical realism.

68. It is worth noting also that if we follow Jüngel's argument that divinity is compromised by any primary relationality that requires the participation of any other than God and that therefore self-communication is inherent to divinity, this rules out a monadic conception of God.

69. If, as noted, Need suggests that 'The unity of the two [divine and human] elements in Christ is the root of an epistemological unity between the knower and the known . . . [and] the difference between the two elements in Christ [is] the root of an epistemological distinction between knower and known' (see Need, *Human Language and Knowledge*, p. 203), this co-inherence in relational being that we find in Christ as God-with-us, as Economic Trinity (by virtue of the doctrine of appropriation or attribution), is the same co-inherence in relation that we infer in the Immanent Trinity.

70. Yet this model of divine language-riddenness undercuts the 'we create our reality (including our God) with our words' arguments generated by a postmodern awareness of our inability to escape from language unaccompanied by the generation of an adequate postmodern metaphysic.

Perhaps, however, the main benefit of such a model is in Christian life. In worship and prayer it removes the tarnish of any modern metaphysical anxieties that we might be either bouncing our Godward words back off the boundaries of a language that seems inherently incapable of addressing a God who is outside that language, or discoursing redundantly with one contained within human language. It also counters ecclesial self-certainty and promotes prophetic self-criticism in suggesting that the Spirit's role in the dialectic between Scripture and tradition is to lead us into participation with a God who is always new. But that is the concern of the final chapter.

7

Becoming the Church

It is time to draw the theory into the pragmatic reality in which it is tested: the Church. If the Church has to be realist unless it holds the belief that it constructs its own reality, divine as well as human, it is also faced with engaging with a postmodern world, and in its humanness is, of course, itself a part of that world. Most of this inquiry so far has been concerned with how theology, as Christian theory, might do this engaging. With the shift of focus to practice, the investigation of theory continues as the net of investigation widens to include ecclesiology, for according to the model advanced throughout, the nature of the Church is inseparable from its practice.

The Church as personal

Theological realism has often been labelled exclusivist and imperialist. That this accusation is in part justified is due to the realist tendency to regard Christian facts as true for everyone in the same way. As a corrective to this approach, Lindbeck maintains that as we do not know how much (or whether) our ecclesial forms of life – the 'giant propositions' of our traditions – correspond to a divine reality, we cannot take their doctrines as being absolute immutable truths cast in concrete, but must regard them as 'categorially true' – that is, true for their context.[1] On the other hand, however, he would agree with Lesslie Newbigin and other theological realists that the Christian Church must be universalist (if not exclusivist) in that it 'points unambiguously to Jesus Christ as the one whom God has set forth to be the given centre of human unity, the one

1. Lindbeck, *The Nature of Doctrine*, p. 48.

who "through the blood of his cross" can reconcile all people and all things'.[2] How can the Church be both realist and face a human reality that is language-riddenly postmodern, a reality which is at the same time its own because the Church is also a human form of life?

First of all, the Church is realist in that its constituting reality and rationale is a transcendent God – necessarily transcendent in that if the Church's God were not other than and constituting of the Church, this God would in effect *be* the Church, or a product of the Church. This reality is also an incarnational reality in being christologically constituted. As noted in chapter 5 and elsewhere, while realism requires verification of our human attempts at truth according to the reality with which they claim to correspond, at the same time human attempts at truth cannot be verified other than theistically. Yet if this judgment is to be accessible, it must be available to us on the human level. For this reason, the coherence of realism relies on incarnation. The Church both participates in and represents (or bears) this incarnational reality (and thus participates in divine being) as the locus of Christ's being and agency in the world. That is, it participates in the Economic Trinity. In this sense the Church itself is the verifier and judge of human forms of life, but with the proviso advanced in chapter 5 that a theistic realism is at the same time a critical realism in its provisionality and revisability.

For the Church to participate in God's reality means that it is a personal reality.[3] It is personal in its divine 'vertical' aspect because its reality is christological. Again, personal being has been argued to be relational. In Christ the Church participates (in patristic parlance)[4] in the dialectic between the two natures in the one person in Christ which reflects and indwells the self-relationality of the Immanent Trinity, the incarnational seam joining divine transcendence and human contingency. Therefore, the Church as personal may be understood first and foremost as relational.

It is also relational in its human 'horizontal' aspect where this human relationality is that of true human personhood in God's image. As noted, Gunton suggests that a relational model best describes the complex pluriformity of contemporary reality because everything is constituted as what it uniquely is in relation to everything else. In addition, human

---

2. L. Newbigin, 'The Christian Faith and the World Religions', in Wainwright, *Keeping the Faith*, pp. 310–40, pp. 337–8.
3. This personal definition is consistent with other relational models of the Church, such as Body of Christ, People of God, and Communion of Saints.
4. See Need, *Human Language and Knowledge* and the discussion in the previous chapter.

personhood is created by God as relational in God's image. We are truly persons insofar as we are in relation with one another and participate in God's personhood in this way.[5] Human personhood-in-relation both participates in and anticipates its fulfilment in Christ, in whom, as created image, it is radically contingent upon the One whom it images. In its human membership also, then, the Church participates in divine relationality.

Ecclesial becoming

As personal and accordingly relational, the Church draws in all that pertains to divine and human personhood. To begin with, the Church's being as personal and relational is agential. It is a *perichoresis* of being and doing. This agency is expressed fundamentally in the divine self-relatedness which, according to Jüngel, is to be 'understood as a *becoming peculiar* to [God's] *own* being, a becoming which allows us to comprehend God's own being as a "being in act"'.[6] (Thus Jüngel suggests that we might read the Economic Trinity as *becoming* the Immanent Trinity, and vice versa, in a sort of diachronic coinherence summed up in the reciprocal processions of *kenosis* and *theosis*, sending forth and receiving back.) This being-as-becoming also represents the nature of the Church as a human form of life, both as created in God's image and as christologically redeemed and realized.

The Church's being-as-agent means that its nature and function are inherently ethical. Yet as persons human beings are good or otherwise in a way that is indefinably more than the sum of their beliefs and actions. This recognition gives rise to a more wholesale notion of good as reposing in personal character, or virtue, where these are an interweaving of being and doing that embraces all the people we are and language-games we play in our various situations. On a personal level the good that we are is judged and fulfilled in Christ's person and therefore also by the Church as the bearer of revelation. The ethics of the Church are christological, as Dietrich Bonhoeffer has said, because we find in Christ our definition of the Good. Yet the Church as personal is inherently ethical in a way that is more than the sum of its parts in that it possesses

---

5. For this reason John Zizioulas sees the Church as the *imago Dei*. Our true being is in communion, that is, ecclesial. 'The life of the eucharist is the life of God Himself... the life of communion with God, such as exists within the Trinity and is actualized within the members of the eucharistic community.' John Zizioulas, *Being as Communion* (London: Darton Longman & Todd, 1985), p. 81.   6. Jüngel, *The Doctrine of the Trinity*, pp. 99–100.

and enacts in its Christology, and offers in its witness, a prophetic vision of the Good. As Hauerwas has said,

> Modern moral philosophers have failed to understand that moral behaviour is an affair not primarily of choice but of vision. They see all moral agents as inhabiting the same world of facts: thus they discriminate between the different types of morality only in terms of acts and choices. But differences of moral vision or perspective may also exist. When we assess other people, we do not consider just their solutions to particular problems; we feel something much more elusive which may be called their total vision of life . . . Our morality is more than adherence to universalizable rules; it also encompasses our experiences, fables, beliefs, images, concepts, and inner monologues.[7]

That is, the Church-as-ethical is the keeper of a vision of the Good. As knowledge of the Good (as informing practice) includes vision which is a seeing of the world in a way that imagines truly the world's future as well as its present, then the Church's practice or way of being the Church is dependent upon its seeing the world through Christ – that is, imagining itself christologically in relation to the world.

> A Christian does not simply 'believe' certain propositions about God; he learns to attend to reality through them. This learning requires training of our attention by constantly juxtaposing our experience with our vision. This means that there is an unmistakably pragmatic aspect to the Christian life, not in the sense that 'it is true because it works', but because it is always being tested by our encounter with reality.[8]

This means that the Church's being is creatively constructive in imagining reality as future as well as present. Imagination is a part of its nature as personal. As Green argues, imagination is central to human personhood for it is the agent of revelation by which we construe ourselves christologically.[9] Imagination creates the visionary 'seeing as' which reads the world in terms of a christological grammar. For if this grammar rules our ecclesial language-games, then 'It is not a matter of transforming the language to fit the world in the name of relevancy; but it is a matter of transforming the [ecclesial] self to fit the language. The problem is to become as we see.'[10]

This emphasis on ethical vision underlines that the Church as

---

7. Hauerwas, *Vision and Virtue*, p. 35.   8. Ibid., p. 46.
9. Green, *Imagining God*, pp. 106–8.   10. Hauerwas, *Vision and Virtue*, p. 46.

incarnationally personal is also an eschatological reality. It is eschatological in imagining its own and the world's true potential and possibility christologically in drawing into its being-in-Christ all of human reality past, present and future. In this way, the Church-as-christological participates in a divinity whose immanent being is in becoming. What then is implied is a provisionality to present ecclesial actuality that allows us to infer a continuing creation and re-creation of the Church's being without going outside of a trinitarian Christology and all that implies. That the Church's own being-as-christological is in becoming is expressed in an underdeterminedness which is its freedom to become itself.

That this becoming includes its becoming redeemed indicates that in its humanness it is not only incomplete but also fallen. This is shown in its capacity to create false and distorted worlds that are diminishing and destructive of the relationality on which personhood depends, as the historical record shows. As noted in chapter 6, imagination co-opted by sin becomes destructive of personhood, producing false images and misrepresenting the partial as the whole of ecclesial being.[11] The Church misrepresents reality, however, not only in deceiving itself with illusions and fantasies but also in believing its present and past tradition to be exhaustive of its reality. Ecclesially as well as individually, it seems, 'We cannot long look directly at reality, so we use past formulations of the truth as a defense against the constant struggle to pierce through the veil.'[12]

In this way the Church's christological being as eschatological embraces everything that is human. If, as Surin suggests, 'speech about human suffering is in some sense speech about divinity's very own history', it is also about humanity's encounter with evil and sin.[13] 'The salvation of human beings is enacted by God in the realm of humanity', which is the realm of the Church.[14] It is as the Church's own language-games of suffering and overcoming become truly christological that it comes, in its radical identification with those caught up in sin and evil, to know sin and evil for what they are in its own life and at the same time bring effective salvation to others.

Becoming ecumenical

The dynamic relation between redeemedness and unredeemedness at the heart of the Church occurs within an underdeterminedness within

---

11. Green, *Imagining God*, p. 90.   12. Hauerwas, *Vision and Virtue*, p. 32.
13. Surin, *Theology and the Problem of Evil*, p. 149.   14. Ibid., p. 161.

the Church. The Church's freedom humanly to become itself creates a hermeneutical dialectic not only between scriptural norm and tradition, but also between the norm as interpreted at any given time and place and the norm as it may truly become when Christ is all in all. For this reason it is only through a mutual indwelling of traditions and contexts that the Church is able provisionally and progressively to discern an 'objective' Gospel. If such a *perichoresis* of local contexts with one another and with the Gospel is to occur, each tradition or ecclesial context will operate with a mixture of appreciation for its own unique qualities coupled with a recognition of its incompleteness and unconvertedness in falling short of, and in some respects opposing, the totality which is Christ. The opposite occurrence, as is evidenced by both sectarian and intra- and transdenominational ideologies, is the lack of that sense of incompleteness and sinfulness in the exclusivist view that *this* alone is the real world, the true salvation. Another form of this exalting of context is exhibited in postmodern theologies whose critique of universals exhibits a positivism that has effectively eliminated any possibility of a context-transcending reality – including a divine one.

Both of these very different varieties of sectarianism exclude the sort of perichoretic interplay that enables different ecclesial forms of life to be self- and other-critical in the light of the Gospel. As the Gospel is never without a cultural expression and no cultural expression is exhaustive of it, it may only be reached for provisionally and progressively through the comparison of family resemblances displayed in its various figurative vehicles, its ecclesial traditions and contexts. From the reciprocal interaction of these vehicles comes a gain to ecclesial reality. As Kathryn Tanner observes, this complementarity assists in the hermeneutical task of interpreting the biblical norm in which we need to preserve 'the tension between the obvious sense of a scriptural text and its use in changing circumstances'.[15] The dialectic between interpretations enables us to see past our local realities, allowing an ever new and widening appreciation of what is Christianly normative to address and revise the excesses and shortcomings of our contexts. In the process the Bible as the common norm behind the ecclesial practice provides the basis from which Christian traditions begin to understand one another.[16] Upon the bedrock of this common reference the dialectic

---

15. Tanner, 'Theology and the Plain Sense', p. 71.
16. Foucault has pointed out that indigenization is a complex and abuse-prone process in which power considerations may determine which features are selected and which

between text and reader in various contexts (within the underdeterminedness of a christological reality that includes but is not exhausted by the text) enables the Church to evaluate critically age-old 'sedimented Christian practices' which in some instances may have distorted the Gospel beyond recognition.[17] This reconciliation may be able to relate partially incommensurable postmodern worlds, for the model is that of assimilation by a primary and transcending reality, yet an assimilation that does not obliterate but converts and is then itself refigured in a continuing series of interacting and mutually prophetic indigenizations. In this way, through the complementary mutual involvement of ecclesial forms of life, the Church discovers and becomes what it truly, christologically, is.

Ecclesial language-games

The Church's being-as-personal is, as accordingly relational and agential, inherently communicative. As participant in both divine and human reality the Church is constituted in *communicative* activity, that is, in practices involving language,[18] or language-games. If communication is inherent to God's being, the reality of God's self-communication is prior to and definitive of our own. That divine communication is then 'indigenized' in Christ into human communication. It is thus in participating in divine communication that human language becomes what it truly is. From a human perspective, according to Wittgenstein, the language-using activity through which we relate to each other and to the world (where that activity relies on particular agreements as to how words link up with the world) is fundamental to human personhood.[19] It follows from this pragmatic basis that ecclesial (as with human) being and doing, being and knowledge, and belief and practice are all coinherent. This has already been noted in connection with ecclesial being as agency.

Yet as player of language-games the Church is more than the sum of its parts. And the way in which it is more than the sum of its parts reflects

dominate, as feminist and other liberation theologians will vouch. If the Church's being is in becoming redeemed, in its yet-to-be-redeemedness it is the oppressor of the powerless. See Madan Sarup, *An Introductory Guide to Poststructuralism and Postmodernism* (Athens, GA: University of Georgia Press, 1989), p. 57.

17. Tanner, 'Theology and the Plain Sense', p. 75.

18. Again, this is language widely construed to include signs, symbols, gestures, music, art etc.   19. Cathey, *Foundations with Faces*, pp. 328–9. See chapter 6.

its mediation of God's being. As Jüngel argues, God's 'verbal' (*wörtlich*) agency as an integral aspect of both divine self-communication and world-creation may be seen as ontologically prior to and informing of all human activities involving language, so that 'human speech about God . . . owes its being to revelation in which God himself – and that means his being! – manifested itself in human language'.[20] Therefore ecclesial personhood as language-ridden is constituted in 'divine being manifested in human language', that is, preeminently in worship, in the language-games of liturgy, of reading the Scriptures and reciting the creeds, preaching and testimony, confession, communion, and common prayer. As Alan Torrance puts it:

> There is an integral symbiotic link between doxological participation (*koinonia*) in Christ in worship and semantic participation in Christ. Semantic participation, as it includes – and indeed constitutes – our epistemic 'indwelling', is an essential *coefficient* of doxological participation in communion to the extent that worship is cognitive, conceptual and social (ecclesial), and thus grounded in the creative reconstitution in Christ, by the Spirit, of the language-games which constitute our 'capacity' for communion. If worship is 'the gift of participating by the Spirit in the Son's communion with the Father', then this includes semantic participation in such a way that the language–communion link (which parallels the language–world link) is constituted by the Logos. It is 'realised' both *objectively* in the union and communion of the High Priest of our humanity with the Father in the Spirit and also *subjectively* in Christ's union and communion with his Body in the Spirit.[21]

In worship God inhabits the divine gift of praise[22] while, in this 'wondrous exchange', human language-games are drawn into and participate in the divine language-games. 'Christian worship shares in a human–Godward movement that belongs to God and which takes place *within* the divine life. It is precisely into and within *this* that we are brought by the Spirit to participate as a gift of grace.'[23]

It follows that the Church's being is constituted in self-giving agency. The personal relationship between God and humanity involves a kenotic self-emptying on God's part that takes the form of sacrificial love.[24] This love is constituted ecclesially (and language-riddenly) first

20. Jüngel, *The Doctrine of the Trinity*, p. 97.   21. Torrance, *Persons in Communion*, p. 356.
22. See D. W. Hardy and D. F. Ford, *Praising and Knowing God* (Philadelphia: Westminster Press, 1985), Appendix A.   23. Torrance, *Persons in Communion*, p. 314.
24. Surin, 'Some Aspects of the "Grammar" of "Incarnation" and "Kenosis"', p. 106.

in worship of God, and second in drawing the world into its own relationality. David Ford talks about an ethic of love that, when expressed in worship as the central Christian activity, means that this worship is fundamentally 'a social meal-and-world-centered communication informed by the key events of the Christian story'. It is this love ethic involving 'the thrust of present speech, action, suffering, and thought' that, in relating experience to truth, renders Christian truth personal.[25] There is a progression between worship and mission analogous to the kenotic-theotic progression between Immanent and Economic Trinities and in this we are reminded that the Church participates in the Economic Trinity.

Absorbing the world

The Church as personally constituted in worship at the same time encounters and converts others as a missionary Church. According to a theistic realism, the Church as bearer of God's world-embracing incarnational reality must subsume all other human reality. Consistent with this logical necessity, the Church as subject to a normative Gospel is also charged with the commission to go and teach and baptize all nations. Whether subsumption or baptism, the event or process is conversion. It is a process that in its cognitive and linguistic aspects has been described as typological and metaphorical, as including aspect-seeing, transfer of training, and the superimposition of language-games. It is a process that involves both similarity and difference. With the shift to the personal pragmatic context of the Church, the theories of conversion as 'seeing-as', transfer and superimposition are drawn inside conversion as personal event. The cognitive aspects of conversion are to be couched personally if this is not to be a gnostic salvation-by-knowledge. As Surin points out, to be truly salvific, a Saviour must both radically identify with the one to be saved and also, at the same time, transcend the situation necessitating the saving if a raising from that situation is to be possible. The Saviour must descend to the level of the drowning person, grasp her by the arm, and lift her to safety. (It stands to reason that the rescuer cannot save her if s/he also is at the mercy of the tide.) It is Surin's contention that only a personal and incarnate God can effect this salvation.[26]

If a converting encounter requires both personal transcendence and

---

25. Ford, 'System, Story, Performance', pp. 199–205. See also chapter 2.
26. Surin, *Turnings*, pp. 148–50.

personal identification, it is not possible to take the Church as a *human form* (or forms) or life as primary. For the Church to save it must participate in divine transcendence. That is, it must operate with a theistic realism. Theologians such as Don Cupitt who hold an immanentist doctrine of God cannot, on this reckoning, come up with a model of conversion. Cupitt reads the postmodern language-as-universal-medium premise as requiring human contexts (including ecclesial ones) to be their own truth. 'God . . . is the power of language-in-the-unconscious to call life forth into expression and to order the world. God is something like an endlessly self-outpouring Now, a fountain of linguistic meanings that wells up within us and pours out through us on to our world.' Christian language itself is taken as creating the God and Saviour (and hence Church) it proclaims, for 'Like us, God is made only of words.' All meaning and truth is linguistically constituted and 'Only within and by means of language do the world and humanity get constituted as formed and intelligible realities.'[27] The Church invents and reinvents itself according to itself.

In taking human forms of life as primary, this view takes the Church's identity as being exhausted by its membership in the set {human forms of life}. The grammar of incarnation has been displaced by a socio-linguistic grammar that effectively permits neither divine transcendence nor redemption. If salvation is taken to relate to Christ, then Christ (as non-primary in relation to human forms of life as a member of the set {salvific symbols/paradigms in human forms of life}) is immanent in the context in which salvation is needed. Or is it needed? – for if God is identified with the context, from what are we being saved?[28]

Either the Church draws humanity into its world, or the world defines the Church. Lindbeck's dictum, 'Christianity must absorb the world', declares that the Church, if it is to be true to its Gospel, is to see itself as the primary, in fact the only, authentic human form of life. In absorbing the world, as Marshall has argued of Christianity, the Church draws inside itself all that exists humanly. Language-games not unique to Christianity come under a Christian grammar as other forms of life and their grammars (the 'universe of truths') are absorbed. Christianity must absorb the world because the Church is the form of life which, of all

27. D. Cupitt, *Creation out of Nothing* (London: SCM, 1990), pp. 129, x, 10.
28. Yet in claiming *sui generis* relativism as an absolute fact about Christianity, it claims a position ruled out by the very perspective it adopts, a universal eye-of-God view of what is real. See ibid., p. 45.

forms of life, constitutes, in its participation in God's incarnation, the divine form of life that judges and perfects all life. Put simply, Christ is 'the way, the truth and the life'.

So far, as mentioned, conversion has been described mainly in non-personal terms, as the method by which Christianity absorbs the world, a seeing-as involving a transfer of training or knowledge which changes the grammar of reality so that the world is seen through Christian eyes and lived through Christian practices, beliefs and experiences interpreted Christianly. This process has been analysed in terms of the superimposition of secondary upon primary language-games.[29] As noted, parables are an instance of how Christianity takes up the data of what is humanly primary and converts their import and meaning so that they may reveal the fundamental truth about reality. Here, as White has argued, predications of something to God assume ontological primacy over predications of the same thing to a creature or aspect of world,[30] so that the ordinary sense of what is basic is inverted.[31]

As also mentioned, conversion occurs on two levels: the theoretical hermeneutical one of the theological absorption of the universe of truths outside the Church and the personal pragmatic one of the converting of the other to a Christ-shaped personal reality. As the person is the cognitive bearer of theory, the first level of conversion indwells the second, yet at the same time the person as language-ridden indwells a postmodernly theory- or story-laden world. This co-inherence of cognition and personal transformation underlines the co-inherence of theology and evangelism in the life of the Church.

Hauerwas has emphasized the role of training in the making of disciples.[32] Ongoing training in discipleship continually involves further converting training transfer as the convert's world is drawn inside the world of the Church. As training is always at the hands of a trainer, training and transfer of training are the pragmatic personal component in the theory of conversion that hooks the cognitive process into the process of personal transformation.

The link-up with the metaphoric processes of 'seeing-as' and training transfer is a reminder that the results of conversion are always new. Just as a metaphor expresses a new reality from the co-inherence of two old ones, absorbing the world and the world's inhabitants does not leave

---

29. This brief discussion echoes chapter 4's more comprehensive treatment of Wittgenstein.   30. White, 'Notes on Analogical Predication', p. 202.
31. Ibid., p. 210.   32. S. Hauerwas, *After Christendom* (Nashville: Abingdon Press, 1991).

Christianity or the Church unaffected; the absorption is also at the same time reciprocally an indigenization. When Christianity becomes the story of our life, then our reinterpreted, transformed life-stories along with all our understandings of world become parables, positive or negative, of the primary Christian reality. Yet this refiguring is never complete; it must clothe the converter in a new reality that is not iconic of the old.[33] For this reason, as noted, although the final arbiter must nevertheless still be the biblical text however our understanding of that text has been transformed, we cannot regard our reading of the 'plain sense' of the Christian Gospel as fixed.[34]

The convert's imported world refigures the Christian reality. New members represent a gain to ecclesial actuality in more than numbers. Within the incarnational underdeterminedness of a Church that is both transcendent and contingent, the Spirit leads us into new truth. The risk of 'perturbations' in tradition (as a disordering that might lead either to a creative new order or to destruction) comes with every new seeing-as of every new and ongoing refigurer of the Gospel.[35] The risk from other forms of life also arises in connection with the Church's theological and pastoral annexing of 'alien' theories and models to aid its endeavours of self-description, nurture and mission. Again, however, the theoretical is subsumed by the personal; new insights are preached, taught, applied and received. Through such perturbations which disrupt the consistency of belief and practice while rippling outward to establish a new pattern, the Church reinvents itself, but does so un-Cupittly within and in obedience to its redeeming incarnational grammar, for its underdeterminedness is located within a christological reality which absorbs, judges and redeems the present world in all its complexity, and embraces a future which includes the possibility of the Church's becoming and its eschatological fulfilment.

The Church as the converting christological reality that absorbs the world may then be seen to be a Church that is 'indigenized' by those whom it converts, by the bearers of various other traditions and contexts in time and space. Indigenization, in bringing the Church as converter

---

33. Marshall, 'Absorbing the World', p. 82.
34. Marshall comments that 'When supported by persuasive arguments, alien truth claims can lead Christians to change the way they identify and specify the plain sense of Scripture and therefore what beliefs cohere with the plain sense. Encounter with alien truth claims can thus lead Christians to change their vision of the Scriptural world in which they strive to live and think.' Ibid., p. 93.
35. See Hardy, 'Spirit of God', and the discussion in chapter 5.

inside that which is alien to it, is the product of the Spirit's work within a human creativity that brings forth new and surprising truths. With the converting entry which is the human subject's entry into Christ the self receives an incarnational grammar that re-creates it. And in this re-creation which is a creative unfolding of a potential new person – a 'now-but-not-yet' – the subject's imagination has a role. In human personhood the underdeterminedness of creaturely contingency may be understood to be expressed in the freedom granted to us to have a hand in creating ourselves. Yet, as noted, the end of this re-creation that brings the sum of our human activities and relationships within our relationship with God in Christ is the ecclesial one of vocation or discipleship.

Ecclesial apologetics

The inclusion of the other in the Church's being for and saving the other, as has been suggested, modifies the Church in creating perturbations in its tradition. In affording a new perspective on the Gospel these perturbations present the opportunity for prophetic self-criticism. They are enabled by the creative freedom afforded the Church within a Christology that is more than text and tradition. Yet this underdetermined Church is to convince a postmodern world that *it* is the true human reality, the true society. The dilemma in an apologetic or missionary endeavour is the need to find common ground with the other while remaining true to what is Christianly central, where the interpretation of what is Christianly central is not ideologically fixed and yet is christological in a way that will not allow it to be redefined to fit any worldview it encounters. Mission requires both identificational similarity and transcending difference. The terms 'common ground' and 'true' immediately suggest that the Church in relation to its mission in the world is analogous to God's incarnation in the world – or rather, that incarnation includes and is the model for mission. That is, God in Jesus Christ becomes radically identified with humanity in taking on all that is human, while at the same time remaining truly God.

Again, the seam joining divine transcendence to human contingence runs through the middle of Christology. And this incarnational seam is a wavy one that defies 'straight' propositions about the meeting of divinity and world. And it is a seam in the making, sewn by the Spirit. The Christ who is distinctive and unique, the scandal of particularity at the centre of the Church, has his being in becoming. We are unable to determine precisely and finally the way in which Christ is himself as this is a becoming-himself that is for ever revealing new things. The Christ we know in the life, death and resurrection of Jesus is also the Christ who is to come, and is coming, in a new way.

In his becoming, the Christ whose continuing incarnational presence in the world is represented, however flawedly, by the Church is a personal agent offering a salvation that is known in the tasting and thus more than simply a propositional knowledge of the truth although it includes this in its grammar. As noted, this is Surin's view of salvation. The common ground with a postmodern world that he identifies for the Church is that of the (unpostmodern on the face of it) universal human experience of suffering and evil and the need for saving from that evil. On this model those who come to be saved are those who suffer. Evil may be universal but it is experienced personally; it follows that salvation from particular personal evils is particular and personal.

This starting point may be contrasted with the opposite-pole generalist one that takes as its foundation the Christian premise that all of a multifarious humanity are to have access to salvation. Efficacy is also the first consideration in functionalist soteriologies such as those of Schubert Ogden and John A. T. Robinson which suggest that what Christ *does* – that is, his saving *work* – might be construed as universal. On this basis,

> Christ's nature is to be defined by virtue of what God *does* in him, rather than what God *is* in Jesus. And since the saving work that is accomplished in Jesus is for the redemption of God's creation in its entirety, it follows that the uniqueness of Christ cannot be interpreted in a way that excludes those who belong to other religions.[36]

The difference between this view and Surin's is that it requires a definition of salvation that all may agree with – the 'all' being a humanity that includes adherents to other faiths that also offer a way of salvation. Because here the definition of salvation is to match what is taken as the fact (rather than the possibility) of a universal experience of salvation,[37] common ground is sought at a propositional as well as pragmatic level. It follows that the saving function equated with Christ is to be separated from any particular and exclusive (or radically inclusive) vehicle. The result is that christological being and soteriological doing are split apart;

---

36. Surin, *Turnings*, p. 138.
37. This reveals that the agenda in these functionalist soteriologies is interreligious dialogue rather than apologetics as such.

Christ is reduced to 'saving function', a function that may have various vehicles, including that of the person of Jesus Christ. This can only mean that these salvific agents are reduced to salvific models or patterns laid down for us to follow. However, not-yet-saved individuals do not have the ability to follow a salvific pattern; if they did, they would not need saving! Saving agency must be personal as it must embrace persons if persons are to be saved. Mere examples or vehicles cannot save us from the things that are universally beyond human control or comprehension, such as the brute realities of evil and death. At the bottom of this functionalist approach, therefore, lies the Pelagian notion that we might achieve our own salvation by ourselves, independently of what Christ or any other salvific vehicle might do.[38]

Accordingly, Surin argues, for salvation to be efficacious it cannot be abstract in being a doing detached from a being, in the sense of being functional or utilitarian (such a view reflects modernist reductionism), because such a model depersonalizes the agent in a way that makes that agency into a mechanism incapable of being other than abstractly salvific – that is restricted to producing a pattern or model of salvation. If salvation is, as evident, the salvation of persons, this then requires an incarnational model that permits an identification and embracing by a personal Saviour of the person *as* person.[39] Of course the difficulty with the functionalist model, apart from its ineffectual model of salvation, lies in the ecclesiology it implies. If all the world are, or are being, saved either inside or outside the Church, what then do we mean by 'Church' – and 'mission'?

Perhaps, however, it is possible to be incarnational, even christologically incarnational, without asserting 'that the history of Jesus totally expresses, indeed exhausts, the significance of God's saving "identification" with humankind'. This notion may buy into the notion of an underdeterminedness at the heart of an incarnational Christology. Might that underdeterminedness make room for more than the person of Jesus within the person of Christ?[40] This argument misses the point that it is the entire Church of God that, according to the biblical norm, constitutes Christ's continuing incarnation in the world, an incarnation in which Christians, as members of the Church, collectively participate. The propositional grammar, that this one man Jesus is the Christ, the

---

38. Ibid., pp. 147–8.   39. Ibid., pp. 148–50.
40. See (among others) the cosmic christologies of Teilhard de Chardin, Matthew Fox, Rosemary Radford Ruether and Sallie McFague.

Son of God, is a central and indispensible aspect of the Christian intra-systemic logic that rules all our uses of 'incarnation'. This logic requires that the Church, and individuals in the Church, participate in rather than add to incarnation.

Perhaps, even so, the concept of incarnation might be used 'as a rubric for a divine intervenient "identification" with human kind in the person of one or more historical individuals'[41] so that it would be possible to equate the significance of Christ with other incarnational instances outside the Christian Church. This argument hinges on what is meant by salvation and incarnation. The root-premise of such an argument is that all religious contexts in their different ways mediate the same truth. Yet what we mean by incarnation depends on what we mean by such key notions as 'God' and 'the presence of God'.[42] In these respects the Church as bearer of revelation is as particular as its particular incarnational grammar. Where the Church either extends its boundaries to include the 'common ground' of a trans-religious or trans-philosophical 'specification of God', or founds its mission on such common ground, there will be a misleading ambiguity in the use of religious terms in situations where the similarity is close enough to invite an inappropriate equation and not distant enough for one use to be critiqued by the other.[43] The pluralist Church *as* postmodern yet modern (as opposed to the Church that absorbs and refigures the modern and postmodern worlds according to its own grammar) is attempting to be universal by sleight of hand, as it were, for the implication of pluralism is an absorption of Church into world that virtually equates Church with world or humanity; in its conflation of creatureliness and salvation we are all 'people of God'. As theological realist Newbigin reminds us, in a religious-pluralist approach the location of the absolute shifts with the context, with the result that 'that which alone has enabled the churches to relativise their own differences – namely the absolute Lordship of Jesus Christ' – is itself relativized. The consequence is that ecumenism is shipwrecked and the internal logic of Christianity is destroyed.

As noted, the converse approach as illustrated by the Lindbeckian intratextual model requires that the Church absorb the world. The

41. Ibid., p. 153.   42. Ibid., p. 154.
43. This is the case even within the Christian Church where theologies may vary to the extent that they mean different things by 'God' and 'salvation' (as the 'Sea of Faith' movement demonstrates), which raises the question: At what point can it be said that a different Gospel is being proclaimed?

dilemma of mission is here restated according to a different model of radical inclusivism. On this model, the Church still holds that salvation is for all, but as non-negotiably in Christ (if such a model is imperialist it is inclusively rather than exclusively so). The incarnational grammar of ecclesial language-games is always christologically particular (even if our various corporate and individual applications of this grammar modify and expand its meaning) and makes universal claims from within that particularity.[44] On its own terms, Christianity must bring the 'universe of alien truths' within itself even though the meeting will change both participants. As William Placher maintains,

> It is by the criterion of the crucified Christ that Christians can evaluate and provide the framework for assessing the truth claims made by the various religions . . . This particularity does not deny that God has acted elsewhere in history (Israel is testimony to this), but it requires that God's action and nature can be discerned only through a primary focus that then allows all history to appear in its proper perspective. The Christian confronted by religious pluralism – as with any other question – must wear Christological spectacles, so to speak, or is in danger of losing sight and vision.

He goes on to say that

> While Christians claim that Christ was *totus dei* (totally divine), they do not claim that he was the divinity in its totality. Hence, insights and wisdom from the world religions can often be incorporated within a Christological outlook, enriching and deepening the faith of the Christian. But this is a far cry from entertaining truth claims inimical to faith in Christ while at the same time confessing the Christian faith. It is a simple matter of rational coherence.[45]

These comments underline the radically inclusive nature of Placher's postliberal theology. On such a reckoning the Christian world cannot be self-contained, or watertight – or if it is, the tank is cosmic in size, for the claims it makes are not just for Christians but for everyone everywhere. Somewhere the context has to give way to a prior reality, that of God. The story at the bottom of everyone's story is God's story exegeted by God's

---

44. Here the realist claim to a generic rationality may be an unwitting underminer of the Church's incarnational particularity. As Stephen Toulmin points out with respect to scientific realism, the assumption here is that tests of 'rationality' carry over from one context or situation to another, just as they stand. This assumption is built into the traditional realist metaphysic, as was discussed in chapter 1. See Toulmin, *The Return to Cosmology*, p. 21.

45. W. C. Placher, *Unapologetic Theology: A Christian Voice in a Pluralistic Conversation* (Louisville: Westminster/John Knox Press, 1989), pp. 148–9.

own self and that self-exegesis is incomplete until it grounds everyone everywhere in the Gospel of Jesus Christ.

So it then becomes a matter, in the face of the present reality, of arguing that 'the *manner* in which all will be saved *in Christ* will be known in the life to come'.[46] Here the postliberal 'salvation-for-all-in-Christ-in-a-manner-to-be-determined' model has to reckon with its own cultural-linguistic thesis that other religious human forms of life, in being world-defining, are at least partially incommensurable, a thesis which must push oneness in Christ even more firmly beyond the end of human history. A corollary to Lindbeck's eschatological model is his suggestion that we cannot know to what extent other human religious forms of life proclaim Christ because the incommensurability of religious world-views precludes an accessible Gospel. The Day of Judgment lies ahead of all human traditions, even ahead of our partial and distorted Christian-ities. It is when Christ is all in all that the sum of all religious categories will be judged and known for what they are.

Because the world-defining nature of Christianity precludes all but a Christian view of reality, Surin argues that it is only outside this Christian world that the Lindbeckian notion of categorial adequacy can be meaningful.[47] The Christian revelation must, by definition, be primary, requiring that it must be when *Christ* is all in all that salvation is complete, according to *Christ* that all are judged. Yet, as hinted in chapter 2, categorial adequacy may be brought inside a Christ-shaped world in being related to underdeterminedness. Ecclesial traditions are traditions-in-becoming and, incomplete and in part unredeemed, cannot be taken to be the final word on the representation of the Gospel which, in any case, has been interpreted by themselves. The need for such a concept as categorial adequacy to convey in some sense the uncertainty or unreliability of the Church's use of its freedom to participate creatively in Christ, is borne out in connection with what otherwise might be deemed a sophisticatedly fundamentalist understanding of the Church and Christianity as world-absorbing. To claim to know and represent Christ fully – that is, to maintain that *our* particular version of a Christ-shaped world is correct and complete – is to pretend to an ideol-ogy or an idolatry. A world-absorber 'without chinks', that is, that does not allow the possibility of or acknowledge the fact that it is continually modified by what it absorbs in a way that may be a gain to its true being,

---

46. Surin, *Turnings*, p. 174.   47. Ibid., pp. 172–3.

has no need of a theistic realism, for its parameters of truth are the internal ones of coherence and comprehensiveness.

As Ferré has argued, the end-point of an internally watertight explanatory system is not truth as such but unfalsifiability, for such a model in accounting for 'in principle, all real or possible events, cannot be disproved by any real or possible event that comes to pass'. By its very nature it has 'already, in germ, accounted for anything that might occur, and accounted for it within an interpretative framework that cannot possibly be tested independently of that framework, since any test – and any outcome of that test – that is real or possible is already accounted for within that framework!'[48] This is not to dispute the certainty that comes with faith or the need we have to exempt certain beliefs from inquiry if we are to investigate others. Nor does it gainsay that knowledge rests on commitment. What it does question is the assumption that the formulations we profess at any one time have reality all sewn up.

Accordingly, this account argues that it is vital that Lindbeck's notion of categorial truth, as here related to underdeterminedness, accompany the key postliberal insight that, quite apart from biblical truth claims, Christian self-consistency requires that the Church read Christian Scripture as pertaining to Christ and reciprocally take the biblical witness to Christ as the key not only to Scripture and Christian tradition but to the whole of human reality. If, as Frei suggests, to read a text as Scripture is for that text to tell the story of our lives both comprehensively and authoritatively, that is, as the exhaustive truth about us, then, as he also points out, the ordinary worldly details of our life become figurative, parabolic of the textual reality and to the extent to which they do so truly, they participate in and extend the reality they figure. If we take revelation to be complete in the interplay of biblical text and ecclesial use of text, of Scripture and its various interpretative traditions, then we not only equate the Church as it presently is with its perfected eschatological being, but we also ignore the revelatory potential of the narratives of ordinary human living. As Rowan Williams points out, we need to see that our telling extends the revelation:

> The Church may be committed to interpreting the world in terms of
> its own foundational narratives; but the very act of interpreting
> affects the narratives as well as the world, for good and ill, and it is
> not restricted to what we usually think of as the theological

48. Ferré, 'Mapping the Logic of Models', p. 81. (See also ibid., p. 91, Toulmin, *The Return to Cosmology,* p. 28 and Marshall, 'Absorbing the World', p. 85.)

mainstream. Something happens to the Exodus story as it is absorbed into the black slave culture of America. Something still more unsettling happens to Abraham and Isaac when they have passed through Kierkegaard's hands – or the hands of the agnostic Wilfred Owen, writing in the First World War of how the old man refused to hear the angel 'and slew his son, and half the seed of Europe, one by one'. Where are we to locate this kind of reflection? It is not purely intratextual, conducted in terms fixed by the primal narrative, nor is it in any very helpful sense a 'liberal' translation into an extraneous frame of reference. It is, much more, a generative moment in which there may be a *discovery* of what the primal text may become (and so of what it *is*) as well as a discovery of the world.[49]

The world outside the text helps the text to become what it is. The skewing of the world into a Christ-shape may be non-negotiable but that Christ-shape cannot yet be construed as Church-shaped. The Church's being is in becoming.

Demonstrating

Surin's point was that, in the face of evil and suffering, both the need for and the demonstrable efficacy of any model of salvation will out. As our encounter with evil and suffering is a personal one, only a personal God who is both so radically at one with human suffering as to encompass it and so transcendent of it as to remove it is able truly to save. This is both the nature and the model, therefore, of the Church's salvific agency. While, as argued, the Church's role in salvation includes the proclamation of its incarnational grammar, this grammar is co-inherent with soteriological language-games. What the Church proclaims it also shows in both first-order language-games of nurturing, healing, reconciling and restoring (where these, on a personal model, involve the holistic saving of both soul and body) and second-order language-games of liturgical practice such as baptism, absolution, communion and unction. The former come under the grammar of the latter and so indwell them that the two types of activities are interwoven. Everything done to save is done in the context of worship, just as worship represents and offers up everything salvific.

Endorsing a pragmatic starting point along these lines, postliberal theologians William Werpehowski and William Placher, have developed

---

49. Williams, 'Postmodern Theology and the Judgment of the World', p. 94.

Hans Frei's notion of an *ad hoc* apologetics.[50] Werpehowski offers a sort of 'limited licence' approach in which a meeting point between Christians and others on a common project addressing a particular and local practical concern (such as homelessness, poverty or violence) becomes a position from which to offer a Christian apologetic. According to Werpehowski, we do not need to be able to map competing beliefs on to a common grid of intelligibility, or measure them by some supposedly neutral norm of rationality in order to be able to make a rational comparison.

> The task of apologetics . . . is to unearth the particular storied character of the variety of human commitments and trusts in order to disclose and appreciate how they may contain within them some witness to an all-embracing promise that is relevant to all and that is made meaningful in the solidarities of thought and action. The task has a heuristic character, in that it bears the hope of concretely engaging anew in new contexts the world that is God's, in the service of God and neighbor.[51]

We can be intelligible or rational on a 'limited licence' basis in which we compare and contrast analyses and prescriptions around some point of common agreement. To deny this possibility, Werpehowski argues, 'requires the implausible assumption that there are no areas of overlap in different interpretative schemes and that these schemes hermeneutically imprison their adherents within them'. The real issue, as he sees it,

> is not that comparison between competing warrants for a belief cannot take place but, rather, that the warrant finally adopted for the purposes of common life and action may function in different ways for Christian and non-Christian. The latter takes up the Christian's proposal without conceding its presupposition . . . In that case, the non-Christian adopts what can only be an approximation of the Christian belief. If the apologetic is to proceed, conversation would have to move to another level, one concerning the warrants for the background belief just found helpfully to order our moral sensibility.[52]

For example, Christians may endorse personal self-respect in common with liberal humanism, but where a Christian anthropology enables this self-respect through a co-human model of personhood as relational, an

50. See W. Werpehowski, 'Ad Hoc Apologetics', *Journal of Religion*, 66/3 (1986), 28–30 and Placher, *Unapologetic Theology*.   51. Werpehowski, 'Ad Hoc Apologetics', 300–1.
52. Ibid., 292–3.

individualistic rights-centred humanist model fails to show how this self-respect may be achieved. To demonstrate that this is so 'involves showing that certain beliefs held by non-Christians presuppose other particular beliefs in turn warranted by the terms of Christian faith', but all on the common ground of human creatureliness. On this ground 'a particular vision of power in connection with suffering', or of human nature as inherently relational, is proposed for rational acceptance, given the relation of each, respectively, to 'deeply held judgments about ... the exigencies of social justice'.

> The presupposed beliefs ... lend greater coherence to the non-Christian's set of beliefs about some area of human life and may also explain the errors of other less plausible accounts. But the task of testing and revising a system of beliefs does not end at this point. One may go on to consider whether the beliefs to be presupposed are more plausible than alternatives that also appear to support the original judgments ... At that point theological apologetics must engage in a conversation about the more ultimate Christian beliefs upon which the presupposed beliefs rests.[53]

So there are three stages to this procedure: first, coming together on a point of common practical concern; second, agreeing on a proposal yet differing in the doctrinal or hermeneutical presuppositions or warrants with which the 'players' support the proposal; then third, discerning and discussing those differences. While in the latter stage each side in the conversation will resist challenge to their respective beliefs, if disagreement fuels an apologetic debate then in the addressing of the common concern the *fruits* may determine what it is rational (on the basis of that shared concern) to believe.[54] Let the best anthropology or ethic stand up. That is, the Church's proclamation of the Gospel rests on the Church's demonstration of its adequacy. In the face of other secular and religious theories about the nature of humanity and how it might be saved, which is able to offer the more fruitful model, and then according to what doctrinal warrant?

This raises for Werpehowski one of the questions this account has been considering: might not things go the other way? Might not the Church itself be altered by such an apologetical encounter? As suggested, through a challenging that leads to self-critique the Spirit may work in our cognitive processes to reinforce what is central to faith through creating a new understanding which constitutes a gain to eccle-

53. Ibid., 293–4.   54. Ibid., 298.

sial being. As Werpehowski points out, the critical exchange needed to advance common human commitments of human creatures may lead to the discovery of some long-buried or previously unrevealed aspects of Christian faith.[55] The various insights offered by liberation and green theologies are a good case in point.

The key to this apologetic's workability is its limited scope. Agreement between a few coming together from a couple of different places on a single issue does not require the positing of semi-generic anthropologies or rationalities. Its basis may still be particularity, necessarily so, as the Gospel is particular. As noted, Surin has a similar line of argument. The Church is able to demonstrate in a way that is verified in its results what salvation really is when it meets with particular others in the face of particular manifestations of intractable evils. When, he suggests, it has to ask itself and the others it engages with apologetically: what will save these people here? – and then: what sort of God could save these people here? – it will both practise and justify an incarnational soteriology.[56] Again, to reiterate, for the Church to avoid the danger of becoming sub-theologically humanist in taking a human condition as the apologetic common denominator, the first-order soteriological language-games must come under the grammar of the second-order-yet-primary ones that lift everything into the context of worship, and progressively (in gathering up the Church's encounter with the other as a gain to its actuality) carry the Church further into its life in God.

Conclusion

It must be concluded that if the Church expresses and represents personhood as christological, human personhood as christological is completed and perfected ecclesially. As theistic realism is personal, the Church is able both to be realist and to gather up a humanity that is postmodernly language- and context-ridden. If the image of God in humankind is the image of Christ, it is in the context of the Church – of relation both to God and other human beings – that this image has its being in becoming. Ecclesial becoming is a refiguring or indigenizing that creates as many metaphors and parables of Christ as there are Christian contexts. This view of the Church as the christological bearer of God's image breaks with the individualist modern worldview which

55. Ibid.   56. Surin, *Turnings*, pp. 136ff.

understands Christianity primarily in terms of a personal relationship with God (as *my* personal Saviour embraced through *my* personal decision for Christ). Such a view is incompatible with the christological requirement that our personal being be completed and perfected in participation with the corporate personhood of the Church. By grace we become ourselves as we truly are ecclesially as worshippers of God. We grow in discipleship, as the goal of our being, through the vision, training and encouragement of other Christians in the context of worship, the dimension of our personhood that is only to be had ecclesially. In this way, therefore, the reading back of the personal into theistic realism is completed in ecclesial, vocational personhood.

Again too, in the Church the pragmatic shift from the theoretical to the practical required by an understanding of divine (and therefore human) reality as personal hence agential is brought inside the wider and deeper agency of corporate ecclesial personhood. Yet the Church is not just another human society. Its communal personhood represents – is becoming – that of Christ's in a way that is more than the way human personhood becomes itself in Christ, although it includes that. The Church participates in christological personhood in its divine as well as human aspects. It is not locked into present and past formulations of tradition and readings of the Gospel, for it participates in the metaphorical incarnational becoming at the heart of Christ in the dialectic of the two natures. Therefore its underdeterminedness is not simply the underdeterminedness of a contingency that participates in the humanness of Christ and thereby hooks into the christological dialectic between contingence and transcendence. As well as possessing this underdeterminedness with its baggage of imperfection and sin, the Church as God's Church also participates in the becoming of God's own being. It participates in the Economic Trinity's co-inherence with the Immanent Trinity. Accordingly, the coming of God's Kingdom on earth in the eschatological Church is a breaking through of divine transcendent reality that gathers up into God those whose humanity is in Christ.

Conclusion

In the process of this inquiry three strands or levels of argument have been knitted and cabled together into a sort of theological Aran sweater. Hopefully, the inevitable loss in theoretical elegance accompanying the complex task of trying to think together models and schools that have traditionally been kept separate has been compensated for by a gain in theological comprehensiveness and explanatory force, so that the resulting pattern is at least interesting and useful if not stylish.

The first strand has been the meta-theological one of integrating schools of theology. Here a critical/postcritical realism now expanded and complicated, has come to subsume and incorporate postliberal and revisionist insights. In the process this realism has itself been modified but, it is contended, not critically. The second strand has been the shift from the theoretically non-pragmatical (theological realism and language-riddenness) through the theoretically pragmatical (language-games and agency) to the practically pragmatical and then corporately pragmatical (ecclesial practice). The third strand has been the shift from an impersonal and static perspective to the personal and dynamic view of reality already present in theological realism but, for the purposes of this inquiry's incorporation of the weak postmodern thesis, allowed to come progressively into focus.

The contention was put forward in the introduction that if progress is to be made in theology it will not be by digging existing lines of thought deeper, but by developing lateral and synthetic approaches that aim to overcome the shortcomings of realist, liberal-revisionist and postliberal approaches while building on their strengths. In endeavouring to develop these approaches this inquiry began with two premises. The first one was the minimalist monotheistic requirement that God's reality and truth be absolute together with the Christian corollary that this divine reality and truth be revealed christologically. In revealing God's absolute reality and truth in human terms, Christianity as pre-eminently christological may be said to absorb the world in providing the ultimate parameters of humanly knowable reality.

The second premise was that the human reality with which theology engages is a postmodern one – that is, according to a weak postmodern thesis which while maintaining the particular and linguistic nature of human existence, at the same time allows the possibility of meta-narratives or master-stories that are trans-contextual. If the first premise entails that realist Christian theology in a postmodern age involves the incorporation of that postmodern age within realist theology, the second premise requires that a realist Christian theology take on board the implications of that incorporation, positive and negative – that Christian (as well as creaturely) reality be understood as particular and language-ridden while at the same time offering a master-story that draws the rest of human reality inside its linguistic particularity. That this incorporation is possible is pointed up by Christianity's own insis-tence on particularity and its textually and liturgically storied nature, as Loughlin has indicated.[1] That mutual modification must also occur is pointed up by Marshall and Werpehowski as well as by the very model of conversion and 'indigenization' used in this inquiry to describe the interaction of contexts or philosophies that gives rise to new truths.

The connection between Christianity and postmodernity in these respects has already been developed by postliberal theologians. Yet the seminal work of Lindbeck and Frei, in its attempt to take postmodern insights about language seriously, has tended to be ambiguous about truth in its assimilation (or at times the reverse) of the Wittgensteinian-Geertzian cultural-linguistic model to the postliberal Barthian christo-centric theology. In other words, postliberal theology has tended to lose self-consistency through getting trapped within the linguistic turn. It has been suggested that if modern theological realism has not been linguistic enough, postliberal theology has not been realist enough. Yet perhaps postliberal theology, like many programmatic innovations, has suffered more from lack of articulation than lack of realism, a lack that more recent work has remedied. Lindbeck certainly implies a theistic realism in his notion of categorial adequacy. That a recasting of his argument may make

1. See Loughlin, *Telling God's Story*.

the pieces fit has been suggested by construing a link between the categorial model and Hardy's notion of underdeterminedness.

It has been argued that the incorporation of a weak-thesis postmodernity within theological realism does not negate realism or render it a contradiction in terms so much as expand it. This it does in two ways. First, while endorsing the theological adoption of the shift from naive to critical and postcritical realism instigated by science's recognition of the theory-laden and personal nature of observation, it expands theological realism in the middle, as it were, in challenging it to take seriously the implications of a constructive element in human knowing. At the same time it takes on itself the personal aspect of postcritical realism in understanding language-ridden particularity as inherently personal. This constructive element is able to be linked with theological models of human freedom and creaturely contingence.[2] A secondary philosophical model is used to assist in the articulation of this element on the grounds that a Wittgensteinian view of language-using activity as primary, as well as recasting the postmodern weak thesis in a pragmatical mode as postliberal theologians have noted and appreciated, may usefully annotate an incarnational theistic realism. In this connecting, or hingeing, capacity it is able to annotate the one-way semantic *analogia entis* proposed by Eberhard Jüngel and Alan Torrance.[3] While we inevitably have to work within language in addressing all the concerns of our existence, we are not dealing with an exclusively linguistic reality. It is we, as personal agents, who use language, who link signs with world.

Second, this incorporation of an inextricably language-ridden world forces the expansion of critical and postcritical realism upward, as it were. If all human attempts at establishing truth are 'contaminated', as Putnam puts it, realism must be theistic to be coherent. Then for truth to be accessible, this theistic-realist model must be incarnational. Of course, theistic realism's upholding of a personal reality is consistent with and is seen to inform (as a further expansion of the *analogia entis*) the postcritical realist insistence on knowledge as personal and dynamically ongoing. In this way reality comes to include its progressive coming to be known in a way that is consistent with linguistic creativity.

Up to this point such an expansion of theological realism may seem to have been little more than a reinvention of the Torrancean, Polanyian and Jüngelian wheel. However, there are further implications of this

2. See Hardy, 'Spirit of God'.
3. See Jüngel, *Theological Essays*, p. 142 and Torrance, *Persons in Communion*, pp. 325–6, 356.

two-way expansion. The first is to do with the personal pragmatic nature of theistic realism. If reality as (in the first instance) divinely personal is also inherently communicative, it follows that there is no need to encase language within a human framework. If God's being as personal (and therefore communicative) is in becoming, this becoming includes God's becoming known and coming to speech, as Jüngel argues. Yet there is a provisionality and revisability to becoming that suggests the need to retain a critical as well as a postcritical element in a theistic realism. On the one hand, reality as postcritically personal is more than language-riddenness. We (and God) are not simply 'life narratives with a future' or the sum of our language-games. Lives and games must be lived and played, If we indwell our histories and practices, so they indwell us. It is this co-inherence that establishes the weak-thesis postmodern perspective within realism rather than the other way round. On the other hand, if God's being as trinitarian is in becoming, and this divine freedom to become is, on the one-way analogy of being, of a piece with yet constitutive of the human freedom to become built into our creaturely contingence, then there is an underdeterminedness to all reality including God's. All tends to an eschatological finality when Christ (and God) is all in all. It is in this contention of revisability that liberal-revisionist theology has found a place in this inquiry. The revisionist emphasis on the dialectical relationship between old truth and new truth, text and user in both hermeneutics and Christian life is a valuable one that this study has sought to bring inside its theistic-realist utilization of the postcritical and critical-realist notions of becoming and underdeterminedness.

In case the exposition of these notions has been less than clear, it remains to be said that 'underdeterminedness' is in no way advanced as a new-version 'God of the Gaps' thesis in which we participate in a divine perfecting and fulfilling of creation rather than being ourselves confounded and transformed along with the rest of creation. Nor is 'becoming' a postcritical version of anthropocentrism that, in maintaining a co-inherence of knowing and being, reads a provisional divine being from a provisional human reality. This inquiry's development of the Wittgensteinian superimposition model allied with White's predication and Marshall's absorption models to explicate an understanding of conversion as a christological re-creation of world should put paid to any such suspicions.[4]

4. Ibid., p. 355. The study Torrance refers to suffers from a misleading lack of exposition rather than a 'theology from below'.

Finally, theology itself has been drawn inside its exponent, the Church. Here human reality as personal is brought inside the wider and deeper agency of corporate ecclesial personhood. Yet the Church's communal personhood participates in christological personhood in its divine as well as human aspects, in the christological dialectic between contingence and transcendence which is the Economic Trinity's co-inherence with the Immanent Trinity. This participation grants the Church the space to 'invent itself in Christ by the Spirit'. This self-invention in which the Church in the Spirit becomes itself is subsumed in worship which is the primary constituting by God of ecclesial being, and which is therefore the ground of discipleship and mission.

Select bibliography

Abraham, William S. and Holtzer, Stephen W. (eds.) *The Rationality of Religious Belief*, Oxford: Clarendon Press, 1987

Anderson, Ray S. *Historical Transcendence and the Reality of God*, Grand Rapids: Eerdmans, 1975

Auerbach, Erich *Mimesis: The Representation of Reality in Western Literature*, trans. Wm R. Trask Princeton: Princeton University Press, 1953

Barth, Karl *Church Dogmatics,* ed. and trans. G. W. Bromiley and T. F. Torrance 2nd rev. edn, Edinburgh: T. & T. Clark, 1975 and 1977, vol. 1/2

Burnham, Frederick B. (ed.) *Postmodern Theology*, San Francisco: Harper & Row, 1989

Cathey, Robert Andrew *Foundations with Faces: A Prolegomenon to a Postliberal Doctrine of God*, Ann Arbor, MI: UMI, 1990

Coleridge, Samuel Taylor *Biographia Literaria*, ed. J. Shawcross, Oxford: Clarendon Press, 1907

Cupitt, Don *The Sea of Faith*, London: BBC, 1984

   The Long-Legged Fly: A Theology of Language and Desire, London: SCM, 1987

   Creation Out of Nothing, London: SCM, 1990

Davidson, Donald and Harman, Gilbert (eds.) *Semantics of Natural Language,* Dortrecht: D. Reidel, 1972

Dummett, Michael *Truth and Other Enigmas,* London: Duckworth, 1978

Ferré, Frederick 'Mapping the Logic of Models', in D. M. High (ed.) *New Essays on Religious Language*, Oxford: Oxford University Press, 1969, pp. 54–96

Ford, David 'System, Story, Performance', in S. Hauerwas and L. G. Jones (eds.) *Why Narrative? Readings in Narrative Theology*, Grand Rapids: Eerdmans, 1989, pp. 191ff

Ford, David (ed.) *The Modern Theologians*, 2 vols., Oxford: Blackwell, 1989, vol. 1

Frei, Hans W. 'Apologetics, Criticism and the Loss of Narrative Interpretation', in B. D. Marshall (ed.) *Theology and Dialogue : Essays in Conversation with George Lindbeck*, Indiana: University of Notre Dame Press, 1990, pp. 50ff

   '"Narrative" in Christian and Modern Reading', in B. D. Marshall (ed.) *Theology and Dialogue: Essays in Conversation with George Lindbeck*, Indiana: University of Notre Dame Press, 1990, pp. 149ff

   The Eclipse of Biblical Narrative: A Study of Eighteenth and Nineteenth Century Hermeneutics, New Haven, CT: Yale University Press, 1974

   Theology and Narrative: Selected Essays, William C. Placher and George Hunsinger (eds.) Oxford: Oxford University Press, 1993

Types of Christian Theology, George Hunsinger and William C. Placher (eds.) New
    Haven, CT: Yale University Press, 1992
Gill, Robin (ed.) *Readings in Modern Theology*, London: SPCK, 1995
Gillett, Grant *Representation, Meaning and Thought*, Oxford: Clarendon Press, 1992
Goldstein, Arnold P. *The Prepare Curriculum: Teaching Prosocial Competence*, Champaign,
    IL: Research Press, 1988
Green, Garrett '"The Bible As . . .": Fictional Narrative and Scriptural Truth', in G.
    Green (ed.) *Scriptural Authority and Narrative Interpretation*, Philadelphia:
    Fortress, 1987, pp. 79ff
    Imagining God, San Francisco: Harper & Row, 1989
Green, Garrett (ed.) *Scriptural Authority and Narrative Interpretation*, Philadelphia:
    Fortress, 1987
Gunton, Colin E. 'Trinity, Ontology and Anthropology: Towards a Renewal of the
    Doctrine of the *Imago Dei*', in C. Schwöbel and C. Gunton *Persons, Divine and
    Human*, Edinburgh: T. & T. Clark, 1991, pp. 47ff
    The One, the Three and the Many: God, Creation and the Culture of Modernity, Cambridge:
    Cambridge University Press, 1993
    A Brief Theology of Revelation, Edinburgh: T. & T. Clark, 1995
Hardy, Daniel W. 'Man the Creature', *Scottish Journal of Theology*, 30 (1977), 111–36
    'Rationality, the Sciences and Theology', in G. Wainwright (ed.) *Keeping the Faith*,
    Philadelphia: Fortress/Pickwick Publications, 1988, pp. 274–309
    'The Spirit of God in Creation and Reconciliation', in H. Regan and A. J. Torrance
    (eds.) *Christ and Context*, Edinburgh: T. & T. Clark, 1993, pp. 237ff
Hardy, Daniel W. and Ford, David F. *Praising and Knowing God*, Philadelphia:
    Westminster Press, 1985
Harré, Rom and Lamb, Roger (eds.) *The Encyclopaedia Dictionary of Psychology*,
    Cambridge, MA: MIT Press, 1983
Hauerwas, Stanley *Vision and Virtue*, Indiana: University of Notre Dame Press, 1981
    After Christendom, Nashville: Abingdon Press, 1991
Hauerwas, Stanley and Jones, L. Gregory (eds.) *Why Narrative? Readings in Narrative
    Theology*, Grand Rapids: Eerdmans, 1989
Hebblethwaite, Brian and Sutherland, Stewart (eds.) *The Philosophical Frontiers of
    Christian Theology*, Cambridge: Cambridge University Press, 1982
Hintikka, Merrill B. and Hintikka, Jaakko *Investigating Wittgenstein*, Oxford:
    Blackwell, 1986
Jeanrond, Werner G. *Textual Hermeneutics: Development and Significance*, New York:
    Crossroad, 1991, pp. 94–5
Jüngel, Eberhard *The Doctrine of the Trinity: God's Being is in Becoming*, trans. Horton
    Harris, Edinburgh: Scottish Academic Press, 1976
    Theological Essays, trans. and with introduction by J. B. Webster, Edinburgh: T. & T.
    Clark, 1989
Kelsey, David H. *The Uses of Scripture in Recent Theology*, Philadelphia: Fortress, 1975
    'Whatever Happened to the Doctrine of Sin?', in R. Gill (ed.) *Readings in Modern
    Theology*, London: SPCK, 1995, pp. 236ff
Kerr, Fergus *Theology After Wittgenstein*, Oxford: Blackwell, 1986
Kort, Wesley 'Reading a Text as Though it were Scripture', paper presented at the
    Center of Theological Inquiry, Princeton, March 1994
Kripke, Saul 'Naming and Necessity', in D. Davidson and G. Harman (eds.) *Semantics of
    Natural Language*, Dortrecht: D. Reidel, 1972, pp. 253–355

Kuhn, Thomas S. *The Structure of Scientific Revolutions*, 2nd edn, Chicago: University of Chicago Press, 1970

Lash, Nicholas 'How Large is a Language Game?', *Theology*, 87 (1984) 19–28

Levin, Samuel 'Standard Approaches to Metaphor and a Proposal for Literary Metaphor', in A. Ortony (ed.) *Metaphor and Thought*, Cambridge: Cambridge University Press, 1979, pp. 124–135

Lewis, C. S. *God in the Dock: Essays in Theology*, Glasgow: Collins, 1979

Lindbeck, George A. *The Nature of Doctrine: Religion and Theology in a Postliberal Age*, Philadelphia: Westminster Press, 1984

Loughlin, Gerard *Telling God's Story*, Cambridge: Cambridge University Press, 1996

McCrone, John *The Myth of Irrationality: The Science of the Mind from Plato to Star Trek*, London: Macmillan, 1993

McFadyen, Alistair 'The Doctrine of Sin and the Sexual Abuse of Children', paper presented at the Center of Theological Inquiry, Princeton, Summer 1993

Macintyre, Alasdair *After Virtue: A Study in Moral Theology*, 2nd edn., London: Duckworth, 1997

Marshall, Bruce D. 'Absorbing the World: Christianity and the Universe of Truths', in B. D. Marshall (ed.) *Theology and Dialogue: Essays in Conversation with George Lindbeck*, Indiana: University of Notre Dame Press, 1990, pp. 69ff

Marshall, Bruce D. (ed.) *Theology and Dialogue: Essays in Conversation with George Lindbeck*, Indiana: University of Notre Dame Press, 1990

Milbank, John *The Word Made Strange: Theology, Language, Culture*, Oxford: Blackwell, 1997

Moltmann, Jürgen *God in Creation: an Ecological Doctrine of Creation*, London: SCM, 1985

Mulhall, Stephen *On Being in the World: Wittgenstein and Heidegger on Seeing Aspects*, London/New York: Routledge, 1990

Murphy, Nancey *Theology in the Age of Scientific Reasoning*, Ithaca, NY: Cornell University Press, 1990

Murphy, Nancey and McClendon, James Wm Jr. 'Distinguishing Modern and Postmodern Theologies', *Modern Theology*, 5/3 (1989), 191–214

Need, Stephen W. *Human Language and Knowledge in the Light of Chalcedon*, New York: Peter Lang Publishing, 1996

Newbigin, Lesslie 'The Christian Faith and the World Religions, in G. Wainwright (ed.) *Keeping the Faith*, Philadelphia: Fortress/Pickwick Publication, 1988, pp. 310–40

Ortony Andrew (ed.) *Metaphor and Thought*, Cambridge: Cambridge University Press, 1979

Osgood, Charles E. *Method and Theory in Experimental Psychology*, Oxford: Oxford University Press, 1953

Patterson, Sue 'The Theological Implications of the Relationship Between a Wittgensteinian Understanding of the Relationship of Language to World and the Role of Metaphor as an Agent of Revelation', unpublished doctoral thesis, University of Otago, Dunedin, New Zealand, 1991

    'Word, Words and World', *Colloquium*, 23/2 (1991), 71–84

    'Creation and Postmodernity', in V. Pfitzner and H. Regan, (eds.) *The Task of Theology Today: Doctrines and Dogmas*, Adelaide: Australian Theological Forum 1998, pp. 62–80

Pfitzner, Victor and Regan, Hilary (eds.) *The Task of Theology Today: Doctrines and Dogmas*, Edinburgh: T. & T. Clark, 1999

Placher, William C. 'Paul Ricoeur and Post liberal Theology', *Modern Theology* 4 (1987), 35ff

    Unapologetic Theology: Christian Voices in a Pluralistic Conversation, Louisville: Westminster/John Knox Press, 1989

Polanyi, Michael *Personal Knowledge*, London: Routledge, 1958

    The Tacit Dimension, London: Routledge, 1966

Putnam, Hilary *Mind, Language and Reality*, Cambridge: Cambridge University Press, 1975

    Realism and Reason, Cambridge: Cambridge University Press, 1983

    Reason, Truth and History, Cambridge: Cambridge University Press, 1981

    Representation and Reality, Cambridge, MA: MIT Press, 1991

    The Many Faces of Realism, La Salle, IL: Open Court, 1987

Ramsey, Ian 'The Systematic Elusiveness of "I"', *Philosophical Quarterly*, 5 (1955), 193–204

Regan, Hilary and Torrance, Alan J. (eds.) *Christ and Context*, Edinburgh: T. & T. Clark, 1993

Ricoeur, Paul *The Rule of Metaphor*, London: Routledge, 1978

Rorty, Richard *Objectivism, Relativism and Truth. Philosophical Papers,* vol. 1, Cambridge: Cambridge University Press, 1991

Ryle, Gilbert *The Concept of Mind*, New York: Barnes & Noble, 1962

Sarup, Madan *An Introductory Guide to Poststructuralism and Postmodernism*, Athens, GI: University of Georgia Press, 1989

Schwöbel, Christoph *God, Action and Revelation*, Kampen: Kok Pharos, 1991

Schwöbel, Christoph and Gunton, Colin E. (eds.) *Persons, Divine and Human*, Edinburgh: T.& T. Clark, 1991

Soskice, Janet Martin *Metaphor and Religious Language,* Oxford: Clarendon Press, 1985

    'Theological Realism', in W. S. Abraham and S. W. Holtzer (eds.) *The Rationality of Religious Belief*, Oxford: Clarendon Press, pp. 105–119

Surin, Kenneth 'Atonement and Christology', *Neue Zeitschrift für Systematische Theologie und Religionsphilosophie,* 24 (1982) 131–49

    Theology and the Problem of Evil, Oxford: Blackwell, 1986

    (ed.) *Christ, Ethics and Tragedy,* Cambridge: Cambridge University Press, 1989

    'Some Aspects of the "Grammar" of "Incarnation" and "Kenosis"', in K. Surin (ed.) *Christ, Ethics and Tragedy,* Cambridge: Cambridge University Press, 1989, pp. 94ff

    The Turnings of Darkness and Light: Essays in Philosophical and Systematic Theology, Cambridge: Cambridge University Press, 1989

Tanner, Kathryn 'Theology and the Plain Sense', in G. Green (ed.) *Scriptural Authority and Narrative Interpretation*, Philadelphia: Fortress, 1987, pp. 59ff

    God and Creation in Christian Theology: Tyranny or Empowerment?, Oxford: Blackwell, 1988

Thiemann, Ronald *Revelation and Theology: The Gospel as Narrated Promise,* Indiana: University of Notre Dame Press, 1985

Thorndike, E. L. and Woodworth, R. S. 'The Influence of Improvement in One Mental Function upon the Efficiency of Other Functions (I); II The Estimation of Magnitudes; III Functions Involving Attention, Observation and Discrimination.' *Psychological Review* 8 (1901), 247–61, 384–95, 553–64

Torrance, Alan J. *Persons in Communion: Trinitarian Description and Human Participation,* Edinburgh: T. & T. Clark, 1996

Torrance, T. F. *Space, Time and Incarnation,* Oxford: Oxford University Press, 1969
  Theological Science, Oxford: Oxford University Press, 1969
  God and Rationality, Oxford: Oxford University Press, 1971
  Divine and Contingent Order, Oxford: Oxford University Press, 1981
  Reality and Scientific Theology, Edinburgh: Scottish Academic Press, 1982
  'Theological Realism', in B. Hebblethwaite and S. Sutherland (eds.) *The Philosophical Frontiers of Christian Theology,* Cambridge: Cambridge University Press, 1982, pp. 169–96
  The Christian Doctrine of God, Edinburgh: T. & T. Clark, 1996
Toulmin, Stephen *The Return to Cosmology: Postmodern Science and the Theology of Nature,* Berkeley: University of California Press, 1982
  Cosmopolis: the Hidden Agenda of Modernity, Chicago: University of Chicago Press, 1990
Tracy, David *Plurality and Ambiguity: Hermeneutics, Religion, Hope,* San Francisco: Harper & Row, 1987
Wainwright, G. (ed.) *Keeping the Faith,* Philadelphia: Fortress/Pickwick Publications, 1988
Werpehowski, William 'Ad Hoc Apologetics', *Journal of Religion,* 66/3 (1986), 28–30
White, Roger 'Notes on Analogical Predication and Speaking About God', in B. Hebblethwaite and S. Sutherland, (eds.) *The Philosophical Frontiers of Christian Theology,* Cambridge: Cambridge University Press, 1982, pp. 197–226
Williams, Rowan D. 'Postmodern Theology and the Judgment of the World', in F. B. Burnham (ed.) *Postmodern Theology,* San Francisco: Harper & Row, 1989, pp. 92ff
Wittgenstein, Ludwig *The Blue Book, Blue and Brown Books,* Oxford: Blackwell, 1958
  Philosophical Investigations, 2nd edn., Oxford: Blackwell, 1958
  On Certainty, G. E. M. Anscombe and G. H. von Wright (eds.) (San Francisco: Harper & Row, 1972
  Remarks on Colour, ed. and trans. G. E. M Anscombe, Oxford: Blackwell, 1977
  Remarks on the Philosophy of Psychology, vol. 2, G. H. von Wright and Heikki Nyman (eds.), trans. C. G. Luckhardt and M. A. E. Aue, Oxford: Blackwell, 1980
  Last Writings in the Psychology of Philosophy, vol. I, G. H. von Wright and Heikki Nyman (eds.), C. G. Luckhardt and M. A. E. Aue (trans.), Oxford: Blackwell, 1992
Wolterstorff, Nicholas *Reason within the Bounds of Religion,* 2nd edn. Grand Rapids: Eerdmans, 1984
Zizioulas, John *Being as Communion,* London: Darton Longman & Todd, 1985

Index of names

Index of subjects